ADULT EDUCATION AND THEOLOGICAL INTERPRETATIONS

ADULT EDUCATION AND THEOLOGICAL INTERPRETATIONS

EDITED BY
PETER JARVIS AND NICHOLAS WALTERS

KRIEGER PUBLISHING COMPANY
MALABAR, FLORIDA
1993

Original Edition 1993
Printed and Published by
KRIEGER PUBLISHING COMPANY
KRIEGER DRIVE
MALABAR, FLORIDA 32950

Library of Congress Cataloging-In-Publication Data

Adult education and theological interpretations/edited by Peter
  Jarvis and Nicholas Walters.
        p.   cm.
     ISBN 0-89464-587-0 (alk. paper)
     1. Adult education—Philosophy. 2. Learning—Religious aspects—
Christianity. 3. Church and education. 4. Education (Christian
theology) I. Jarvis, Peter, 1937–   . II. Walters, Nicholas.
LC5219.A295   1992
374'.001—dc20   92-8562
                                                                    CIP

10 9 8 7 6 5 4 3 2

CONTENTS

PART 3

LEARNING

PART 4

THE INDIVIDUAL

Contents vii

PART 5

COMMUNITAS

Chapter 12 Foundations of Community Education and the
Dangers of Asceticism 187
Ruud van der Veen

Chapter 13 Contract Learning and the Covenant 203
Reg Wickett

PART 6

SOCIETY

Chapter 14 Open Multicultural Society—Access and Election 221
Nicholas Walters

Chapter 15 Beyond God the Father and the Mother: Adult
Education and Spirituality 237
Mechthild Hart and Deborah Horton

Chapter 16 Moral Issues in Adult Education: From Life
Problems to Educational Goals and Postmodern
Uncertainty 259
Walter Leirman and Luc Anckaert

Chapter 17 Prophecy: Radical Adult Education and the Politics
of Power 273
David Deshler

Chapter 18 And I Saw a New Heaven and a New Earth 309
Peter Jarvis

PART 7

REFLECTIONS

Preface

There is a well worn adage that declares "no-one has ever been argued into the kingdom of heaven," and yet beside the kerygmatic tradition of the preacher, religions have a didactic teaching tradition of importance to the educator of adults. In practice religions appeal for a change of heart as well as a change of mind. Adult Education by definition practices a didactic tradition, but innovative approaches are increasingly described in kerygmatic terms. Such words as "pioneer" and even "mission" appear on conference agendas and in literature relating to adult education outreach activities.

This book is based on several premises and it is important to identify these before proceeding to the debate itself. Theology has been described as a systematic study of religious experience and traditions. This study is about a theistic interpretation of everyday living. How this is done reflects the current philosophy and the results are expressed in contemporary cultural concepts. The study of adult education is not based on theistic premises. In practice it can be argued that it is most influenced by Pragmatism and a pragmatic critique of Platonic ideals. It is a pragmatism that claims to respond to both individual and societal need and concern, and this duality runs as a theme throughout this study. From a theological point of view it is humanistic rather than theistic. The first premise of the volume is that the experience of the human condition is a unity. There is not one set of experiences of everyday living that needs addressing by theologians and another set that needs the adult educator. There is not a divide between the secular and sacred, the former being the province of adult education and the latter the legitimate concern of theology. It follows that any divide between adult education and theology is a divide about interpretation of life experience. There is a historical tradition of theologians as adult educators, and while this is acknowledged, this study is not about outlining this history and its significance; it is rather about examining and explaining the two traditions of interpretation of the one life experience.

In this sense the authors are writing from a position of reflective learning. They are not writing from a faith perspective as a contribution to Adult Religious Education. The debate is a discussion about values, universals and perceived dilemmas rather than a comparison of different theological solutions. This kind of reflection implies there are no predetermined solutions, rather there is an ongoing search for meaning. Theology after the Second World War emphasized the secular nature of society. This has now been overtaken by the growth of individualism and fundamentalism, both offering solutions to the human predicament. The authors write within this tension, but they are not attempting to proselytize, nor are they promoting a baptism of adult education. They are not involved in an attempt to secularize or demythologize theology. All the contributors have a personal and professional interest in both theological and adult education's interpretation of life experiences, rather than writing in the interest of one particular ideology. The book then is an exercise in debating and exploring the significance of such interpretations. The premise of the book can be modelled thus:

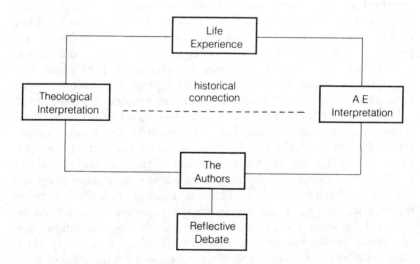

The volume opens with a debate about the nature of learning as a religious phenomenon. There follows a collection of contributions based on the theme of the relationship between faith and knowledge, which leads to a discussion on interpretations of learning. The theme then changes to explore the implications for the individual and the nature and role of the individual person in the debate. Both adult education and religion practice in groups and the next theme to be taken up is that of "community." Finally there is a series of authors looking at differing analyses and interpretations of societal issues. The final chapter is a contribution from an academic theologian which reviews the volume and identifies a possible agenda for future debate.

The Contributors

Luc Anckaert	Assistant Lecturer in Moral Theology, Catholic University of Leuven, Belgium
Carolyn Clark	Assistant Professor. Texas A & M University USA
Bradley Courtenay	Professor and Head of the Department of Adult Education, College of Education, University of Georgia, Athens, USA
David Deshler	Associate Professor, Department of Education, College of Agriculture and Life Sciences, Cornell University, USA
Trenton R Ferro	Assistant Professor and Co-ordinator for the Adult and Community Education Program, Indiana University of Pennsylvania, USA
Mechthild Hart	Assistant Professor, School for New Learning, DePaul University, Chicago, USA
Deborah Horton	School for New Learning, DePaul University, Chicago, USA
Peter Jarvis	Professor of Continuing Education, Department of Educational Studies, University of Surrey, Guildford, UK
Walter Leirman	Professor, Department of Social Pedagogy, Catholic University of Leuven, Leuven, Belgium
Tony McCaffry	Lecturer in Regious Studies, St Mary's College, Twickenham, Middlesex, UK
Nicola Slee	Lecturer in Theology, Roehampton Institute of Higher Education, London UK
Harold Stubblefield	Associate Professor of Adult Education, Virginia Polytechnic Institute and State University, North Virginia Graduate Center, Virginia, USA
Ruud van der Veen	Senior Lecturer in Adult Education, Institute for the Study of Adult Education, Catholic University of Nijmegen, The Netherlands.

David Walker	Founding Director, Educational Centre, College for Christian Adult Education, Sydney, Australia
Nicholas Walters	Senior Staff Tutor, Department of Educational Studies, University of Surrey, UK
Michael Welton	Associate Professor, Department of Education Dalhousie University, Halifax, Nova Scotia
Reg Wickett	Professor, Department of Communications, Continuing and Vocational Education, College of Education, University of Saskatchewan, Canada
Peter Willis	Centre for Human Resource Studies, University of South Australia, Australia.

Part One

A Religious Phenomenon?

CHAPTER 1

Learning as a Religious Phenomenon?
PETER JARVIS

THE PARADOX OF THE QUESTION—WHY?

Learning has been defined by many as "a relatively permanent change in behavior that occurs as a result of practice" (Hilgard and Atkinson, 1967, ed., p 270) and definitions, such as this one, have reflected the behaviorist practices in education whereby the teacher sets the learning objectives, operationalizes the teaching plan and expects the learner to have acquired precisely what the teacher determines by the end of the session. In precisely the same way, in the work situation, there has grown up a "scientific management" school which assumes that the actual role demands can be determined precisely and that the worker merely acquires those techniques through practice which produce the most efficient and effective performance outcomes. For many, this is their conception of learning. This is the way they perceive that their employees or their students should learn. But there are other implications to this approach, one of which provides a focus for this paper. Examine the conception of the human being implicit in it—malleable and mindless! Is this the human being that the psalmist could wax lyrical about, when he wrote:

What is man that thou art mindful of him,
    and the son of man that thou dost care for him?

Yet thou hast made him little less than God,
    and crowned him with glory and honour.

Thou has given him dominion over the works of thy hands:
  thou has put all things under his feet.

                                          (Ps. 8:4–7)

However, the question posed by this paper is: which perspective seems nearer to reality about the human being? Are the majority of humankind merely cogs in a large machine or is there more to human beings than this? Is learning merely the acquisition of predetermined knowledge and skills or is there more than this to learning?

In order to explore these questions it is necessary to examine the human condition, and thereafter to apply that analysis to the questions that have been posed.

The Human Condition

Human existence might be characterized as being in time (Heidegger, 1962), space, society and culture, but one of the crucial factors of human being for human beings is that being is itself an issue. Human beings cannot and do not take themselves for granted and yet their quest to understand themselves is always ultimately doomed to some form of disappointment, for however hard they search, existence seems to be full of contradictions.

> Man can only react to contradictions by annulling them through his own action; but he cannot annul existential dichotomies, although he can react to them in different ways. He can appease his mind by soothing and harmonizing ideologies. He can try to escape from his inner restlessness by ceaseless activity in pleasure or business. He can try to abrogate his freedom and turn himself into an instrument of powers outside himself, submerging his self in them. But he remains dissatisfied, anxious and restless. There is only one solution to his problem: to face the truth, to acknowledge his fundamental aloneless and solitude in a universe indifferent to his fate, to recognise that there is no power transcending him which can solve his problem for him. Man must accept the responsibility for himself and the fact that only by using his powers can he give meaning to life. But meaning does not imply certainty; indeed, the quest for certainty blocks the search for meaning. Uncertainty is the very condition to impel man to unfold his powers. If he faces the truth without panic he will recognize that there is no meaning to life except the meaning man

gives his life be unfolding his powers, by living productively; and that
only by constant vigilance, activity, and effort can keep us from failing
in the one task that matters—the full development of our powers within
the limitations set by the laws of our existence. Man will never cease to
be perplexed, to wonder, and to raise new questions. (Fromm, 1949, pp
44–45)

Here in this full passage, Fromm depicts the heart of the human
condition; humankind is a restless wanderer (Fromm, 1949, p 41),
always seeking meaning for existence and knowing that every experience is meaningless, unless it has meaning given to it. Naturally this is
a debatable conclusion and one which those with a deep faith might
wish to dispute, but it is not one upon which this chapter dwells—for
the significance of this passage in this chapter is the endless quest to
discover meaning.

Throughout history every tribe and people of the world have trod-
den this path and sought meaning for their existence. There have
grown up profound stories, beautiful myths and complex theologies, all
of which have become embedded in the cultures of the peoples of the
world. Yet all have started from the same point, all have posed questions about existence. At the start and the heart of every complex
theology and profound myth lies a simple word—why?

Individual human beings, therefore, are not alone—"no man is an
island"—and every person is a member of a society and since every
society has evolved its own answers to those questions about the unknowns of human existence, these systems of meaning have become
part of the cultures of the people. As children are born into a society
so they go through this same human process of asking questions and
gaining answers from their sociocultural environment. Every parent is
aware of those perpetual "why" questions and every adolescent has
been plagued by that same question. At the heart of human existence
lies that questions—why? Whenever this question is posed a variety of
answers may be produced, many of which relate to the cultural milieu
into which the questioner is born, some of which may be regarded as
religious and other as nonreligious.

Thus it may be seen that much human learning starts from this
question. Perhaps it is the genesis of all knowledge and belief, and that
all religious systems also start here. The chapter seeks to map a theory

of learning that parallels it to the religious quest of humankind and it has seven parts: the birth of the self; why?; creation of order; conversion; growth and development; utopia; molding the human mind. Finally, there is a brief concluding discussion in which it is pointed out that this chapter seeks only to relate human learning to some profound questions of human existence rather than to produce definitive answers. Before embarking upon these issues it is necessary to clarify one major point. Religion, as a concept and as used in this chapter, refers to religious systems in general rather than Christianity in particular, although many of the references here are to Christian thought, and religiosity is the individual belief system that has emerged as a result of trying to answer some of these questions of human existence. Indeed, religiosity was defined elsewhere as a system of meaning about existence which relates it to a perceived general order of the cosmos (Jarvis, 1983).

The Birth of the Self.

The human being is not born with a self. Peter Berger (1966, p 117) makes the point that "identity is not something 'given,' " while Mead (Strauss, 1964) highlights the fact that the self emerges through social interaction. It might be clearer to suggest that children are born with brains but not fully developed minds. It is through interaction and the use of language and gesture that the mind is formed and only then can the self begin to emerge. This has been more fully discussed elsewhere (Jarvis, 1987), but note the significance of the idea of word. It is through social interaction that questions of meaning are posed and answers provided, so that individuals gradually acquire their own system of meaning, or as Luckmann (1967, p 50) suggests:

> ... human organisms do not construct "objective" and moral universes of meaning from scratch—they are born into them. This means that human organisms normally transcend their biological nature by internalizing a historically given universe of meaning, rather than constructing universes of meaning.

He argues that human beings become selves by constructing with others an "objective" and moral universe of meaning and in so doing transcend their biological nature. The significance of this is that with the birth of the mind and the emergence of the self, the human being is no longer merely a biological organism. This is the wonder of life and birth, it is the birth of something that is not only biological but intangible—almost spiritual. Luckmann develops this point in a very significant manner by arguing that this process of transcending the human being's own biological nature and becoming a self is fundamentally a religious process, but it is also a learned process. Hence at the heart of one of the most fundamental elements in the birth of every human being there lies a process of learning which might also be regarded as religious in itself.

According to the interactionist school of thought the self is a product of social interaction and the birth of the self is related to the beginnings of the acquisition of a system of meaning. The earliest belief system is a learning process and is itself involved in the formation of the mind from whence develops the self—which, for Luckmann, is a religious process.

Why?

Human beings do not go through the whole of life asking questions, rather the opposite. Schutz and Luckmann (1974, p 7) write:

> Every implication within the life-world goes on within the milieu of affairs which have already been explicated, within a reality that is fundamentally and typically familiar. I trust the world as it has been known by me up until now will continue further and that consequently the stock of knowledge obtained from my fellow-men and formed from my own experiences will continue to preserve its fundamental validity. . . .From this assumption follows the further and fundamental one: that I can repeat my past successful acts. So long as the structure of the world can be taken to be constant, as long as my previous experience is valid, my ability to operate upon the world in this and that manner remains in principle preserved.

From the above it may be seen that many experiences of life do not result in any form of learning. Indeed, nonlearning is an important feature of human living and without it there could be no social stability (Jarvis, 1987, pp 133–146). However, time and tide await no man and human beings change as they grow—they have different questions of meaning; society and culture change and their questions change with those changes; experiences change and the questions emerge yet again, why?

Many scholars, for example, Mezirow (1981), Jarvis (1987) *inter alia*, regard this process of questioning as the beginning of all learning, for if the meaning is taken for granted rarely does the experience evoke a question. For Mezirow it is a disorientating dilemma and for Jarvis it is disjuncture. Individuals enter every experience with their own biography, that is with a stock of knowledge, beliefs, attitudes and values gained as a result of previous experiences, and if that stock of knowledge and belief is sufficient then they enter a meaningful situation and are able to operate on the world in a nonlearning manner. But when that reservoir is insufficient then there is a disjuncture between the biography and the experience. It is the experience of disjuncture which stimulates the question—why? The question constitutes the start of the learning process—for once asked it demands an answer. Sometimes the question can be answered from the perspective of one of the disciplines of knowledge, sometimes there is an ideological response and sometimes the answer comes from another form of belief or religious system.

The significance of the question cannot be lost in any consideration of religion, since it is that question that occurs throughout life in this quest for ultimate meaning. While humankind longs for stability and even seems to assume that the static is the normal, in fact the world is dynamic and change is endemic and the human being is a restless wanderer within it for about three score years and ten, or a little longer. For most people, seeking to understand their existence is an intermittent, but lifelong, quest—at times they take it for granted but at other times that question emerges again—why? why? Questions are asked about the past and metahistorical past, about the future and the metahistorical future, about the present, about the self, people and the cosmos. (Jarvis, 1983) All are questions about the meaning of human experience. But the ability to ask questions about these "unknowns" neither makes an individual religious nor describes the phenomenon of religion. It simply depicts the human condition. To have answers, however, is the expression of people's religiosity.

Human beings have to make sense of their experiences—for human beings are meaning seeking animals, so that not only is the self formed through this meaning-seeking process, people sustain their humanity through it. It is at the root of all knowledge and all belief. Being able to provide an answer to those questions of meaning indicates both a belief system and that the thinker has at least tried to respond to those questions. It is not knowledge, it is belief—but in order to be meaningful it has to be learned. If there were no genuine questioning there could be no authentic human being. It was William Temple who wrote somewhere that if eating of the forbidden fruit from the tree of knowledge led to a fall—then it was a fall upwards!

The Creation of Order

Religious systems of the world have all tried to impose order on the apparent chaos of creation. The Genesis story is not alone in the Old Testament that seeks to do that, the abominations of Leviticus are also a system of order imposed by early thinkers upon an apparently unstructured world (Douglas, 1966). Trying to impose meaning upon an apparently meaningless world is part of that human condition described so cogently by Fromm and cited above. But what happens when the meaninglessness of a situation becomes apparent and oppressive? What happens when events seem disordered and the problems of life become apparent? That question is posed again—why?

The question leads to the start of the learning process but in a great deal of recent writing about human learning the process of reflection has become a central concern (Mezirow, 1981, Boud et al., 1985, Jarvis, 1987). However, it is perhaps significant that many years ago Dewey (1958 ed., p 66) wrote:

> When thinking is successful, its career closes in transforming the disordered into the orderly, the mixed-up into the distinguished or placed, the unclear and ambiguous into the defined and unequivocal, the disconnected into the systematized. . . .
>
> Reflective inquiry moves in each particular case from differences to unity; from indeterminate and ambiguous position to clear determination, from confusion and disorder to system. When thought in a given case has reached its goal of organized totality, of definite relations of distinctly placed elements . . .

Here, then, Dewey is suggesting that as a result of reflection order is created out of chaos. Like the early thinkers who suggested theologies that related the imposition of ordered meaning upon a disordered physical cosmos, so the reflective learning process does the same on a disordered subjective experience of the world. The question is answered and a system of meaning is created out of disorder and the parallel between the biblical and the learning process is complete. Reflection—meditation—is at the heart of the process of religious growth and further reference is made to this below.

Conversion

Over recent years the work of Mezirow has been significant in adult learning theory and it is to one of his earlier papers on this topic that attention is focused here. In it he (1978) first discussed the idea of perspective transform which he (1978, p 101) describes in the following manner:

> A meaning perspective refers to the structure of cultural assumptions within which new experience is assimilated to—and transformed by—one's past experience.

Mezirow's position and the thesis of this paper are close in as much as the personal meaning perspective is cultural and assimilated by the individual within the process of socialization. It is by using the biographical store of culture that enables the person to give meaning to an experience but also when a major life change is experienced it enables the learner to see experiences differently, that is, to derive a different sense of meaning from them or impose a different sense of meaning upon them. However, through the process of maturation human beings have a variety of experiences some of which might intergrate creatively with the previous biography but sometimes a process of restructuring occurs. Mezirow suggests that it occurs in three stages: alienation from previous perspectives, reframing and reconceptualizing and, finally, re-integration.

Mezirow admits that he was greatly influenced by the work of Paulo Freire who also regarded learning as transformation, but he used the term *conscientization*, which refers to "the process in which men, not as recipients but as knowing subjects, achieve a deepening awareness both of the sociocultural reality which shapes their lives and of their capacity to transform that reality." (Freire, 1972b, 51n) But Freire's work arose within the context of liberation theology (Gutierrez, 1974) with its exciting synthesis of Christian thought and Marxism.

Indeed it was Karl Marx who considered that because of the structures of society, the socialization process resulted in a false class consciousness. This has led critical theorists, such as Habermas (1972), to postulate that people acquire a false consciousness and one of the main forms of learning is emancipatory learning, which is the process of "emancipation from seemingly 'natural' constraint" (Habermas, 1972, p 311).

Thus it may be seen that in learning theory people can come to themselves, see the world differently and be emancipated from the structures into which they are born. Or, in other words, "he came to himself" (Luke, 15:17), he saw the world differently and changed direction, which is the meaning of the Greek work μετανοω, to change one's mind, to see things differently or to be converted.

Growth and Development

For Dewey (1916), education is growth. By this he meant that life itself is a process in which human beings develop and grow because it is a process of having new experiences, new learning and continuous transformation of experiences and systems of meaning. There is a volume of literature on the stages of adult development and it is significant that learning is not always seen as crucial because it is taken for granted within the process. Gradually there is also emerging a literature of faith development in which Fowler (1981) relates faith development to the quest for meaning. At the very heart of growth lies certain forms of learning—learning that is reflective, learning that is encouraging human autonomy and responsibility in thought and action. Indeed, learning from the experiences of living is at the very foundation of growth. Learning is growth and maturation. There can be no maturation without learning, although there can be physical growth merely through imbibing food and drink. But "man shall not live by bread alone but by every word that proceeds from the mouth of God" (Matt. 4:4). That is, man is matured by learning, and in this case, it is learning from the established religious answers to those questions of meaning.

It was pointed out earlier that an intrinsic part of some learning experiences is reflection/meditation and there are many accounts in religious literature of the mystics who spent their time contemplating the mysteries of the world in order to mature and seek holiness. For other religious people, contemplation is not the answer to Christian maturity—living a good life is more important and for them there may apparently be little time in their lives to spend in contemplation. However, recent learning theorists have begun to recognize that there is a process of reflection-in-action (Schon, 1983), which itself suggests that the good life lived may also be underpinned with the process of learning from experience. Freire (1972a, pp 56–57) suggests:

> Problem-posing education affirms men as beings in the process of *becoming*—as unfinished, uncompleted beings in and with a likewise unfinished reality. Indeed, in contrast to other animals who are unfinished, but not historical, men know themselves to be unfinished; they are aware of their incompleteness and this awareness lies at the very roots of education as an exclusively human manifestation. The unfinished character of men and the transformational character of reality necessitate that education be an ongoing acticity. (Freire's italics)

For Freire, then, a particular form of education, and of learning, is important for the growth and development of the human being, so that the human being can be and become in this world.

Utopia

What should be the outcome of learning? Perhaps the quotation from Paulo Freire (1972a) begins to provide an answer when he discusses the idea of an unfinished reality. Elsewhere, he (1972b, p 51)) continues with this theme when he writes:

> It is as conscious beings that men are not only *in* the world, but *with* the world, together with other men. Only men, as 'open' beings, are able to achieve the complex operation of simultaneously transforming the

world by their own action and grasping and expressing the world's reality in their creative language. (Freire's italics)

For Freire, human beings have both to grasp and understand creatively this complex reality of the world but also they have to transform it, to humanize it in the way that "it reveals the presence of men" (ibid. p 55) who have grown and are capable of creating a utopia on earth. This, then, is the human ideal—throughout history humankind has looked to the future, a metahistorical future, when the world will be utopian—be it heaven on earth, the Kingdom of God or the classless society.

Molding Humankind

There is a paradox to this analysis which is contained in this final section. Once the self has formed and the mind become a relatively independent entity it is able to contemplate the very process by which it was formed. It is able to be critical of the very culture that has made it what it is and being itself becomes problematic. The restless search for meaning has begun, but for others there is another process: if there are potential learners then there might even be teachers. Often they start with another approach to learning; Freire calls it the banking approach to education and elsewhere it has been called "education from above" (Jarvis, 1985). This is when the information to be learned is presented to people in a fixed curriculum and in an authoritative manner. Then, the learning does not start from disjuncture or from questions of why, then there need be no reflection, only an endeavor to memorize what has been given.

Much education is like this and the processes which have been described above may be viewed from a different perspective. There is no disjuncture until it is deliberately created, there is no question before an answer is given, there is no freedom to reflect only the opportunity to memorize and there is no independent growth only an acceptance of the answers which are provided. The freedom of the quest for meaning is replaced by a certainty that is provided by others which as Fromm suggests might actually intrude into the quest and hinder it. But as he (1984 ed.) writes elsewhere, there is a fear of freedom and a need for authority in many people and so they welcome the answers that are provided and sometimes they cling to them. This is not to suggest that there is not a place for teachers—there certainly is—but the role might require some form of reconceptualization within the context of humankind's quest for meaning.

Some analysts see this as a process of cultural and social reproduction (Bourdieu and Passeron, 1977), and reproduction is a much lesser form of creation if it is creative at all. The outcome is a molded person. But this raises questions about the nature and morality of teaching, which is being considered in another paper. Since oftentimes teaching is an imposition of thoughts and ideas upon another person and since they do not necessarily stem from the learner's questioning process, they have to be presented with care, but without care and consideration the teaching process might well be regarded as one of symbolic violence (Bourdieu and Passeron, 1977). Then it is the process of invading the person in order to mold and reproduce a person, like everybody else, so that people fit into the machine—cogs in a complicated machine—which was part of the question raised at the outset of this paper.

All who proclaim, whether teacher or preacher, have to be aware of this criticism and also be aware that in seeking to mold individuals, a very dangerous and responsible undertaking has been embarked upon: the making of the person in the image of the person. But in order to do it either learning has to be seen from within the behaviorist approach or the person has to be seen as mindless and malleable and irresponsible.

CONCLUSIONS

This paper started with a question: to what extent is learning itself a religious process and that question must now be answered. Is learning a religious phenomenon? Clearly it may be but in some cases it may not be. Perhaps it is important to separate the elements in order to elaborate on this conclusion. Learning has two elements: a process and a content. The process might be regarded as religious in certain situation, irrespective of whether the content is religious or not. However, there may be times within a religious context that the teaching and learning process may not be religious, even though the content may be.

Such a conclusion raises other issues and just two of these are touched upon here.

It is clear from the above discussion that learning is fundamentally about the human being and, therefore, such definitions of learning that do not take the human person into account contain implications for humanity that require a great deal of consideration. This raises fundamental questions about the nature of some of the most widely cited definitions of learning itself and about many of the practices of teaching and learning.

One other point that needs to be made is that because learning is about the achievement of personhood and even utopian ideals, it requires a great deal of consideration from those who purport to speak on behalf of religious organizations—but as yet, unfortunately, there is no theology of learning.

In order to live life to the full human beings have to learn that underlying all meaningful living lies learning and the search for meaning is itself a learning quest, one that might be inhibited if answers that claim a degree of certainty are taught, discovered or professed. This is one of the religious paradoxes of learning and so the question— why?—may never be answered with certainty, if human beings are to achieve the fullness of their own humanity.

REFERENCES

Berger, P. 1966, *Invitation to Sociology*. Harmondsworth, Penguin.
Boud, D., Keogh, R., and Walker, D. 1985, *Reflection: Turning Experience into Learning*. London, Kogan Page.
Bourdieu, P. and Passeron, J-C. 1977, *Reproduction—in Education, Society and Culture*. London, Sage.
Dewey, J. 1916, *Democracy and Education*. New York, The Free Press.
Dewey, J. 1958, *Experience and Nature*. New York, Dover Publications.
Douglas, M. 1966, *Purity and Danger*. Harmondsworth, Penguin.
Fowler, J. W. 1981, *Stages of Faith*. New York, Harper & Row.
Freire, P. 1972a, *Pedagogy of the Oppressed*. Harmondsworth, Penguin.
Freire, P. 1972b, *Cultural Action for Freedom*. Harmondsworth, Penguin.
Fromm, E. 1949, *Man for Himself*. London, Routledge and Kegan Paul.
Fromm, E. 1984, *The Fear of Freedom*. London, ARK Books.
Gutierrez, G. 1974, *A Theology of Liberation*. London, SCM Press.
Habermas, J. 1972, *Knowledge and Human Interests*. London, Heinemann.
Heidegger, M. 1962, *Being and Time*. London, SCM Press.

Hilgard, E. R. and Atkinson, R. C. 1967, *Introduction to Psychology*. New York, Harcourt, Brace and World, Inc.

Jarvis, P. 1983, Religiosity: Man's Responses to the Problem of Meaning, *Bulletin of the Institute of Worship and Religious Architecture*. Birmingham, University of Birmingham.

Jarvis, P. 1985, *The Sociology of Adult and Continuing Education*. London, Croom Helm.

Jarvis, P. 1987, *Adult Learning in the Social Context*. London, Croom Helm.

Luckmann, T. 1967, *Invisible Religion*. London, Collier-Macmillan.

Mezirow, J. 1978, Perspective Transformation in *Adult Education*, Vol. XXVIII, No. 2.

Schon, D. 1983, *The Reflective Practitioner*. New York, Basic Books.

Schutz, A. and Luckmann, T. 1974, *Everyday Structures of the Life World*. London, Heinemann.

Strauss, A. ed. 1964, *George Herbert Mead on Social Psychology*. Chicago, University of Chicago Press.

Holy Bible. Revised Standard Version. London, Nelson.

PART II
FAITH AND KNOWLEDGE

CHAPTER 2

Truth, Belief, and Knowledge

CAROLYN CLARK

Home is where one starts from.

—T. S. Eliot, "East Coker"

Any task, no matter how abstruse or theoretical, has as its point of origin a personal horizon, those sets of experiences, values, and beliefs which define our perspective, or, in Eliot's terms, our home. This book is no exception. The preface, describes the purpose of this book as providing a kind of binocular vision of life experience, viewing that experience through the dual lenses of theology and adult education and placing those lenses or interpretations of experience in dialogue with one another. It is possible to do this, or at least to make a good attempt, because each of us contributing to this dialogue has experience and some degree of expertise in both realms. Most of us have advanced degrees in both theology and in adult education; many of us are ordained or have ministerial experience. These dual backgrounds mean that the examination and exploration of "the two traditions of interpretation of the one life experience" are not themselves two distinct tasks but rather one interrelated task, since our perspectives have been shaped by both traditions. Our vision, in a real sense, is binocular and what we see when we look at life experience is colored by our experience in both arenas.

While the above is an argument for the selection of this particular group of contributors rather than inviting pure adult educators to dialogue with untainted theologians, it also provides another starting point which I consider even more interesting, and that is that this particular binocular vision is such a common one. When I began my doctoral studies in adult education I was struck by the number of people in the field with theological backgrounds. In my own program at the time there were three other students who were either ordained or had advanced degrees in theology, and the department chair was an ordained minister. Further, it was possible to name others prominent in the field with similar backgrounds. Why is this so common? What is this intrinsic and yet unexamined connection between theology and adult education?

I have a hunch the connection lies in the most fundamental of arenas, namely in how we think about our experience and make sense of it. I believe people in both fields think relationally, by which I mean that they view the world in relational terms and understand those relationships as dynamic and interactive. Let me illustrate this in several ways, first with a piece of my own experience and then by examining the relational assumptions underlying both fields.

In addition to my dual experiences of the ministry and adult education, I also have had professional experience in another field—addictions treatment. It is the different way of thinking characteristic of the third field which highlights for me the similar approach to the world shared by the first two. My religious tradition is Roman Catholic, and I worked for more than fifteen years in various ministerial positions within the Church. My particular focus was on adult spiritual development, though I also addressed issues of leadership formation and the development of a faith community. To say that I understood my ministry in terms of relationship seems to belabor the obvious: for the religious person the fundamental relationship that exists is between each person and God, with that finding expression within the bonds of the faith community; all ministry is a manifestation of that primal relationship and the minister is understood as an enfleshment of God's loving presence. I was conscious of both the transcendant relationship that encompassed all of what I did with people, as well as the relationships that I established with them personally; in fact, I saw the quality of our relationship as central to my work. Similarly, as an adult educator I have an abiding interest in the relationships I establish with learners, believing that the character of those relationships has a direct impact on the quality of learning which results. Furthermore, I see the learners themselves as situated in multiple relationships—with the subject matter, with themselves, with one another, with their particular social contexts, with the future—and that these relational layers are interactive.

My experience as an addictions counselor was very different, however. It is not that I could not think relationally in this context; certainly the relationships I established with clients were an important feature of their recovery and an aspect I gave serious attention to. Further, the addictions process can be understood as a relationship which a person develops with a chemical, and that relationship has a significant impact on all other relationships the person has. What is different is how this reality is understood by the field itself. Here the thinking is not relational but objectified. The dominant explanatory model is medical, one which sees the client as having a disease which must be treated. The counselor stands on the outside of this objective reality and seeks to manipulate the environment in such a way as to encourage the client to make the changes needed to counter the disease process. It is a very different way of thinking from the relational mode shared by the fields of theology and adult education. Not surprising, it is not one I found congenial for long. In fact, I moved into adult education after working with addicted clients for several years because I came to understand clients as learners who needed to find a totally new way to make sense of their experience, and I found few resources in the addictions field that helped facilitate that kind of learning. My relational way of thinking was not a good fit within a field that thought in more objective ways, and I chose another field which I found more congenial.

If my experience suggests a connection between theology and adult education that arises from a relational way of viewing the world, an examination of the foundational assumptions or beliefs of each field will illustrate more clearly how the relational view is constructed and how it functions to organize and give meaning to experience.

VIEWING LIFE THROUGH A RELATIONAL LENS

The View of the Theologian

The Christian tradition is rooted in scripture, and in those scriptures relationship is a central concept. I would even argue that it is *the* central concept. From the biblical point of view, relationship is essential to life. Both Old and New Testaments make the assumption that being is unity and that its source is in God. To be alive is to be connected to God, and loss of that unity, imaged in the scriptures as separation, is death. Further, connection to God also leads to connection with other human beings and with all of creation. Relationship, therefore, is essential to being.

This original theme of unity is imaged more dramatically in the creation stories of Genesis. In the first, Genesis 1:1–2:4, God carefully creates an organized, harmonious world, then creates human beings in the divine image to exercise dominion over that world. In the second story, Genesis 2:4–25, God is described as more anthropomorphic, creating Adam first out of the clay of the earth, then the garden and all creatures to address the man's needs, and finally creating the woman, Eve, to be his partner. Both stories present a world that is unified both within itself and with its creator. This original unity is broken, however, by the woman and man deciding, apart from God, to eat from the tree of knowledge of good and evil. It is this act of separation which breaks the relationship of unity and leads to death. This first Fall from primal unity is prelude to further acts of separation: the conflict between Cain and Abel (Gen. 4), the story of Noah and the flood (Gen. 5a–9), and the scattering of humankind after the attempt to build the tower of Babel (Gen. 11).

If in Genesis 1–11 we have the creation of unity and its disruption, the rest of the scriptures (Gen. 12–Rev. 22) are essentially the unfolding of salvation as the restoration of that unity. Beginning with Abraham and the calling of the Hebrew people to be in a covenantal relationship with God, God labors for that restoration. The Mosaic law is God's attempt to introduce life into a broken world; the ritual law showed how to be united with God, while the civil law attempted to reestablish human relationships. While these efforts were restricted to the Hebrew people, they were a reflection of the original unity of creation and prefigured the ultimate union to come.

It is with the Incarnation that this theme of the restoration of unity is made most clear and most visible. God became human in order to gather all people to him and reestablish that original state of unity. Jesus espresses this fundamental mission in his priestly prayer before his crucifixion: "I pray . . . that all may be one as you, Father, are in me, and I in you; I pray that they may be one in us. . . . that their unity may be complete" (John 17:20–21, 23). The salvific act is at its core an act of love which restores all creation to its original state of unity with God.

This view of God's plan for creation has implications for our understanding of God. If divine activity is directed towards the creation of unity, then the nature of God must be deeply relational. To speak of God is to speak of intimate community, a community whose life principle is love. This conceptualization of God as triune in nature is a central tenet of Christian belief, and the three Persons of the Trinity are defined in terms of their relationship to one another: the Father's love for the Son finding expression in the Spirit. That relationship is most dramatically expressed in the famous Rublev icon. In it we see three angelic figures seated around a small table on which rests a chalice. The three figures are arranged in such a way as to suggest a dynamic movement among them, a circulation of life and love that spills over to include the viewer and all of creation. It is a vivid image of the divine life as loving relationship, and readily suggests that the Christian life is a sharing in that relationship.

Christians hold a corollary belief about the nature of men and women, that they too are relational beings. We cannot exist without one another. "Society is a tissue of personal relationships expressed through mutual confidence and love. . . . Life in common is one of the great answers to the quest for meaning and happiness" (*A New Catechism*, 1967). Ratzinger (1979) draws the theological implications of this belief:

> . . . human beings live and depend in a very real and at the same time very complex sense on one another. . . . The one, whole [person] is deeply marked by his [or her] membership of the whole of [humankind]—the one "Adam". It thus becomes clear that [a person] is a being that can only "be" by virtue of others. (p 184)

Faith in God is likewise understood in terms of relationship. It is not simply a matter of assent to a body of religious beliefs but is rather a personal relationship with a transcendant God. Fowler (1981), in his study of faith development, describes faith as "our way of finding coherence in and giving meaning to the multiple forces and relations that make up our lives. . . . a way of seeing [ourselves] in relation to others against a background of shared meaning and purpose" (p 4).

He suggests that as we mature we locate "centers of value and power" which give coherence to our lives, and that our relationship to these centers is one of trust and loyalty. In a purely religious context the center of value and power is God, and while Fowler's conceptualization includes more than expressions of religious faith, it nonetheless captures the essential relational character of faith in all contexts.

It is clear, then, that theology has a relational perspective since, as we have seen, salvation history, the nature of God and human beings, and faith are all conceptualized in relational terms. Further, these relationships are always understood as dynamic and interactive.

The View of the Adult Educator

There are parallels in the adult education universe to the major theological categories we have considered. Analogous to salvation history is the theoretical or philosophical framework that guides the adult educator. The conceptualization of God and human beings is paralleled in how we understand the teacher/facilitator and the learner. And faith is analogous to learning in that both are shaped by the theoretical frame and the conceptualization of the major actors. All of these are relational in character.

Elias and Merriam (1980) identify six different philosophical orientations found in adult education: liberal, progressive, behaviorist, humanistic, radical, and analytical. While each philosophical position understands the purpose of adult education differently, there is a common thread which unites them. Each conceives education as a process which occurs within a social and cultural context and, while it involves and benefits the learner, it also has an impact on those elements to which the learner is related. In some cases this relational aspect is explicit. In behaviorism, for example, the immediate purpose is to promote a change in the learner's behavior, but the larger view is societal: "Since most of society's problems involve the behavior of humans living in them, controlling human behavior can result in a better society. . . . Skinner is convinced . . . that a 'technology of behavior' is the only means of solving social problems and ensuring survival of the human species" (Elias and Merriam, 1980, p 85–86). In both progressive and radical adult education the goal of societal change is even more explicit. In other philosophical frameworks the relational aspect is more implicit. Humanism falls in this category with its primary emphasis on the enhancement of personal growth. That growth, however, is facilitated by a relationship of acceptance and total positive regard on the part of the teacher towards the learner, and it is meant to stimulate the same attitude in the learner towards others. The outcome, while not overt social change, does involve more than the individual learner.

There is also a relational foundation to the conceptualization of the teacher and learner in adult education. Here too there is a range of positions: the teacher can be manager, organizer, facilitator; the learner can be self-directed, knowledge-oriented, critically reflective (to suggest only a few of the options). What unites all these positions, however, is the degree of interaction between the teacher and adult learner. Unlike the traditional pedagogic model where the teacher's focus is on the transmission of subject content to a passive learner, in adult education the learner is active and the teacher's role is to facilitate that learning process. We have moved from what Freire (1970) called the banking model, to what Belenky, Clinchy, Goldberger, and Tarule (1986) call midwifing the learning process. Brookfield (1989) argues that the roles of teacher and learner begin to overlap and interpenetrate: "At its base is a vision of education that assumes the equality of teachers and learners and the interchangeability of teaching and learning roles" (p 201).

Finally, the learning process itself has a relational component. Most definitions of learning focus on instrumental gains resulting from "changes in knowledge, attitudes, values, or skills" (Darkenwald and Merriam, 1982, p 9). Such a narrow focus misses the relational dimension which is most visible when questions of significance are raised. Ingham (1990) asked learners to talk about the most important things they had learned in their lives, and from these data he concludes that "learning is a change in the actual or potential relationship a person has with some aspect of the world" (p 1). This is somewhat different from the theological realm where faith is itself a relationship. Here learning is understood as shaping the relationships the learner has with the world.

The relational way of thinking which characterizes both theology and adult education is important to understand, not only because it demonstrates a fundamental link between the two fields, but even more because it shapes how both approach important questions about knowledge, belief, and behavior. We turn to some of those questions now, beginning with how theologians and adult educators go about knowing, as well as what each means by knowledge.

KNOWING THE KNOWN

If relationality is a major component of perspective in both adult education and theology, then the process of knowing must also be relational in character. This has been conceptualized by others in several ways. Belenky et al. (1986) distinguish between separate and connected knowing, with separate knowing maintaining distance between the person and the object of inquiry, while connected knowing posits a relationship between the two based on empathy. This echoes the distinction between positivist and interpretative paradigms of inquiry. Postmodernists like Weedon (1987) argue for a connection between knowing and particular sociopolitical contexts, a connection which makes all knowing necessarily partial and incomplete. Bateson and Bateson (1987) construe knowing in terms of systems theory and argue that knowing is at its core "a matter of relationship" (p xii) as a person interacts with the material world. All these perspectives posit various types of relationship within the process of knowing.

I want to suggest that knowing for the theologian and for the adult educator is similarly relational. My interest here is not so much the philosophical arenas in both fields but rather the practical realm. In everyday practice, how do we go about the business of knowing? And what are the relational dimensions of that activity? While differing from one another in process, I believe that knowing for the adult educator and the theologian is similar in its relational dimension. For both that relational quality is personal, dynamic, and highly interactive.

For the theologian these qualities are particularly straightforward. Palmer (1983), reflecting various ways of knowing, notes that objectified knowing sees the world as an object to be manipulated and is expressed as power over. Its source is in the desire to control. For the Christian, however, there is another source, that of love, and it is expressed in relational terms. "A knowledge that springs from love will implicate us in the web of life; it will wrap the knower and the known in compassion, in a bond of awesome responsibility as well as transforming joy; it will call us to involvement, mutuality, accountability" (p 9).

This web or series of connections has a strong biblical base. Leon-Dufour (1973, p 296) notes that "knowledge for the Semite is more than a recondite process of understanding because it involves an existential relationship." The source of knowledge here is the self-revelation of God. Arising out of love, its purpose is to invite humanity to share in the divine life (Ezek. 36:26). The connection between knowledge and God is especially clear in the Genesis story, where the Fall is precipitated by Adam and Eve trying to obtain knowledge apart from God. That effort, in its distortion of the divine order, results in separation from God. Subsequent knowledge, or self-revelation of God, is directed towards restoring the original relationship of unity and oneness. Today it is easy to think of this divine revelation as static, residing in a sacred canon of texts, but it is important to see this revelation as dynamic and rooted in the experience of believers. One of the things that distinguishes the Christian faith from other religions is the Christian belief in the intimate engagement of God in human affairs. In the Old Testament, the Hebrew people viewed God as intimately involved in their history and they read their life experience as a theological text. This is extended in the New Testament when the presence of God in history becomes literally incarnate in the Christ, and that presence continued in the community of believers, the Church. Knowing, then, in biblical terms, was a function of being in relationship with God and it was mediated by human experience.

There is also an existential dimension to this religious way of knowing. Jarvis in Chapter 1 speaks of the question "why?" lying at the heart of human existence. With Dunne (1981) I would prefer to image that in a less cognitive way, speaking instead of the human experience of wonder which leads us beyond our immediate knowing. At a profound level we can see how wonder, in the sense of the restlessness St. Augustine spoke of, leads us to God, the One who planted the wonder within us, leading us into Mystery, and therefore in a real sense into unknowing. This is developed in a systematic way by St. Ignatius of Loyola into a specific method of prayerful knowing he called the Spiritual Exercises (Fleming, 1978). Significantly, the Exercises evolved out of his own experience of prayer and his efforts to discern God's will in his life. God remains the source of knowledge, then, in the religious domain but God can be manifested both in history and in internal experience.

If knowing for theologians is rooted in revelation within human experience, for adult educators it is rooted in exploration or discovery. Experience here is also central to the process. Knowles (1980), as part of a series of assumptions about adult learning, argues that in adulthood personal experience becomes a major resource for learning. While the other assumptions he proposes are not supported by empirical research, the preeminent role of experience in adult learning has become what Brookfield (1986, p 98) calls "a 'given' in the literature of adult learning." Brookfield goes on to claim that "the development of critical reflection on experiences, along with the collaborative interpretation and exchange of such experiences, is . . . one of the most significant forms of adult learning in which individuals can engage."

The relational character of knowing in adult education is somewhat obscured, at least in the United States, by the emphasis placed on self-direction in the learning process and by the individualistic goal of increased autonomy. On the surface this does not look relational in character. It is my belief, however, that it is highly relational. Even in Knowles's (1975) rather linear conceptualization of the self-directed learning process, the learner takes responsibility for the process but seeks out information and insight from multiple sources. And the facilitator's role is to enable that learning by providing support, encouragement, and vision. Brookfield (1986), in his study of successful self-directed learners, enriches the concept further by developing the collaborative aspect. He suggest that the concept of field dependence, with its emphasis on context and on the holistic view, is more descriptive of the self-directed learner than the individualistic, analytical thrust that characterizes field dependence. It is this awareness of and sensitivity to context which enables the learner to develop critical reflectivity, an ability that for Brookfield is central to self-directed learning. He connects this with autonomy, which he defines as "the possession of an understanding and awareness of a range of alternative possibilities" (1986, p 58). Autonomy then can exist only within a context of relatedness.

If this relational quality is essential to the concept of self-directed learning, which outwardly appears individualistic, then it is even more evident in more collaborative expressions of adult learning. Whether involving connections with other people, with various content areas, with prior and current experience, or with particular contexts, knowing for the adult educator is a relational process that is personal, interactive, and highly dynamic, just as it is for the theologian.

CLAIMING THE TRUTH

Given the relational way of knowing shared by theology and adult education, how are we to understand the object of that knowing? How do we know what is true? Again, I want to situate that question within the context of our everyday experience as much as possible, and not in philosophical discourse. The answers are both easy and difficult.

In the theological realm the easy answer is that truth is not so much propositional as personal, enfleshed as it is in the Person who said "I am the way, and the truth, and the life" (John 14:6). To know the truth, therefore, is to know the One who is Truth. But what does that lead us to? Is certainty possible? Obviously not, or there would be no need for faith. Dunne (1981) argues persuasively that, while certainty is not possible, assurance for the believer is. Assurance arises from within a relationship of trust, imaged in the relationship between Jesus and the Father. It is the death/resurrection experience which Dunne (1981, p 49) sees as the source of assurance, the source of faith: "Because he acted as one Assured, and because that Assurance was justified in that uncanny event we call the 'resurrection,' Jesus himself becomes God's Assurance to us that we are never abandoned." For believers the ultimate truth lies in this assurance that God will always be with us, the assurance that our relationship is trustworthy.

For adult educators the easy answer about truth is that it is relative, depending on how the process of inquiry is understood. For positivists there is objective truth, knowable through empirical means; for postpositivists, those who espouse an interpretive approach, truth is highly contextual and personal, a social construct that is knowable through subjective means (Deshler and Hagan, 1989). But just as we did in the religious realm, we can ask if certainty is possible here, and again it is clear that it is not. The whole process of inquiry, whichever paradigm is used, builds on itself and is unending; research findings and theories are replaced by new findings and theories that claim to be better until they too are supplanted. Where is the assurance here? I believe the assurance lies within the process itself, with the ongoing thought and practice that characterizes any viable field of inquiry. It, too, like the trust of the believer in God, is relational and based on trust. We place our trust in the intellectual integrity of the process as well as those who engage in it.

There is a problem in knowing what is true, however, which both adult education and theology share. Relying as both do on experience, the problem lies in how experience is understood. Dewey (1938) understood experience as the way in which we explore and participate in the world, and he saw that process as complex but straightforward. However, poststructuralists argue that experience contains a significant problematic which makes it less reliable as a way of knowing the world and engaging in it. That problematic lies within the nature of subjectivity; we must think about our experience before it can be "ours," yet our thought is not purely our own, but is shaped by language and culture, both of which are socially constructed. Hawkesworth (1989, p 544) points to "the manifold ways in which all human experiences, whether of the external world or of the internal world, are mediated by theoretical presuppositions embedded in language and culture." And this construction is not neutral; it reflects and supports the position of the dominant group in society. We understand our experience in terms devised by the dominant culture, a structuring that takes place apart from our awareness. We are, in this significant arena of interpretation, distanced and possibly alienated from that which we consider to be uniquely our own, our personal experience. For women and for others who stand outside the dominant culture, this separation is most visible, though it affects us all.

Saiving (1979) illustrates this problem of distancing and alienation from personal experience within the context of theology. It is the function of any religious system to reflect on the human condition and render it meaningful, and most do so in overtly patriarchal terms. In the Christian tradition the male innate sense of separation defines the human condition, and it is upon this foundation that the pivotal definitions of sin and virtue are structured. Sin is thus defined as the act of self-assertion at the expense of others; virtue is defined as self-giving love. These are the constructs of the dominant male culture. But women have an innate sense, not of separation, but of connectedness. Saiving suggest that, at the level of experience, women are diminished by selflessness, where they can lose their identity in service to others, and expanded by self-assertion, through which they can redress the balance and extend care to themselves. Yet they must think of their experience in terms established by the dominant culture, in this case by male theologians writing over the centuries, so that what diminishes them is called virtue and what expands them is called sin. This is a dramatic example of the power of ideology to dominate, but my point is that it does so by determining how we think about our experience. It is precisely in this juncture between experience and thought that the problem of subjectivity is located.

I raise this issue not to suggest a way around or through it but rather to illustrate some of the limits within which both theology and adult education function as they go about knowing and making claims to the truth. It is to suggest, in fact, another layer of relationality in knowing which is largely unrecognized in either field but which has serious implications in both. The relationship between the sociocultural norms contained within language and how that shapes personal perceptions of experience is a critical one. To assume there is no dysjuncture between the two is to foster the perspective of the hegemonic culture, often unknowingly, and to thereby perpetuate a distortion of truth. There are voices in adult education (see, for example: Freire, 1970; Mezirow, 1991; Brookfield, 1987) and in theology (the preeminent liberation theologian is Gutierrez, 1973) who argue for a more critical perspective, but they are marginalized in both arenas. Inclusion of their voices into the mainstream discourse of both fields would only enrich the knowledge base and claims to truth in both.

BECOMING WISE

The overlapping issues of truth, belief, and knowledge merge into a single concept: wisdom. I will conclude by examining how wisdom is understood by theologians and by adult educators. As with the other concepts, they share a relational perspective on this ultimate form of knowledge.

The Christian tradition of wisdom is mixed, having elements of Greek philosophy as well as Hebrew spirituality. Drawing from the Greek tradition, Christian theology recognizes both practical wisdom, concerning right action in human affairs, and philosophical wisdom, directed towards understanding the ultimate nature of things (Clayton and Birren, 1980). This duality parallels the dichotomy within Christian thought between the profane and the sacred, this world and the next. Philosophical or divine wisdom is considered a manifestation of the presence of God. Because of its divine nature, it is recognized as a gift from God rather than an achievement of the intellect. However, the gift is not random. Reflecting the influence of Hebrew spirituality, Christians believe that all the spiritual gifts, including wisdom, are an outgrowth of the relationship maintained between the individual and God. This relationship is developed most commonly in this tradition through a life of prayer and asceticism. To receive the gift of divine wisdom is to share in the life and vision of God (Leon-Dufour, 1973). Wisdom in the Christian tradition, therefore, was understood in trans-cendant terms; as such it was defined by and served a religious system.

In adult education the focus is placed more on the process of be-coming wise and it is understood in terms of learning. The most useful theory to help us understand how experience produces learning and how that learning effects growth and change in the individual is the work of Mezirow (1981, 1991). In his study of women returning to college in the 1970s, he identified a ten-step process of the change in consciousness which these women experienced, a process he called per-spective transformation. Mezirow suggests that all human beings func-tion within meaning structures, and he understands learning as changes in these structures. A meaning structure functions as a lens or filter through which personal experience is mediated and by which it is interpreted, thereby bringing coherence to those experiences. As an experience passes through the meaning structure, it becomes assimilated into it, either reinforcing the original structure if it was completely congruent with past experiences, or gradually reshaping the structure if less congruent. A radically new experience, what Mezirow calls "a disorienting dilemma," is too different to be assimilated into the cur-rent structure; it is either rejected altogether, or it stimulates the for-mation of a new meaning structure that can assimilate it. This process of transformation can be sudden or gradual, but the direction of growth is towards greater autonomy and responsibility as the meaning structure becomes steadily more inclusive. Mezirow describes this more authentic or superior perspective as:

> not only one that is a more inclusive or discriminating experience of integrating but also one that is sufficiently permeable to allow one access to other perspectives. This makes possible movement to still more inclu-sive and discriminating perspectives. (1981, p 9)

In this description of the superior meaning perspective we recognize the expansive horizon of the wise person. What Mezirow does, I believe, is give us a way of understanding the developmental process, and particularly how wisdom develops through the process of perspective transformation over time. The steady expansion and even transformation of the meaning structure leads to that wider perspective which characterizes the wise person in all cultural traditions.

What both adult education and theology share in their conceptualizations of wisdom is an expanded sense of being in relationship. Fowler (1981), in describing the final stages of faith development, illustrates this relational quality. In the penultimate stage, paradoxical-consolidative faith, the person recognizes the integrity and truth in other positions and belief systems, and identifies with a community beyond tribal, racial, class, or ideological boundaries. The ultimate, and rare, stage of universalizing faith is characterized by a sense of oneness with all people. This is fully congruent with Mezirow's superior meaning perspective.

Wisdom, then, the capstone of knowing, has the same relational foundation in theology and in adult education. And it is one final piece of evidence that the intrinsic connection between the two fields arises from a shared relational perspective on life experience.

REFERENCES

A New Catechism, 1967, New York, Herder and Herder.

Bateson, G., and Bateson, M. C. 1987, *Angels Fear: Towards an Epistemology of the Sacred.* Toronto, Bantam Books.

Belenky, M., Clinchy, B., Goldberger, N., and Tarule, J. 1986, *Women's Ways of Knowing.* New York, Basic Books.

Brookfield, S. 1986, *Understanding and Facilitating Adult Learning.* San Francisco, Jossey-Bass.

Brookfield, S. 1987, *Developing Critical Thinkers.* San Francisco, Jossey-Bass.

Brookfield, S. 1989, Facilitating Adult Learning. In *Handbook of Adult and Continuing Education.* S. Merriam & P. Cunningham, Eds., San Francisco, Jossey-Bass.

Clayton, V., and Birren, J. E. 1980, The development of wisdom across the lifespan. In *Lifespan Development and Behavior*, Vol. 3, P. Baltes and O. Brim, Jr., eds., New York, Academic Press.

Darkenwald, G., and Merriam, S. B. 1982, *Adult Education: Foundations of Practice.* San Francisco, Jossey-Bass.

Deshler, D. and Hagan, N. Adult Education Research: Issues and Directions.

34   ADULT EDUCATION AND THEOLOGICAL INTERPRETATIONS

In *Handbook of Adult and Continuing Education*, S. Merriam and P. Cunningham, eds., San Francisco, Jossey-Bass.

Dewey, J. 1938, *Experience and Education*. London, Collier-Macmillan.

Dunne, T. 1981, *We Cannot Find Words*. Denville, NJ, Dimension Books.

Elias, J. L., and Merriam, S. B., 1980, *Philosophical Foundations of Adult Education*. Huntington, NY, Krieger.

Fleming, D. L. 1978, *The Spiritual Exercises of St. Ignatius: A Literal Translation and a Contemporary Reading*. St. Louis, Institute of Jesuit Sources.

Fowler, J. 1981, *Stages of Faith*. San Francisco, Harper and Row.

Freire, P. 1970, *Pedagogy of the Oppressed*. New York, Herder and Herder.

Gutierrez, G. 1973, *A Theology of Liberation*. New York, Orbis.

Hawkesworth, M. E. 1989, Knowers, knowing, and known: Feminist theory and claims of truth. *Signs: Journal of Women in Culture and Society*, Vol. 14, pp. 533–557.

Knowles, M. 1975, *Self-Directed Learning*. New York, Cambridge.

Knowles, M. 1980, *The Modern Practice of Adult Education: From Pedagogy to Andragogy* (2nd Ed.). New York, Cambridge Books.

Ingham, R. J. 1990, *Learning as Relating*, unpublished manuscript.

Leon-Dufour, X. ed., 1973, *Dictionary of Biblical Theology*. New York, Seabury.

Mezirow, J. 1981, A critical theory of adult learning and education. *Adult Education*, Vol. 32, pp. 3–24.

Mezirow, J. 1991, *Transformative Dimensions of Adult Learning*. San Francisco, Jossey-Bass.

New American Bible. Nashville-New York, Nelson.

Palmer, P. 1983, *To Know as We Are Known: A Spirituality of Education*. San Francisco, Harper and Row.

Ratzinger, J. 1979, *Introduction to Christianity*. New York, Seabury Press.

Saiving, V. 1979, The human situation: A feminine view. In *Womanspirit Rising: A Feminist Reader in Religion*. C. Christ & J. Plaskow, eds., San Francisco, Harper and Row.

Weedon, C. 1987, *Feminist Practice and Poststructuralist Theory*. Oxford, Basil Blackwell.

CHAPTER 3

The Authority of the Word

TRENTON R. FERRO

Every religion has an authoritative source from which it receives inspiration and guidance and to which it appeals for answers and direction. For most of the major religions of the world this authoritative source is the Godhead or Divinity which is the center of that religion's awe and worship. This Divinity, in turn, reveals itself to, and establishes communication with, its human adherents. These revelations and communications are recorded in written documents which, because of their divinely inspired contents, have gained authoritative status as well. I will discuss this topic, the authority of the Word, within the Judeo/Christian framework. Readers of other religious persuasions should transfer the major developments of this chapter to their various belief systems.

Although much has been written about authority (Moltman & Küng, 1981; Quebedeauz, 1982; Penaskovic, 1987), Word/word (see, for example, Campbell, 1950; Debrunner, Kleinknecht, Proksch, & Kittel, 1967; Bergman, Lutzmann, & Schmidt, 1978), and the combination of these two concepts, the authority of the Word/word (including Dodd, 1960; Barr, 1973, 1980; Jodock, 1989; Fiorenza, 1990), the intention of this chapter is neither to review this vast literature in depth nor to add significantly to the theological discussion to which most of this literature is devoted. Rather, I wish to explore the meaning and implications of the concept, "the authority of the Word/word," within the framework of adult education, paying particular attention to the relationship between the role of hermeneutics (the art and science of interpreting meaning) and such constructs as the teaching/learning transaction and various theories of adult development.

AUTHORITY AND THE TEACHER

When we attend our place of worship, participate in a group studying Scripture, or turn on the radio or television, we often hear the preacher or teacher say something of this sort: "The Scripture says," or "The Lord says." Such a statement appeals to the Word as authority. By what or whose authority, however, is that leader actually speaking?

That is the important question: By what or whose authority do religious leaders teach? While the appeal to "Scripture" or "the Lord" implies that Scripture or the Lord is the authoritative source to which appeal is made, is that truly the case? Such appeals are made, quite often, to bolster a position already taken or to support an argument being made. Whose authority is the leader really asking hearers or learners to accept, that of "the Word," some other source of authority, or a combination of the two?

An analysis of the teaching/learning transaction provides evidence that there are actually a number of elements present, in addition to the Scripture or Word to which appeal is made, which bear upon the question of authority. Christian teachers work from within a certain theological tradition—Anabaptist, Anglican, Calvinist, Lutheran, Orthodox, Roman Catholic, and so forth. Whether or not these teachers realize and acknowledge it, some tradition has influenced their own conceptions of, and attitudes toward, the Word and their understanding of its message (see Moltmann & Küng, 1981). These conceptions and attitudes are evident in the training that pastors, teachers, and other leaders receive and in the prepared materials made available to them from denominational publishing houses. They are part of the teacher's theological milieu.

Added to this is the perceived role, function, or status of religious leaders within a particular religious tradition (How does the church teach authoritatively today, 1979; Moltmann & Küng, 1981). By performing such rites as certification, ordination, investiture, or holy orders a church body transmits a special status to those persons so elevated. Those set apart now can speak "with authority" by right of their position in the church body. If that church possesses a hierarchical structure, it may imply as well that authority also attends those persons who hold ecclesiastical office—or may even overtly expect or require respect for such leaders. The higher the position the person holds, the greater is the authority with which she can speak. The authority of the Word and the authority of the office are joined, and the line of demarcation between the two may become hazy or be lost altogether. In fact, many religious systems and leaders demanding the unquestioning obedience of their adherents make no distinction between the two: that which the leader speaks by virtue of her office *is* the authoritative word.

Furthermore, the question of authority is raised by the philosophical position the teacher holds regarding the purpose of education and the role of students in the educational process (Zinn, 1990). If the teacher views his role as one of transmitting knowledge (referred to by Elias & Merriam, 1980, as the "liberal" position) or changing attitudes and behaviors ("behaviorist"; Elias & Merriam, 1980), he accepts responsibility for both the content and process of the educational situation and perceives the learner as passive and the recipient of the content, attitudes, and behaviors he transmits. The role of the learner is to accept and conform. On the other hands, if the teacher views his role as more facilitative ("progressive," "humanistic," or "radical"; Elias & Merriam, 1980), he expects the participant to be much more active in the learning process and even to take major responsibility for her learning experiences and her personal development and growth.

Another, and very significant, aspect of authority deals with the role and function of the interpretive process. What methods do teachers utilize in determining the meaning and application of the authoritative source? Furthermore, what are their expectations of their learners? Do they expect learners to accept their interpretation, which might have been received in turn from others, without question? Or do teachers concentrate on helping learners develop the skills necessary to draw their own understandings from Scripture? Obviously, the stance teachers take on these questions is governed by their theological tradition, their attitude toward church hierarchy and authority, and their philosophical position. This question of interpretation, or hermeneutics, will be discussed further below.

Related to the previous discussion, but deserving of separate mention, is the matter of teaching style. Some teachers view their task as that of organizing and presenting information on skills to be learned. It is the responsibility of students, in turn, to remember and rehearse what has been presented so that they can reproduce what they have been taught. Students are usually expected to be quiet, attentive, and often unquestioning. Many who teach in this manner do so because that is how they were taught, and they have never examined their role, purpose, or function as teachers and how they might best help their students grow and develop.

Other teachers foster openness, often characterized by the freedom to discuss and question, and they provide both the atmosphere and the materials which allow and encourage learners to be inquisitive, to try novel and different interpretations, and to arrive at tentative conclusions which may not be those held by the teachers. Thus the actual ways in which teachers operate in and manage their classrooms—their teaching style—convey a message about the locus of authority. Controlling teachers expect acceptance of what they say because they represent authority, while facilitating teachers allow learners to draw their own conclusions.

By what or whose authority, then, do teachers teach? Although the explicit appeal is made to God or the Scriptures, the implicit appeal may well include one or more of the levels or types of authority discussed briefly above. Teachers may actually be asking, or even expecting, learners to accept what they are saying on the basis of one or more of these levels of authority: theological tradition, ecclesiastical status, philosophical position, interpretive stance, and/or teaching style. These levels of authority may actually be layered, as illustrated in Figure 1. Teachers may be making appeal to several levels of authority when they say, "Thus says the Lord," and participants may be expected to accept as "the Word of the Lord" teaching which has actually passed through several filters or screens of authority.

To what authorities are teachers actually making appeal when they ask learners to accept their teaching? To what levels of authority are learners actually exposed? Through how many filters has the teaching passed? The answers to these questions reflect the position and attitude of teachers, of those persons who, operating from an authoritative position, also use the appeal to authority to support their interpretation and teaching. Frequently, the expectation, whether implicit or explicit, is that learners will accede to the teachers' explications, without question or challenge, because of the teachers' appeal to authority.

ADULT DEVELOPMENT AND AUTHORITY

Just because teachers expect learners to accept what they say because they have appealed to authority does not necessarily mean that the

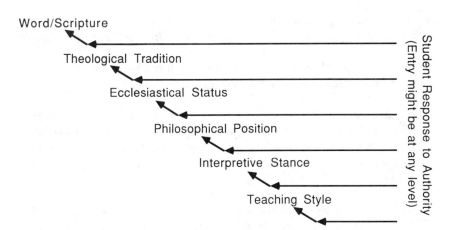

To what levels of authority are learners asked to respond?
To what levels of authority are they actually exposed?
Through how many filters does the teaching pass?

FIGURE 1
Authority Filters or Screens

learners will do so. Increasing understanding of adult or lifespan growth and development processes provide unique insight into the various ways adults respond to their environments, collect and process information, and react to and deal with authority (for overviews, see Lasker and Moore, 1980; Cross, 1981 pp 168–185; and Merriam, 1984).

Of particular interest and utility are those investigations which have produced descriptions of what Lasker and Moore (1980) and Cross (1981) label as developmental *stages* in adulthood (see also Ferro, 1991). In contrast to phase theories, which are organized around the metaphors of seasons and life journeys and which emphasize environmental influences on the process of adult development, stage theories emphasize epigenetic factors and are, consequently, grounded in biological conceptions of development. Drawing upon Kitchener (1978), Lasker and Moore outline the major characteristics of stage theories:

• Development is internally organized. That is, the emerging processes are guided by an intrinsic system of organization, such as the genetic code. . . .

- Development proceeds through identifiable stages, and the stages represent discrete and relatively stable developmental plateaus.

- The direction of development is toward increasing complexity of form and increasing differentiation of parts. . . .

- At each identifiable stage of development, the organism displays emergent qualities that were not present at the previous stage. . . . Higher stages of psychological development enable persons to function in ways that cannot be anticipated at earlier stages. (1980 p 15)

Building variously upon the work of John Dewey, Jean Piaget, and Erik Erikson, several researchers have utilized this epigenetic or stage approach to explore and delineate ego development (Loevinger, 1976; Weathersby, 1981), intellectual and ethical development (Perry, 1970, 1981), moral development (Kohlberg, 1969, 1973), and faith development (Fowler, 1981) throughout the adult lifespan. These theorists attempt to describe, on a hierarchical basis or model, the series of personality and cognitive stages through which adults *may* (but not necessarily *must*) pass as they mature. Each stage is, in effect, a psychological set which frames how each adult views the world and perceives herself in relationship to that world.

Each of the theorists mentioned have developed hierarchies containing six to nine stages which can, for the sake of convenience and the purposes of this discussion, be grouped into three major categories or levels: (1) egocentric, (2) sociocentric, and (3) allocentric (Okun, 1984 p 60; see Figure 2). In the *egocentric* stages, individuals make decisions based upon the perceived effect of a decision upon the self, e.g., "How can I avoid punishment?" or 'What actions will cause others to like me?' Persons in the *sociocentric* stages make decisions based on established group norms, with their rationale for adherence to these norms ranging from a "law and order" perspective on the one hand to the perception, on the other, that the well-being of the greatest number of people depends upon the voluntary submission to accepted community standards. According to stage theorists, the large majority of adults operate at levels which are classified as sociocentric. Finally, a smaller number of adults can be described as *allocentric* in their stage development. These persons are able to subject themselves to what they perceive as the higher good, to universals. They consider these over-arching principles so important that personal life and well-being are no longer dominant. They are ready and willing to give themselves over to—even to sacrifice themselves for—these ultimate ideals.

These levels or stages of adult development suggest implications for adult education which are outlined in Figure 2. In each of the categories there is not only a progression toward autonomy on the part of learners as they proceed from egocentric to sociocentric and, potentially, allocentric stages. There is also a movement from a more static to a more dynamic view of the learners' role and function. Stage theory predicates that the full complement of adult learners will be spread over all stages, with the greatest number concentrated toward the middle sections.

AUTHORITY AND THE
TEACHING/LEARNING TRANSACTION

The significance of the progression or movement implicit in Figure 2 is that adult learners' attitudes and reactions toward those who exercise authority will vary depending on the learners' current level of stage development. This observation is of extreme importance for religious leaders or teachers. If teachers expect participants whose stage levels fall within the allocentric and higher sociocentric categories to accept what they say simply because they say so (bringing into play the various filters or screens of authority discussed above and presented in Figure 1), they will be startled, if not actually angered, by the failure of their learners to follow meekly. Participants will challenge and question their teachers' interpretations because of their need to examine their teachers' viewpoints in terms of their own worldviews—worldviews which may differ from, or even be at odds with, their teachers' perspectives. On the other hand, learners operating from an egocentric or "law and order" stance will be uncomfortable, or even find fault, with teachers who attempt to be facilitative when the learners want answers or, to be more precise, the right answers.

The discussion to this point, then, has raised for consideration several dynamics which are at play in those situations in which appeal is made to the authority of the Word. One set of dynamics related to the number of authority filters or screens which are in place (see Figure

1). The more both teachers and learners share in common the filters or screens they accept and with which they work, the more compatible they are likely to be. For example, they may view the authoritative source from a similar theological tradition but are unencumbered by several of the other screens discussed above; conversely, they may share an understanding of the Word which is influenced as well by a common understanding of ecclesiastical status, philosophical position, and interpretive stance. On the other hand, the greater the difference, both in terms of the number of filters with which the teachers and learners work and the understanding or meaning attached to those filters, the greater will be the dissonance in the teaching/learning transaction. For example, teachers and learners may be from significantly different theological traditions or hold disparate interpretive stances.

Another set of dynamics relates to the developmental stages, respectively, of teachers and learners. If both are, say, at a "law and order" stage (toward the egocentric side of the sociocentric portion of the developmental spectrum), the worship or learning setting should be highly comfortable. The same analysis would hold if both were moving from sociocentric to allocentric stages. On the other hand, if one is at the "law and order" stage and the other is approaching the allocentric level, dissonance is more likely to occur. This is especially true if the learner is the one moving in the allocentric direction. One of the characteristics of stage theory is that an individual can comprehend the levels he has already experienced, but he is unable to appreciate stages through which he has not already passed. This means that teachers should be able to understand their learners' perspectives if learners are operating at developmental stages through which the teachers have already passed, even if these teachers are no longer at those levels. Conversely, teachers who have not experienced as many developmental stages as their learners are less likely to appreciate and understand their learners' frames of reference.

Figure 3 presents a schema or graph which attempts to visualize the dynamics just described. In effect, each person involved in a teaching/learning transaction can be plotted on this graph with respect to her developmental stage and according to the number of authority screens she utilizes. The more scattered the participants, the more diverse are the viewpoints and perspectives in the educational situation and the greater the potential for disagreement. The more closely the participants bunch, the greater the chance of compatibility.

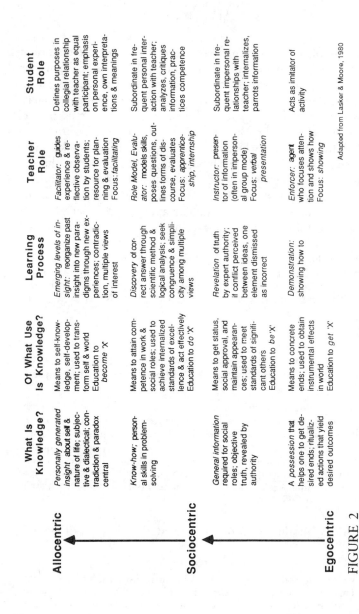

	What Is Knowledge?	Of What Use Is Knowledge?	Learning Process	Teacher Role	Student Role
Allocentric	*Personally generated insight* about self & nature of life; subjective & dialectical; contradiction & paradox central	Means to self-knowledge, self-development; used to transform self & world. Education to *become* 'X'	*Emerging levels of insight:* reorganize past insight into new paradigms through new experiences; contradiction, multiple views of interest	*Facilitator:* guides experience & reflective observation by students; resource for planning & evaluation. Focus: *facilitating*	Defines purposes in collegial relationship with teacher as equal participant; emphasis on personal experience, own interpretations & meanings
	Know-how: personal skills in problem-solving	Means to attain competence in work & social roles; used to achieve internalized standards of excellence & act effectively. Education to *do* 'X'	*Discovery of* correct answer through scientific method & logical analysis; seek congruence & simplicity among multiple views	*Role Model, Evaluator:* models skills, poses questions, outlines forms of discourse, evaluates. Focus: *apprenticeship, internship*	Subordinate in frequent personal interaction with teacher; analyzes, critiques information, practices competence
Sociocentric	*General information* required for social roles; objective truth, revealed by authority	Means to get status, social approval, and maintain appearances; used to meet standards of significant others. Education to *be* 'X'	*Revelation* of truth by expert authority; if conflict perceived between ideas, one element dismissed as incorrect	*Instructor:* presentor of information (often in impersonal group mode). Focus: *verbal presentation*	Subordinate in frequent impersonal relationships with teacher; internalizes, parrots information
Egocentric	*A possession that* helps one to get desired ends; ritualized actions that yield desired outcomes	Means to concrete ends; used to obtain instrumental effects in world. Education to *get* 'X'	*Demonstration:* showing how to	*Enforcer:* agent who focuses attention and shows how. Focus: *showing*	Acts as imitator of activity

Adapted from Lasker & Moore, 1980

FIGURE 2
Implications of Stage Development for Adult Education

43

PARADIGMS, HERMENEUTICS, AND AUTHORITY

Two important topics which have received considerable attention in the research and evaluation literature and which must be considered within the context of the present discussion are (1) paradigms and (2) hermeneutics, the art and science of interpreting meaning. Thomas S. Kuhn has contributed to the general awareness of the important role of paradigms in his landmark work, *The Structure of Scientific Revolutions* (1970; see also Schwartz and Ogilvy, 1979; Polkinghorne, 1983; Lincoln & Guba, 1985; Guba, 1990). He speaks of the need, from time to time, to make a shift in how people view the world and how they organize their knowledge about that world because new questions, new information, and new understandings no longer fit into a previous way of thinking and doing things:

> Scientific revolutions are inaugurated by a growing sense . . . that an existing paradigm has ceased to function adequately in the exploration of an aspect of nature to which the paradigm itself had previously led the way. . . . The sense of malfunction that can lead to crisis is prerequisite to revolution. (Kuhn, 1970 p 92)

The term "revolution" is well chosen because the emergence of new paradigms is seldom met with open arms. As with almost any change, such new perspectives are resisted. As Kuhn points out, the choice

> between competing paradigms proves to be a choice between incompatible modes of community life. Because it has that character, the choice is not and cannot be determined merely by the evaluative procedures characteristic of normal science, for these depend in part upon a particular paradigm, and that paradigm is at issue. When paradigms enter, as they must, into a debate about paradigm choice, their role is necessarily circular. Each group uses its own paradigm to argue in that paradigm's defense. (1970 p 94)

Burke provides another way of looking at the concept of paradigm shift:

> Today we live according to the latest version of how the universe functions. This view affects our behaviour and thought, just as previous versions affected those who lived with them. Like the people of the past,

we disregard phenomena which do not fit our view because they are 'wrong' or outdated. Like our ancestors, we know the real truth.

At any time in the past, people have held a view of the way the universe works which was for them similarly definitive, whether it was based on myths or research. And at any time, that view they held was sooner or later altered by changes in the body of knowledge. (1985 p 9)

Much of the resistance to the acceptance of new ideas is caused by the perception that paradigm shifts have never happened before, that the understanding or interpretation now being posed is the first effort at fundamental change ever proposed. This occurs, says Kuhn, when previous revolutions become invisible because of the manner in which the history of scientific investigation has been codified:

> There are excellent reasons why revolutions have proved to be so nearly invisible. Both scientists and laymen take much of their image of creative scientific activity from an authoritative source that systematically disguises . . . the existence and significance of scientific revolutions. . . . By the source of authority, I have in mind principally textbooks of science together with both the popularizations and the philosophical works modeled on them. . . . They address themselves to an already articulated body of problems, data, and theory, most often to the particular set of paradigms to which the scientific community is committed at the time they are written. . . . Textbooks thus begin by truncating the scientist's sense of his discipline's history and then proceed to supply a substitute for what they have eliminated. (1970 pp 136–137)

This observation has direct bearing on the topic being treated in this chapter. In an effort to make subject matter as clear as possible to learners, teachers tend to reduce the processes leading to significant discovery and understanding. When teachers see their task as that of transmitting knowledge as content, they convert the processes of discovery as well. They replace discovery with a schema that can be memorized and reiterated (some would say, less elegantly, swallowed and regurgitated). Thus the process of discovery and the content of what might be discovered are both pablumized. The learners, consequently, as strictly passive recipients of this minimalist product, do not grasp the full significance of either the content or the process that led to its discovery. The holistic picture is lost. Furthermore, the participants have not really learned the process because they have not practiced it. They, in effect, are asked to accept the description of both the

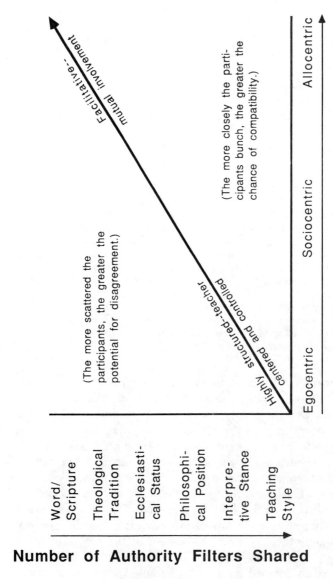

Number of Authority Filters Shared

Word/
Scripture

Theological
Tradition

Ecclesiasti-
cal Status

Philosophi-
cal Position

Interpre-
tive Stance

Teaching
Style

(The more scattered the
participants, the greater the
potential for disagreement.)

Facilitative--
mutual involvement

(The more closely the participants bunch, the greater the
chance of compatibility.)

Highly structured--teacher
centered and controlled

Egocentric   Sociocentric   Allocentric

D e v e l o p m e n t a l   S t a g e

FIGURE 3
Dynamics Present in the Teaching/Learning Situation

process and the content, handed down ("tradition") in authoritative fashion, on faith. The material presented must be right, because the teacher said so.

Such an attitude makes both learning and the development of knowledge appear to be a static activity, one that is not to be examined or modified but, rather, one that consistently operates within the same framework or paradigm. This approach assumes that the current worldview has always existed and will continue to do so. Such is the insidious consequence of the use of authority in teaching. When the current perspective is cast back on the authoritative source, that source is taken out of its original context and forced into the presently accepted paradigm. As a consequence, not only is the Word altered by the paradigm currently in vogue; the Word is depicted as having possessed the present meaning, message, and application throughout the period of its existence in writing.

This interaction between the authoritative Word and those who appeal to it introduces the second point, hermeneutics. Whenever teachers appeal to their authoritative source, they must enunciate what that source is saying and define (some might even say, "divine") the meaning of what has been said. This is the hermeneutical or interpretive task, a task which comprises both a stance and a process.

Until the last few decades those who attempted to meet the hermeneutical challenge sought to arrive at the "right" or "correct" interpretation of the Word. If the proper key could be discovered to unlock the secrets of the authoritative source, then those who possessed that key might also share in that authority. The assumption was that if they found and utilized the correct tools, they would properly interpret the Scripture. Right interpretation, or truth, was an object to be sought. It had a separate, identifiable existence apart from that of those who sought that truth. From this perspective, the correct interpretation and the proper application of the Word never changes because the Word never changes. The Word is unaffected by either the interpreter or the hermeneutical process.

Many no longer hold this static view of arriving at the meaning of the authoritative Word. Philosophers, scientists, theologians, and others have come to recognize that the truth one finds and the understanding one gains depends on the stance of the interpreter. Interpreters cannot stand outside of, and apart from, that which they are seeking to understand. They are limited in what they can see by their attitudes, their context (historical, cultural, religious, scientific, social, etc.), and the actual questions they ask and the methodology they use. Their very allegience to the Word they seek to interpret renders impossible the discovery of "objective truth."

One philosopher who has devoted considerable attention to this hermeneutical question or problem is Hans-Georg Gadamer, whose philosophical ancestry can be traced back through Martin Heidegger to Edmund Husserl and whose paradigmatic contemporaries in the realms of theological and biblical hermeneutics include Rudolf Bultmann, Gerhard Ebeling, and Ernst Fuchs. Gadamer's views are presented in his *magnum opus, Truth and Method* (1975), and in several very helpful and useful discussions both of Gadamer's work and of current investigations into hermeneutical theory, hermeneutic philosophy, and critical hermeneutics (including Robinson & Cobb, 1964; Palmer, 1969; Hoy, 1978; Rabinow & Sullivan, 1979; Bleicher, 1980; Bubner, 1981; Hollinger, 1985; Mueller-Vollmer, 1985; Weinsheimer, 1985; Warnke, 1987).

In his discussion of Gadamer, Bleicher (1980) asks the question, What, then, characterizes [the] hermeneutic experience? His understanding of Gadamer's response is:

> The central task of the interpreter is to find the question to which a text presents the answer; to understand a text is to understand the question. At the same time, a text only becomes an object of interpretation by presenting the interpreter with a question. In this logic of question and answer a text is drawn into an event by being actualized in understanding which itself represents an historic possibility. The horizon of meaning is consequently unlimited, and the openness of both text and interpreter constitutes a structual element in the fusion of horizons. In this dialogical understanding the concepts used by the Other, be it a text or a thou, are regained by being contained within the interpreter's comprehension. In understanding the question posed by the text we have already posed questions ourselves, and, therefore, opened up possibilities of meaning. (1980 p 114)

Hermeneutics, then, is a dialogical process which brings interpreters into a relationship with that which is being interpreted. The interpreters' own experiences and histories, as well as the cultural and historical environment in which they move, shape, define, and limit (as well as establish the paradigm underlying) their understanding of, in this case, the Word:

> Over against the myth of purely conceptual and verifiable knowing, Gadamer places his carefully enunciated historical and dialectical concept of "experience," where knowing is not simply a stream of perceptions but a happening, an event, an encounter. (Palmer, 1969 pp 194–5)

The implication of this hermeneutical approach is that the Word does not always speak the same message. Each time interpreters bring their questions to the Word, their experience of that encounter changes them. The next time they encounter the Word, they are not the same person (shades of Heraclitus!). Because of their previous experience, they have changed, and they have been changed. They view the Word from an altered perspective. Likewise, their questions have changed. Consequently, any subsequent encounter with the Word is a different experience than was the previous encounter, albeit the current encounter has been conditioned by that previous one.

Furthermore, each person's encounter with the Word is different from that of any other individual. Questions, history, experience, and culture differ from one person to the next. This would mean that in the teaching/learning situation, the authoritative message which teachers perceive and wish to transmit may differ considerably from those which the learners perceive. For teachers to impose their understanding of the text on the learners would give the impression that teachers do not recognize and value the concerns and experiences of the learners.

Realizing and appreciating the contextual nature of the hermeneutical process changes the understanding and use of authority. No longer are teachers persons who possess "the truth," who know all the right or correct answers. Rather, as, presumably, those more experienced in the process of encounter with the Word, they serve the learners as guides, as facilitators, even as midwives. Theirs is not the task of sharing their encounters with learners in such a way that teachers expect that sharing to be the sum of the learners' experience with the Word. Theirs is the responsibility of bringing each learner into an authentic encounter with that Word. Then each participant, learner and teacher alike, can share the meaning and significance of that encounter which every other participant accepts as valid and authoritative for the one who has had the experience. As a result, participants benefit and grow in three ways: from their actual contact with the Word, by sharing their experience with others, and by gaining new insights as others, in turn, share experiences with them.

REFERENCES

Barr, J. 1973, *The Bible in the Modern World*. San Francisco, Harper & Row.

Barr, J. 1980, *The Scope and Authority of the Bible*. Philadelphia, The Westminster Press.

Bergman, J., Lutzmann, H., and Schmidt, W. H. 1978, *dābhar, dābhār*. In G. J. Botterweck & H. Ringgren, eds., *Theological Dictionary of the Old Testament*, Vol. III, pp. 84–125; J. T. Willis & G. W. Bromiley, trans., Grand Rapids, MI, Eerdmans.

Bleicher, J. 1980, *Contemporary Hermeneutics: Hermeneutics as Method, Philosophy and Critique*. London, Routledge & Kegan Paul.

Bubner, R. 1981, *Modern German Philosophy*, E. Matthews, trans.. Cambridge, Cambridge University Press.

Burke, J. 1985, *The Day the Universe Changed*. Boston, Little, Brown.

Campbell, J. Y. 1950, Word. In A. Richardson, ed., *A Theological Word Book of the Bible*. New York, Macmillan, pp. 283–285.

Cross, K. P. 1981, *Adults as Learners*. San Francisco, Jossey-Bass.

Debrunner, A., Kleinknecht, H., Proksch, O., and Kittel, G. 1967, *lego, logos, rhēma, laleō*. In G. Kittel, ed., *Theological Dictionary of the New Testament*, Vol. IV, pp. 69–136; G. W. Bromiley, trans.. Grand Rapids, MI, Eerdmans.

Dodd, C. H. 1960, *The Authority of the Bible* (rev. ed.), London, Nisbet.

Elias, J. L., and Merriam, S. 1980, *Philosophical Foundations of Adult Education*. Malabar, FL, Robert E. Krieger.

Ferro, T. R. 1991, Adult development: An integrative model for practice. In *Conference Proceedings: The Tenth Annual Midwest Research-to-Practice Conference*. St. Paul, University of Minnesota, pp. 58–63.

Fiorenza, F. S. 1990, The crisis of Scriptural authority: Interpretation and reception. *Interpretation: A Journal of Bible and Theology*, Vol. 44, No. 4, pp. 353–368.

How does the church teach authoritatively today? 1979, *The Ecumenical Review*, Vol. 31, No. 1, pp. 77–93.

Fowler, J. W. 1981, *Stages of Faith: The Psychology of Human Development and the Quest for Meaning*. San Francisco, Harper & Row.

Gadamer, H.-G. 1975, *Truth and Method* (translation edited from 2nd German ed. of 1965 by G. Barden and J. Cumming). New York, Seabury.

Guba, E. G., ed. 1990, *The Paradigm Dialog*. Newberry Park, CA, Sage.

Hollinger, R. ed. 1985, *Hermeneutics and Praxis*. Notre Dame, IN, University of Notre Dame Press.

Hoy, D. C. 1978, *The Critical Circle: Literature, History, and Philosophical Hermeneutics*. Berkeley, University of California Press.

Jodock, D. H. 1989, *The Church's Bible: Its Contemporary Authority*. Minneapolis, Fortress.

Kitchener, R. F. 1978, Epigenesis: The role of biological models in developmental psychology. *Human Development*, Vol. 21, No. 3, pp. 141–160.

Kohlberg, L. 1969, Continuities and discontinuities in childhood and adult moral development. *Human Development*, Vol. 12, No. 2, pp. 93–120.

Kohlberg, L. 1973, Continuities in childhood and adult moral development revisited. In P. B. Baltes and K. W. Schaie (eds.), *Life-Span Developmental Psychology: Personality and Socialization.* New York, Academic Press, pp. 179–204.

Kuhn, T. S. 1970, *The Structure of Scientific Revolutions*, 2nd ed., enlarged. Chicago, The University of Chicago Press.

Lasker, H., and Moore, J. 1980, Current studies of adult development: Implications for education. In *Adult Development and Approaches to Learning.* Washington, DC, National Institute of Education, pp. 1–41.

Lincoln, Y. S., and Guba, E. G. 1985, *Naturalistic Inquiry.* Newberry Park, CA, Sage.

Loevinger, J. 1976, *Ego Development.* San Francisco, Jossey-Bass.

Merriam, S. B. 1984, *Adult Development: Implications for Adult Education.* Columbus, OH, ERIC Clearinghouse on Adult, Career, and Vocational Education.

Moltmann, J., and Küng, H. eds. 1981, *Who Has the Say in the Church?* New York, The Seabury Press.

Mueller-Vollmer, K. Ed. 1985, *The Hermeneutics Reader: Texts of the German Tradition from the Enlightenment to the Present.* New York, Continuum.

Okun, P. 1984, *Working with Adults: Individual, Family, and Career Development.* Monterey, CA, Brooks/Cole.

Palmer, R. E. 1969, *Hermeneutics: Interpretation Theory in Schleiermacher, Dilthey, Heidegger, and Gadamer.* Evanston, IL, Northwestern University Press.

Penaskovic, R. ed. 1987, *Theology and Authority.* Peabody, MA, Hendrickson.

Perry, W. G., Jr. 1970, *Forms of Intellectual and Ethical Development in the College Years.* New York, Holt, Rinehart and Winston.

Perry, W. G., Jr. 1981, Cognitive and ethical growth: The making of meaning. In A. W. Chickering, ed., *The Modern American College.* San Francisco, Jossey-Bass, pp. 76–116.

Polkinghorne, D. 1983, *Methodology for the Human Sciencies: Systems of Inquiry.* Albany, NY, State University of New York Press.

Quebedeaux, R. 1982, *By What Authority: The Rise of Personality Cults in American Christianity.* San Francisco, Harper & Row.

Rabinow, P., and Sullivan, W. M. eds. 1979, *Interpretive Social Science: A Reader.* Berkeley, University of California Press.

Robinson, J. M., and Cobb, J. B., Jr. eds. *The New Hermeneutic.* New York, Harper & Row.

Schwartz, P., and Ogilvy, J. 1979, *The Emergent Paradigm: Changing Patterns of Thought and Belief.* Palo Alto, CA, Stanford Research Institute.

Warnke, G. 1987, *Gadamer: Hermeneutics, Tradition and Reason.* Palo Alto, CA, Stanford University Press.

Weathersby, R. P. 1981, Ego development. In A. W. Chickering, ed. *The Modern American College.* San Francisco, Jossey-Bass, pp. 51–75.

Weinsheimer, J. C. 1985, *Gadamer's Hermeneutics: A Reading of 'Truth and Method'*. New Haven, CT, Yale University Press.

Zinn, L. M. 1990, Identifying your philosophical orientation. In M. W. Galbraith, ed., *Adult Learning Methods*. Malabar, FL, Robert E. Krieger, pp. 39–77.

CHAPTER 4

The Priesthood of the Teacher—
Language and the Teaching
of the Word

TONY McCAFFRY

Put people for the first time on to video or sound tape and many will disclaim the result: it is not them, they claim; they do not look/sound like that—do they? The problem is one of perception. Being aware of oneself, one's looks and sounds, from the inside out, is not the same as from the outside in. Less is revealed and the experience remains superficial; it does not do us justice.

The same would seem to apply in attempting to interpret one discipline in terms of another, in this case theology and adult education. Jarvis (1987) indicates the close relationship between this century's major thinkers in adult education and the influences of institutional religion, particularly Christianity.

Interpretation of their ideas is helped by knowledge of the influences to which they were subject in their formative years. To move from that to a meaningful juxtaposition of theology and adult education is to go from the chronological to the interpretative with the intention of gaining fresh perceptions. Unexpected alliances can produce interesting results, if only by calling into review the perceptions which until that point had been considered safe and secure. Metaphor is the figure of speech which links the seemingly unrelated and disturbs the apparent calm of the view of reality as it is. The language used (in words and the evocations aroused by their structural patterns) provides a particular environmental perception, a new and challenging context in which meanings can be explored and interpretations attempted. The title of this chapter uses language which demands exploration: it is not immediately clear that the usage is worthwhile because of the added meaning it conveys. The sharing of language between disciplines is a risky endeavor: on the one side we risk confusion; on the other we risk meeting fresh insights which will call for readjustment in our perception of what *is* across a broader spectrum. As a practitioner in both Christian theology and adult education, I lay professional claim to use both sets of specialist language: my particular individual perception can be taken to be the common denominator throughout. Can that perception be stretched, deepened and shared?

Hermeneutics is the word often used in biblical studies to describe the systematic exploration of meaning in a text. In this chapter we shall examine some meanings of adult education in the light of theology, and theology in the light of adult education, with a view to locating any common ground. To put the matter in propositional (but still metaphorical) form: to what extent does adult education provide the hermeneutics of the text of human existence?

The chapter will proceed cumulatively through five phases, examining first the meaning of *teacher*; second, questioning *teaching*; third, reflecting on *priesthood*; fourth, checking the *content* ("the Word"); fifth and last, *language and learning*.

Teacher is an ambiguous word in the sense that it describes both a function and the person who exercises that function. The professionalism of the teacher can be a cultural limitation on the appreciation of teacher as a function rather than as an individual: it could be argued, for example, that the function need not necessarily be personalized, that the "teacher" could be contained in an environment, a learning situation of whatever sort, independent of particular persons. This becomes the more important to remember as the content is broadened to take in the whole of humankind's quest for meaning (cf. Jarvis in Chapter 1).

Personally identified or not, what is the function of the teacher? Knowles (1970) offered the distinction between pedagogue and andragogue. The pedagogue is the teacher of the school child—the authoritative transmitter of essential information, the upholder of due social order and the judge of things that are of worth. The andragogue, on the other hand, is the teacher of the adult—helper; guide; encourager; consultant resource. That Knowles simplifies to make his point is clear from his later writing (e.g., Knowles, 1980; 1984a; 1984b): his insistence on there being at least two distinct modes of fulfilling a similar function is nonetheless useful. A teacher can be a pedagogue with adults or an andragogue with children: the mode is not dictated by the recipient but by the agent and the nature of the learning project (Tough, 1971) and its environment.

Elias and Merriam (1980) suggest the complexity of the teacher's situation by their analysis of six possible approaches to adult education: Liberal; Progressive; Behaviorist; Humanistic; Radical; Analytical.

In the Liberal approach, the teacher (a learned and learning person) directs the learner to the best of classical culture through the orderly acquisition of knowledge. Most esteemed are the powers of the intellect and all that has rational, moral, spiritual, or aesthetic merit.

The Progressive approach places less emphasis on tradition and authority as principal ways of arriving at truth, but rather more on the open-ended exercise of reasoned reflection on experience and personal feelings. The Progressive teacher's function is to guide the learner to recognize the questions which life raises for them. Such a teacher seeks for balance between necessary social control and respect for individual freedom.

The teacher in the Behaviorist approach sets the parameters and program of the particular learning environment with a view to ensuring particular, socially significant, learning outcomes.

In the Humanistic approach, the basic premise is the intrinsic worth of each individual person. The teacher works with all the capacities of the individual, the affective as well as the intellectual. The function of the teacher is as facilitator and collaborator.

The teacher using the Radical approach looks beyond the individual learner to developing that person's capacity to be an agent for change in the world, committed to tackling its social, economic and political problems. The teacher encourages a process of dialogue between the teacher, the taught and the present material situation.

In the Analytical approach the teacher pays particular attention to method, insisting on clear use of language and concepts in the construction of a sound philosophical basis to the learning.

This pattern of complexity in the philosophical approaches and foundations of adult education leaves the teacher in a position that is shifting and difficult to determine categorically. Nevertheless, as Elias and Merriam point out:

Whatever the position adopted, it must be held critically. The professional adult educator should be constantly in the process of examining,
evaluating and perhaps rejecting or modifying what has been received
from the past. (Elias and Merriam, 1980 p 206)

This is a clear invitation to question the theories, practices, institutions
and assumptions of others. It is useful to apply the categories offered
by Elias and Merriam in the context of religious education and religious teaching. Often the teacher is the preacher, the proclaimer, in
keeping with the Christian tradition as recorded in Matthew 28:19–20,
that the mission of the disciples, the taught ones, is to teach. In John's
gospel 60 of the 90 titles used of Jesus identify him as a teacher
(Peterson 1984 p 6). Jesus himself from his Jewish tradition would
know the teacher, the rabbi, as a reader, a lawyer, a scholar. It is
interesting to see that the teacher, in this sort of context, is considered
to be one with authority, not necessarily from themselves but with an
empowerment from the tradition. In this sense the teacher is the interpreter, the translator, the mediator, the converser; the approach is a
combination of respect for the content of the teaching, which is hal-
lowed by its origins and development, and respect for the individuality
of the recipient. The syllabus is offered to, rather than created by, the
learners; but the mode in which the learners operate under that syllabus is Progressive, in that it is not dictated in advance.

What has been said about the teacher will, *a fortiori*, apply to
teaching. Teaching can be considered as a content or a process. The
content is a matter we will come back to in section four of this chapter: for the moment we need to highlight some of the questions which
the process of teaching raises. Is there any teaching without learning?
Put in other terms, can teaching be a one way process or does the very
word process imply dialogue, response, a dynamic interaction? Is this
teaching, as the Behaviorists might indicate, a way of imparting ready-
made perspectives to provide predetermined conclusions? And what is
the aim of this teaching? Is it to provide knowledge, or goodness, or
perhaps wisdom? Ultimately, what is teaching for? Is teaching a necessary part of the meaning-seeking process which Jarvis (Chapter 1)
has indicated as the *sine qua non* of humanity? What has teaching to
do with education? A particular question for the teacher in the context
of the search for ultimate meaning is: what is the relationship between
the teacher and the content of the teaching? What is the relationship

between the teacher and the taught? Could it be that priesthood is a concept which might be helpful in our understanding of these interactions?

Priesthood in the Judaeo-Christian tradition generally indicates a dedicated and consecrated defined group with a particular function within the community. However, as Sabourin (1973 p 224) points out, religions do not need priests in this understanding of the term, neither does sacerdotal power necessarily imply priestly status. However, what is apparent from any consideration of priesthood in history is that those who have the function of priesthood are distinctive and prominent and permanent within their communities. In general terms, their function is to bridge from the known to the unknown, a piece of constructive enterprise with which adult religious educators and teachers of all kinds will be familiar. In the religious context associated with priesthood the unknown is the ultimate unknown, the "hidden" which has to be revealed through the operation of rites and the mediation or interpretation of the priest. The priest could link between the received wisdom and the present circumstance, the Divine Will and the present moment of decision. It is interesting to note that the truth claims are more often in the received wisdom than in the personal statement of the priest. To claim to have the answer even before the question is asked is a form of fundamentalism which attacks the very heart of human dignity, the capacity to seek for meaning and ultimately to seek for ultimate meaning. Peterson (1984 pp 4–5) claims that the scene depicted in Genesis 2 showed God as the perfect teacher and the situation a perfect example of adult education practice: highly personalized attention and use of a full range of methods and groups. This interpretation does few favors to the cause of adult education: there is a depth of sophistication in the biblical tradition which such an interpretation ignores. The religious dimension is more demanding than this interpretation would allow.

This dimension, or level of reality, is famously described by Tillich as:

> the dimension of reality which is the ground of every other dimension and every other depth, and which therefore is not one level beside the others but is the fundamental level, the level below all other levels, the level of being itself, or the ultimate power of being. (in Stewart 1980 p 208)

This dimension is both transcendent, being beyond the empirical reality, and immanent, being within the encounter with reality. The way to open up these levels of reality is through the use of symbols; in some religious traditions the word sacrament is used —that by which the sacred, the holy, the ultimate, is reached. The identification of this symbol and the reality symbolized is always a danger.

Sabourin (1973 p 266) notes the tendency within traditions to slide from the charism of priesthood or teacher to being simply administrators of the status quo or of the given regulations, thus marking a shift from the mediator role to one of preserving the tradition and underlining its exclusivity. The key figure in the Christian tradition, Jesus, provides a much more dynamic model.

According to the theology outlined in the documents of Vatican II (Abbott, 1966) Jesus is interpreted as prophet, priest, and king, three godly functions, all with implications for the understanding of teacher. They are three forms of mediation, three dimensions (rather than separate functions) of the office and mission of Jesus. They explain, condition and clarify one another (Flannery, 1982 p 348). Jesus is not priest by office: he is so by nature (Sabourin, 1973 p 228) He is the only totally real priest. In other words, he is not *a* priest but *the* priest. Others are priests by participative function. This Christology will be a key to the understanding of the priesthood of the teacher and the teaching of the word, for it is this same Jesus the Christ who is priest, teacher, and word. The teaching of the word is the teaching of and about the ultimate meaning which is alive and living, not codified and dead.

But what of the content? What is the matter taught or mediated? Two seemingly innocent terms require our attention: language and word. Language is yet another word that describes both genus and species: for our purposes here we will consider it in its broadest aspect. Language is a common factor in questions of meaning, interpretation and learning. It is the material manifestation of the spiritual perception; it covers a whole range of experiences; it is the articulation of a perception. (Saying that, we must always remember that everything perceived is modified by the particular receptive capacities of the receiver.) Language is socially acquired and socially conditioned: it is something learned. Our problem, as humans, is to be aware of the distinction between the way we see and say things and the way others see and say them. As Gadamer puts it:

When a person lives in a language, he is filled with sense of the unsur-
passable appropriateness of the words that he uses for the objects to
which he is referring. It seems impossible that other words in other
languages could name the objects equally well. The suitable word always
seems to be one's own and unique, just as the object referred to is always
unique. (Gadamer, 1975 p 363)

Those who have had the experience of consciously acquiring a language other than that with which they were raised can appreciate the
enrichment that this brings, because of the fresh perspectives which it
affords. Even within our customary languages, a poetic usage or a
theatrical event can shock us with its unusual expression, through the
juxtaposition of previously straightforward but unconnected meanings.

Two other points must be made at this juncture; first language is
socially conditioned; it is meant for communication. Gadamer goes so
far as to state that "Being that can be understood is language" (Gadamer, 1975 p 432). The second point is that language is not always
spoken, it is not always word based. Word-language is only one of the
forms of communication but certainly an important one. Gadamer
again:

Language is not its elaborate conventionalism, nor the burden of pre-
schematisation with which it loads us, but the generative and creative
power to make this whole fluid. (Gadamer, 1975 p 498)

Language implies engagement, connectedness. Put into the religious
context, it is not difficult to see that users of a particular religious
language might all too easily identify that usage with the truth as it is
rather than that language, that usage, as an expression of an understanding of how things are. They fail to appreciate that the language
of all human things "represents only a prismatic refraction in which
there shines the one truth" (Gadamer, 1975 p 397).

The General Catechetical Directory of the Roman Catholic Church
(paragraph 8) looks at the situation from the point of those with a
more finely attuned critical sense and it states:

There are some Christians, of more advanced Christian education, for
whom the language in which the faith is expressed poses a problem.
They believe it to be too tied to an ancient and obsolete formulae or too
closely linked with Western culture. They seek a new language for reli-

gious truths, one in keeping with the modern human condition and which would enable the faith to cast light on the realities which cause concern to people today and would enable the gospel to become incarnate in different cultures. (Flannery, 1982 p 535)

This raises an interesting dynamic which we will explore further in the fifth section. However, the present concern is for the content of the teaching. We have noted that language might raise a few more questions than we might hitherto have thought it solved. Immediately we face the problem: is this Word the Word as appreciated by the Divinity? Or is this the Word as appreciated by the Christian tradition? It is interesting, for example, to remember that the Christ would not have claimed to be a Christian but the Christian would claim to be a follower of the Christ. Likewise, the strength of a tradition is its articulation in the present of appreciations gleaned from past experience. Tradition is a handing down, a given rather than a mere leftover. It is the past and present in creative involvement, very much upon the lines expressed above in the General Catechetical Directory. What comes through in a tradition is a cumulative awareness of the meaningful inter-relatedness of many things in the religious context of the ultimate meaningfulness of experience. In the Christian tradition the Word is the revelation, the Word is the expression of God, a full and meaningful statement in human terms of what and who God is. But this incarnation is not immediately revelatory: we all have experience of language which obfuscates rather than reveals, language which causes mystfication rather than clarification.

A tradition acts as the interpreter of experience: it provides a particular light by and in which to see things, and it has a language which it teaches to its followers. It would claim truth, not necessarily a fixed and absolute truth but a truth of interpretation, a truth of proposal or suggestion rather than of definitive assertion.

This Word, as content, is knowable because incarnate. This Word is no mere verbalization of a particular theology but is a lived and living reality. God is God in the way that the Christ is the man Jesus:

Because he is the image of the invisible God, he is the one by whom this God expressed himself freely in creation and redemption, which are linked by the hymn included in Colossians 1:15−20. (Congar, 1986 p 11)

He is the image of the invisible God, the first born of all creation; for in him all things were created, in heaven and on earth, visible and invisible, whether thrones or dominions or principalities or authorities - all things were created through him and for him. He is before all things, and in him all things hold together. He is the head of the body, the church; he is the beginning, the first-born from the dead, that in everything he might be pre-eminent. For in him all the fulness of God was pleased to dwell, and through him to reconcile to himself all things, whether on earth or in heaven, making peace by the blood of his cross. (Col. 1:15–20)

This Word, then, is no item of mere specific language, but an expression of cosmic and eternal meaning. The gospel, the good news of this Word, is not a mere written account, but a statement of faith and the proclamation of a way of life. God has become the human word and in the process has become vulnerable, as are all human words, open to distortion and misinterpretation. In this Word, past present and future are united, all meaning contained. The Spirit of God enlightens the process of discovering the truth of this Word. The living of the truth implies a radical change of heart. What, then, is the truth of the Word, this plan of God, the God-perception of how things are? The answer has been sought by the tradition, by its movements and its eminent persons. It is, as it were, the mind of God; it is the mystery overarching and underpinning all that is, that has been and that will be. It is the mystery. This mystery does not insult the human intelligence so much as challenge it. It is the reason for the human's irrepressible question: *why*? The good news is that this mystery is not awesome but attractive and realizable through the accessible language of Jesus' life experience, his story, his stories, and his prophetic example in word and deed. As a "fully functioning person" (Rogers, 1983 p 289–290), he demonstrates to his fellow humans what the God wants humans to be. The cumulative consciousness which was his and is shared by his followers is the wisdom, as yet inadequately articulated and appreciated, but on offer for further exploration, consideration and possible commitment.

So we are left now to examine the relationship between the conscious present and the immanent and transcendent mystery, the world of change both within ourselves and in the world around us. Humans have it written into their makeup to ask why this change, this disjuncture between accumulated biography and present impinging experience? Through reflection (or, as the religious might call it, meditation) we reassemble the data and redefine the experience. We grow by learning in this way from the experiences of living. The language that is used often chooses words of freedom, such as emancipation, liberation, transformation, conscientization—all denoting a move from the false or the outgrown consciousness to the truth as it is now perceived. For the religious learner, this implies a change of lived attitude, not simply a change of point of view. The knowing, the believing, the behaving, form one cohesive totality. The truth once claimed satisfies the questioning instinct: the truth, taken as certainty, is comfortably contained. But what then of the mystery? Is the Story (the God plan) reducible to the story (human biographical) dimension? The shared praxis that Groome (1980) expounds is not a simple repetition of ancient doctrine but its reproduction, faithful to its past but adapted to new problems and better understood in the light of the present. This integration or adaptation is in no way a facile harmonization or easy solution: it is a really adult activity, an exercise in autodetermination.

Understanding as Gadamer sees it is "a genuine experience, that is, an encounter with something that asserts itself as truth" (Gadamer, 1975 p 445). This understanding comes through dialogue between that which was perceived to be the truth and the present situation which challenges that truth. There is a conversation, a give and take, a to-and-fro. In this sense, meaning is always a direction of meaning rather than the terminus of meaning. The understanding that the individual reaches is expressed to that individual in a particular language: but it is in the sharing of this articulation with others that real understanding is achieved.

Gadamer (1976 p 64) makes the point that language is the real mark of finitude. It is means rather than end:

> Learning to speak does not mean learning to use a pre-existent tool for designating a world already somehow familiar to us; it means acquiring a familiarity and acquaintance with the world itself and how it confronts us. (Gadamer, 1976 p 63)

The serious question which this leaves us with, then, is: to what extent does language preform thought? For, clearly, if language is conditioned historically, socially and culturally, the paradigms it offers are necessarily restrictive and as such can be outgrown as society, and the conventions of society, are outstripped by human experience. In this sense language conveys the path into the present. It is the patterns of our perception which change with our view of "that there" from our point "here." In this sense Donovan is quite right to emphasize that:

> understanding religious language requires a thorough awareness of the kinds of situation in which it is learned and used. (Donovan, 1976 p 88)

An understanding of this sort implies a consciousness of the past; an awareness of the present experience, and even some anticipation of the future. In religious terms, it is looking to the eschatological, the realm of ultimate meaning. So it is effective learning, owned learning, which is the understanding which is sought. However, even that is not the ultimate answer, for we must understand our very understanding.

More is said of perspective transformation elsewhere (see Chapter 7) but it is useful to identify it in the process of new understanding. There is a movement from a particular position, through alienation to a reframing, reconceptualisation and reintegration into a new position. The similarity with the research of Kubler-Ross (1970) on mourning and bereavement is interesting to note. Could there be parallels between the suffering, death and resurection experience, the paschal mystery, and a possible theology of learning, seen as a creative process begetting new creation?

The search for ultimate meaning is a search for ultimate understanding. It is a quest for what Gadamer calls "the constantly renewed reality of being experienced" (Gadamer, 1975 p xix). Gadamer's contention is that understanding is in the being of that which is understood rather than in the mind of the one understanding. The significance of a statement, record or action is not limited to the intention of the author. History and renewed experience add further significance to the interpreter of this significance. The preeminent skill required is one of hearing (Gadamer, 1975 p 420) and the prerequisite "a disposition of uninterrupted listening" (Gadamer, 1975 p 422). This listening is directed to that relationship which is the conversation between the subject and the object, this subject and object as seen both in the tradition of the past and the contingency of the present. To say that meaning is fixed and immovable is to give free reign to prejudice.

Only the idolator or the bigot claims that the definitive meaning has been interpreted and the last word has been said.

We are left with the problem of how to probe these ultimate realms of meaning. What tools are available to us with which to probe the mystery? We have already mentioned the element of surprise which a poetic use of language can generate. Certainly what we need is a flexibility of language, something which will freshen our awareness of the relationship between things—that is to say, their meanings. We move from the known to the unknown by following a "thread of similarity" (McFague, 1983 p 15), using a figure of speech, a metaphor, which uses the known to express the unknown. Machines do not use metaphors: only the human spirit has the quirky capacity to muddle categories deliberately in order to arrive at a new understanding. There is a wit and wryness implicit in the exercise, if not always in the outcome. The critical problem lies in the interpretation: the mirthless can all too easily take the metaphor as the reality rather than as the indicator of what is real. The strength of the metaphor lies in its capacity for holistic appreciation of experience and the inherent capability for the unusual approach to the accustomed topic. This "indirection" (McFague, 1983 p 16) offers perspectives which could well contribute fresh or revitalised perceptions.

An example from Christianity might be the many and varied reactions in language, thought and practice to the celebration of the incarnation, Christmas. The one event is open to a variety of social, cultural, economic, liturgical, and spiritual interpretations. Yet all of these can contain fresh elements of insight to the mystery at the heart of the liturgical feast. Ricoeur puts it well:

> metaphor is the outcome of a debate between *predication* and *naming*; its place in language is between words and sentences. (Ricoeur, 1978 p 133).

Not all metaphors are worthwhile, metaphors can die while others can be dynamically prophetic; some can be partial others extended; some indicate a single aspect of significance, others go to the root of the matter and offer a paradigm in which the totality can be experienced. In the Christian tradition the parables of Jesus may have this radical significance.

So where does this leave the teacher using language to probe the ultimate mysteries? What is the teacher's role? Perhaps it is to keep the learner to the task, first, of listening to the signs of the times; to be aware of their own questionings and the questionings of others; to build towards a greater understanding of and between all that features in the human experience. It is to facilitate that process of *fides quaerens intellectum* (faith seeking understanding), helping the individual build towards the personally articulated appreciation of ultimate meaning. This facilitation will manifest itself in the encouragement to explore and the offering of reassurance that the risk involved in exploration is worth the while. If the teacher is to be the priest, the go-between, it will only be through offering access to the riches of the tradition and the possibilities of using anew the articulation of language. If the content-Word is also the mystery, then the search for meaning is endless, yet paradoxically achievable through figures of speech naming experience. The teacher will encourage the learner to understand, be it ever so dimly, in the hope and anticipation of ultimate clarification and the eternal realization of and delight in meaningfulness. Adult education, which puts the agenda with the learner; which offers the tradition as a tool for the learner to use, rather than to be used by it; which treats the learning process as open-ended rather than prejudged; which sees human growth as lifelong and understands development qualitatively as well as quantitatively—this indeed would seem to be an ideal hermeneutic vehicle, respectful as it is of human dignity, the richness of accumulative tradition, an awareness of a global and cosmic environment and open to the as yet underknown and underexplored.

REFERENCES

Abbott, W. M. ed. 1966, *The Documents of Vatican II*. London, Geoffrey Chapman.

Congar, Y. 1986, *The Word and the Spirit*. London, Geoffrey Chapman.

Donovan, P. 1976, *Religious Language*. London, Sheldon Press.

Elias, J. and Merriam, S. 1980, *Philosophical Foundations of Adult Education*. Malabar, FL, Krieger.

Flannery, A. ed. 1982, *Vatican Council II: More Postconciliar Documents*. Leominster, Fowler Wright.

Gadamer, H-G. 1975, *Truth and Method*. London, Sheed & Ward.

————1976, *Philosophical Hermeneutics*. Berkeley, CA., University of California Press.

Groome, T. 1980, *Christian Religious Education*. San Francisco, Harper & Row.

Jarvis, P. ed. 1987, *Twentieth Century Thinkers in Adult Education*. London, Croom Helm.

Knowles, M. S. 1970, *The Modern Practice of Adult Education: Andragogy Versus Pedagogy*. New York, Association Press.

————1980, *The Modern Practice of Adult Education: From Pedagogy to Andragogy*, 2nd ed. New York, Cambridge Books.

————1984a, *Andragogy in Action*. San Francisco, Jossey-Bass.

————1984b, *The Adult Learner: A Neglected Species*, 3rd ed. Houston, Texas, Gulf Publishing Co.

Kubler-Ross, E. 1970, *On Death and Dying*. London, Tavistock Publications.

McFague, S. 1983, *Metaphorical Theology: Models of God in Religious Language*. London, SCM Press.

Peterson, G. A. ed. 1984, *The Christian Education of Adults*. Chicago, Moody Press.

Ricoeur, P. 1978, *The Rule of Metaphor*. London, Routledge & Kegan Paul.

Rogers, C. 1983, *Freedom to Learn for the 80's*. Columbus, Ohio, Charles E. Merrill.

Sabourin, L. 1973, *Priesthood*. Leiden, E. J. Brill.

Stewart, D. ed. 1980, *Exploring the Philosophy of Religion*. Englewood Cliffs, N.J., Prentice-Hall Inc.

Tough, A. 1971, *The Adults' Learning Projects*. Toronto, Ontario Institute for Studies in Education.

The Holy Bible (RSV). London, Thomas Nelson.

CHAPTER 5

Teaching: Catechism, Preaching and Indoctrination

PETER WILLIS

INTRODUCTION

Christian Teaching and Life Transition Education

Christian teachers or perhaps more accurately "evangelist teachers" are charged with the task of teaching and proclaiming the word of God "to preach to the Gentiles the unsearchable riches of Christ" (Eph. 3:8). In some cases Christian evangelist teachers are invited to speak by people wishing to hear the gospel. In others they intervene uninvited in people's lives driven by the desire to share the riches of salvation. The educational tasks of the Christian teacher derived from Jesus' commission to the Apostles have traditionally covered, among other things the activities of preaching, teaching, and subsequent further instruction or catechesis (cf. Pope Paul VI 1976, pp 24), together with forms of dialogue. (PCID 1991, p 121–135). The content and processes of Christian teaching are profoundly colored by the sacred and symbolic nature of the information and the use of what can be called challenging or prophetic processes, i.e., processes inviting faith and conversion. Christian teaching involves the whole evangelical agenda comprising *kerygma* or proclamation of the good news calling for a faith response and *catechesis* or instruction about Christian beliefs and practices calling for a deepening of that faith.

Among educators and trainers of adults, there is a field of practice which has similarities to Christian teaching which I have called Life Transition Education (cf. Willis, 1992),. It is concerned to promote personal and social change among learners. It is often practiced by those engaged in forms of community work, religious education, preventative and public health education and some forms of private enterprise self-actualizing programs. Many practitioners in this field seem to possess strong idealistic zeal and to engage in educational activities analagous to many of those carried out by Christian educators and evangelists. Life Transition Educators often intervene in the lives of those they wish to change to offer them a better healthier more interesting life. There are considerable challenges in this kind of education which confront Christian educators as well. By what right does an educator intervene; is there a way to avoid being or being seen as a proselytizer rather than a person caring for the other. In addition there is the question of whether and in what way education can be used as a effective way to promote life transition. The aim of this chapter is to develop a dialogue between ideas of Christian teaching and Life Transition Education seeking illumination from the Christian tradition for current Life Transition Education practice.

The approach in this chapter is influenced by my own background originally as a Catholic missionary priest working with Aboriginal people in outback Australia, subsequently as adult educator and educator of adult educators. In many ways the reflections in this chapter correspond with reflections experienced in my own life generated from events and challenges of Christian and then secular practice particularly in the area of Life Transition Education. It is these that give the chapter some of its shape and guide its direction. Although the brief theological section tends to draw on Catholic interpretative sources particularly those developed as a result of the Second Vatican Council, the themes tend to relate to Christian rather than restrictedly Catholic experience.

Adult educators who are interested in developing liberal and equitable approaches to facilitating human learning may wonder how they could be enriched by interpretative ideas generated from Christian teaching. In the popular and admittedly secular imagination Christian teaching tends to be seen as nonrational and authoritarian indoctrination. In recent years there has been a development of a deeper dialogue between Christians and the secular world through which the theology of Christian teaching has been refined and developed. While still affirming the value of directly promoting the adoption of the Christian

religion, it has validated less overtly proselytizing and more collaborative interaction with non-Christians.

There are three parts to this essay. The first explores some foundational notions of Christian teacher theology; the second looks at the
theory and practice of Life Transition Adult Education. The third part
is a brief dialogue between Christian teacher theology and theories of
Life Transition Education. The emphasis of this study is on Christian
teacher activity primarily as communicative (rather than politically op-
erational or contemplative) action where there are many commonalities
with certain forms of adult education.

THEOLOGY OF CHRISTIAN TEACHING

The theology of Christian teaching or evangelism has moved a great
distance from any simple view that Christian teaching meant telling
nonbelievers about Christ whether they wanted to hear it or not. It is
now perceived as integrated into a creative ministry of service and
witness. Contemporary developments in the theology of Christian
teaching been brought together in an important document issued by the
Pontifical Council for Interreligious Dialogue (PCID) working with the
Congregation for the Evangelisation of Peoples (CEOP) which said:

> ... the evangelising mission of the church is a "single but complex and
> articulated reality." It indicates the principal elements of this mission:
> presence and witness; commitment to social development and human
> liberation; liturgical life, prayer and contemplation; inter-religious dia-
> logue; and finally, proclamation and catechesis. (PCID, 1984, p 817)

Theological Foundations of Christian Teaching

There are five general theological principles which need to inform
Christian teaching practice which have similarites to the kinds of principles relevant to the practice of Life Transition Education: the dignity
of the individual; the essentially *servant* nature of the authority and
mission of Christian teachers; the belief that faith cannot be humanly
generated but is a gift from God; the autonomy and freedom of individuals to make life choices; and the frailty and susceptibility to error

and immoral action of missionaries and converts alike requiring constant vigilance, prayer and frequent renewal.

Christian teaching theology begins with the belief in *God as Father and humans as his children*. The teacher's task of announcing the good news of salvation and attempting to persuade people to undertake personal conversion is colored by the contemporary awareness that evangelizer and evangelized are already God's children whose autonomy and dignity must be respected and in whom God's spirit already resides in a variety of ways.

Theological approaches dealing with persuading people to take on a belief and lifestyle involving considerable personal and social change, stress that the teacher in promoting his or her agenda must respect the dignity of the people he or she wishes to convert. (Paul VI 1976, p 88). This guideline places great emphasis on the spirit which should inspire Christian teachers to use appropriate methods which, while witnessing to the good news respect the people's dignity and do not condemn them (Rom. 14:10).

The theology of Christian education also stresses that teachers do not teach in their own right but in the name of Jesus (Acts 4:18; 5:28). Like Jesus, their doctrine is not their own but of Him who sent them (cf. Jn 7:16). A Christian teacher then must be one with Christ and sensitive to the Holy Spirit.

Christian theology also stresses that faith, wisdom and virtue are given freely by the action of Holy Spirit out of the direct control of humans. This is a salutary reminder that humans cannot directly generate faith within a religious context. The appropriate human response is to work on creating appropriate dispositions of openness, humility and gratitude to God to be ready to respond to his coming.

> Techniques of evangelisation are good, but even the most advanced ones could not replace the gentle action of the spirit. The most perfect preparation of the evangeliser has no effect without the Holy Spirit. Without the Holy Spirit the most convincing dialectic has no power over the heart of man. (Pope Paul VI ibid; p 81)

Christian theology even at its most prescriptive has stressed that all humans have freedom, autonomy and responsibility and that *the power and right to make personal choices rests ultimately with the individual*. The now famous statement of the Second Vatican Council's document

Lumen Gentium validated the individuals right and obligation to "follow the dictates of their conscience" (VII 1966, p 16) The Second Vatican Council in its theology of *aggiornamento* or renewal (Ad Gentes 1966, pp 951), also stressed that in order to be faithful to its evangelical calling, the church needed to be itself evangelized and called to constant conversion. Pope John Paul II said "We cannot preach conversion unless we ourselves are converted anew every day" (1991, p 80).

Christian teachers need to maintain their faith, their calling and their respect for the people they wish to teach. This is the basis for the practice among Christians of prayer and self-examination in order to retain a purity of intention and to avoid falling into any forms of self-serving. As Pope Paul VI said (1976, p 84), the world is calling for teachers to speak to it of a God whom they should know and be familiar with as "if they could see the invisible" (Heb. 11.27). Christian theology also stresses that for those who have taken to heart the teacher's message, their salvation once won can be lost; that converts need to have their faith and virtue constantly renewed; that they should be on their guard against false prophets who may seduce their mind and heart.

In addition to basic theological principles like those outlined above are developments in teacher and evangelizer practice. Motte and Lang (1982, pp. 633–642), point out that dialogue, inculturation and work for liberation are seen as forms of evangelism as well the more traditional proclamation leading to conversion. Proclamation and dialogue (taken here to include inculturation and work for liberation) form the major theme of contemporary theology of teacher practice.

Christian Teacher Practice: Dialogue, Proclamation and Catechesis

Basic Principles

While the Christian church continues to urge its teachers to proclaim the gospel, it has also, particularly under the influence of the Ecumenical Movement, encouraged Christians to include in their teaching repertoire dialogue with other religions as an alternative and complementary form of evangelism. This was stressed in a recent document from the Pontifical Council for Interreligious Dialogue (PCID, 1991).

> Interreligious dialogue and proclamation, though not on the same level, are both authentic elements of the church's evangelising mission. Both are legitimate and necessary. They are intimately related, but not interchangeable. (PCID, p 85)

As the Christian churches developed guidelines for respectful relationships with each other and with members of other religions, there was a need for some resolution of the obvious anomaly between respecting a faith and at the same time attempting to persuade its members to relinquish it. This was one of the catalysts in the generation of the theological development of ideas of dialogue within the general notion of Christian teaching. Amaladoss, a theologian concerned with developing a convergent view of the relationship between teaching and dialogue writes:

> Proclamation leading to conversion is seen only as one aspect of evangelisation, the other aspects being dialogue, liberation and inculturation. . . . .other religions are seen in a more positive light as "ways of salvation" calling for inter-religious dialogue. (1986, p 62)

The development of the theology of dialogue was to generate the beginning of a new theological paradigm through which the dialectic between proclamation and dialogue could be followed through. Amaladoss speaks of

> a new method of theological reflection that does not descend from above, deductively from the truths of faith, but rather starts from below with the experience of the world and, reading the signs of the times, moves on to interpret the perennial tradition in order to make it relevant to the present. (ibid; p 63)

Theological developments have also occurred in the practice of Christian teaching in its two major forms: Dialogue and Proclamation.

Dialogue

In dialogue, the stance of the teacher is of one who celebrates the saving power of God already at work in various religions although experienced and expressed in a different idioms and in different ritual practices, moral teachings and forms of social action. The Pontifical Council for Interreligious Dialogue (op. cit. 1984, pp 28–35) spoke of four forms of dialogue: The first is the *dialogue of life* referring to neighborly living with non-Christians in various communities. The second is the *dialogue of action* referring to shared action for human betterment and liberation.

The third is the *dialogue of theological exchange* between theologians of different religions traditions in which they share the various ways they have of interpreting the religious experience within their own tradition and within the cultural traditions in which their religion is embedded. Theological dialogue has long produced considerable innovations in the way Christians have described their experience and various forms of spiritual exercises. For example Christian theology in Asia and in the West has been enriched by Buddhist and Hundu religious interpretations of their traditions; theological dialogue between Western theologians and American Indian religious teachers and practitioners has brought shamanism into Western religious thought and Aboriginal religious ideas of "the Dreaming" and of the unity of all creation has been welcomed and has served to enrich Western "creation" spirituality and theology.

The fourth is the *dialogue of religious experience*. While retaining centerdness in their own faith, some Christians and non-Christians entering into dialogue with members of other religions, have heard God described and celebrated differently but have discovered that for its adherents their tradition was leading some of its members to forms of human enlightenment and love which seemed similar to the height of spiritual union with God experienced by their own mystics.

Proclamation

The traditional task of the Christian teacher is to proclaim the good news of salvation. It is exemplified in Jesus' words: "I must give the good news of the kingdom of God to the other towns also, for that is what I was sent to do (cf. Luke 4:43). According to the traditional interpretation of Matthew 16.28 this task was then handed onto his disciples who then became his Apostles the "sent ones" whose task was to teach the world by proclaiming the good news of salvation. This remains a major activity of most churches. As the ecumenical movement has gained strength there was call to develop a more sophisticated theology of proclamation that would announce the good news of salvation and invite listeners to be converted which would not appear to put down alternative beliefs held by non-Christians or Christians of other denominations.

Catechesis

Although, under the bridging notions of dialogue the distinction between kerygma and catechesis is less absolute, there are two important aspects of Christian teaching that this concept highlights. One is the concept of the *catechumen* the original recipient of catechesis in the early church. A catechumen is an applicant for baptism, a novice in the church, whose knowledge is rudimentary and, while having made some commitment of faith requires further instruction before being admitted to full membership in the church. Catechesis understood in this way adds a developmental emphasis to Christian teaching. That Christians who live a life committed to Christian ideals and who continue to learn, reflect and meditate on their faith will grow in faith and wisdom and virtue.

The other concept is that of *indoctrination* which carries with it the notion of instruction without freedom, generating blinkered knowledge and rote learning. Current contemporary theology of Christian teaching has focused as we have seen on the freedom of the individual. A direct inference from this is the importance of developing what Neville (1989, pp 15–18) calls indirect ways of teaching, where the focus is on creating a positive environment for learning while safeguarding the freedom of the learner him- or herself. Catechesis would then need to focus on respecting and nurturing positive dispositions in the learner to permit the continued action of autonomous faith and enlightenment wherein lies Christian learning.

Thus Christian teaching in practice involves preparation, kerygma, catechesis and review. These major processes should not be conceived as a linear sequence but rather as a set of overlays which the teacher accesses at different times according to need. This is based on the foundations mentioned above where faith and knowledge and commitment are gifts of the Holy Spirit to be daily formed anew. The following section looks at the development of the theory and practice of Life Transition Education. I have used a grounded theory approach in ordering this section by reflecting on my experience and related reflection during my time as Christian teacher and then later as adult educator.

LIFE TRANSITION ADULT EDUCATION

In the field of adult education there has traditionally been a strong focus on transferring information to learners and providing various forms of skills training. In such programs, the learner is conceived as being assisted to receive information or skills as objective entities apart from the learner. This is not the case to the same extent in Life Transition Education which is aimed directly at the transformation of the learner. Life Transition Education (LTE) is a name given to programs assisting people make and follow life choices which often need to happen during the elective or unavoidable transitions of adult life. Life Transitions include choosing a career, entering or leaving a personal relationship, being retrenched from employment, being sick, being bereaved, adopting a personal philosophy or religion, joining a political or social group, etc. Some educators in these fields work through organized programs which people enroll in. Others intervene to mobilize people to become a learning group to become empowered to choose the transitions they wish to make and work to make them happen.

The idea of life transitions and their implications for theories of adult education and learning is summarized by Merriam and Caffarella (1991, p 108) who point out that transition is a concept used by developmental psychologists who speak of life stages usually in some kind of temporal sequence and those who use transition to refer to life events. This second which has some relevance here, has been addressed especially by Bridgesn (1980) and Sugarman (1986) and their links with adult learning by Aslanian and Brickell (1980) and Schlossberg (1987, p 98). In general Adult Education writers tend to see participation in Adult Education as a way of coping and making sense of life transitions. In this paper, Life Transition Education includes education for coping and making sense of various life transitions but it is extended to refer also to proactive education aimed at generating a particular life transition or attempting to shape the interpretation of and active response to a particular transitional event.

Life transition programs include career guidance programs, consciousness raising workshops, premarriage education programs, bereavement education, educational programs offered by health services particularly to people diagnosed with an illness requiring life-style changes, forms of inspirational staff training offered in industry and certain forms of religious educational programs. Life Transition Education is offered in a variety of ways. Some programs are offered in the traditional contracted way through an advertised course such as a career guidance or bereavement education. Others are more interventionist and are implemented initially through nonformal educational activities through which men and women are engaged and challenged. These are aimed at mobilizing people to become reflective on their personal and social and political life and to engage in various forms of directed learning. They are designed with the aim of generating a life transition choice or, if the life transition choice has already been made, to generate clearer commitment to the implications of the choice and choosing the best way to carry it out.

Some interventionist Life Transition Educational programs are driven by preventative health motives as for example in the Popular Education movement (see Walker and Mays, 1987, p 1). More contractual programs concerned with promoting human personal and social betterment are often offered in Community Education programs (see Clark, 1987, p 50; Willis, 1991, p 71). There are also forms of cultural proselytism usually promoted as an educational way to financial gain by which some self-styled successful entrepreneurs attempt to generate a "conversion" to winning or success oriented thinking among hopeful contracted learners (see Coomb, 1991, p 41).

The distinction between contractual and interventionist adult education has considerable implications in theory and practice. In *contractual education*, the teacher/trainer whether academic, professional or well-informed amateur is expected to share his or her knowledge as an expert, offering information and critique on subjects from history, literature, politics and art. The process of instruction or training is commonly understood to occur within a teaching/learning contract. The teacher or instructor offers information or skilling and advertises a program to impart them. The participant learners by enrolling, agree to submit to the learning process offered and expect to achieve the advertised outcomes. Of course such contracted teaching/learning processes may include areas not expected by the contracted participants. Teachers often challenge learners to come to grips with the frames of reference underlying the information provided which challenges the participant/learner's own position.

In the alternative form, *interventionist education*, the initiative begins with the educator who seeks to influence, challenge, cajole and persuade people who may not even be interested in being learners. Interventionist education may be motivated by the desire to recruit adherents or to manipulate people for gain, much is based on the desire to help. Helping education tends to be offered by agencies such as health and welfare centers, churches, community and neighborhood houses and is of special interest in this paper.

In practice, Life Transition Education whether interventionist or contractual which has a strong helping agenda tends to be linked to religious, health and welfare programs. These tend to focus not so much on the information or skills to be transferred but on the learner in crisis to be guarded against harm or healed according to the ideology and agenda of the teacher/helper.

Life Transition Education purports to provide learning opportunities for people engaged in the transitions such as the ones described. This raises the central question of how this is carried out. In other words what kind of curriculum is employed and how is it managed. The following section explores the dimensions of such curriculum.

Curriculum Dimensions

Brundage and Mackeracher (1980, pp 8–10), identify three major orientations in adult education curriculum based on three basic emphases. The first emphasizes the individual person's needs and goals. *It meets the human need for self-actualization* for which the educator needs to provide a range of learner centered and learner assessed activities with a strong self-actualizing agenda. Examples of this are "participating in new experiences; discovering, extending, and transforming personal models of reality, obtaining feedback about the utility of such models, problem solving, and dialoguing" (p 8). The teaching activities in programs of this kind tend to be facilitative. Some are designed to get learners to create their own representational model of reality and test its utility. Others are concerned to get the learners to fit empathetically into society, to understand the needs and perspectives of others while still meeting their own.

Such processes have an important part in life transition education since one of the agendas is to enable the individuals to identify and articulate their own options and desires and to develop them to their full potential within the real parameters of the society in which they live. This would correspond with one side of the humanistic and pluralistic agenda—as far as possible without exploitation of others, to be in the world as authentically and as fully as possible and to allow others to do the same.

The second approach emphasizes the importance of being familiar with the accepted truths. *It meets the need to be competent and to be seen as competent,* to meet the requirements, of so-called objective reality and ultimate truths of a society. The individual acquires this objective reality through assimilating the standardized and public knowledge, acquiring the related skills and strategies and accepting the approved values (p 8). The educator needs to provide learning programs by which individuals can learn information and skills to accepted standards required in that society. This is the familiar and traditional approach to teaching which is characterized by defining the content to be learned, setting objectives and criteria of performance, presenting and testing comprehension of content and performance skills.

Life Transition Education needs to include this on its agenda since one of the learning requirements adults have is the ability to handle the demands to be placed on them in the life they are about to enter at an appropriate level of competence. Adults involved in career preparation education will need to know and to have gained the skills they will be required to use in their career choice; people attending marriage preparation courses will need to gain the skills they will need in their married life such as communication, conflict resolution and various forms of domestic management.

The third emphasizes the importance of critical reflection and perspective transformation. *It meets the learner's need to be free, wise and critical.* As each individual develops his or her world view during adulthood, distortions can enter and harm social and personal relations. The educator needs to provide "critical," or what Mezirow (1991, p 225) calls "transformative" learning programs to meet these needs.

> to foster learner's reflection upon their own beliefs or meaning schemes through a critical examination of the history, context and consequences of their assumptions and premises.

This emphasis may only be implicit in the life transition learning agenda more as a need partially or hardly understood than as an objective clearly expressed. Freire (1972b), would want to highlight the importance of linking knowing with doing: that emancipation to be real needs to link ways of thinking with ways of acting.

Life Transition Education as we shall see below, should meet to a greater or lesser extent the needs expressed in each of the three orientations. Since Life Transition Education involves personal change and entry into the unknown, the educator often ought to present to the learning group not as a remote or detached instructor but as a supportive yet challenging friend—a mentor.

Mentoring

A mentor is someone engaged in a supportive relationship to people attempting to learn/become something. A mentor is usually a person who has already achieved a measure of success in the matter to be learned. Apart from offering support to aspiring learners, a mentor provides encouragement by providing living proof that the learning tasks being attempted can be achieved.

Laurent Daloz in his book, *Effective Teaching and Mentoring* (1986, p 30), speaks of Virgil in Dante's Inferno as the:

> mentor supreme, alternatively protecting his charge from threat, urging him on, explaining the mysteries, pointing the way, leaving him alone, translating arcane codes, calming marauding beasts, clearing away obstacles and encouraging—always encouraging. A mentor "begins by engendering trust, issuing a challenge, providing encouragement and offering a vision for the journey." (ibid., p 30)

Mentoring moves teaching from any exclusive concentration on detached information transfer to a much more demanding relationship. People may "map themselves onto" the mentor, they will say: "See they can do it and they are just like me; it must be possible." From another perspective, the teacher mentor has a kind of licence to challenge which comes from the inner experience of having achieved the particular learning challenge at hand on the one hand and of a strong feeling of oneness with the new learners on the other. The mentor has the sense of being "one" and "other" at the same time. In a similar vein women have always been able to challenge their sisters to acts of self-liberation in the gender arena, in a way that men cannot do; blacks have been able to challenge and comfort each other in a way that whites cannot do and people who have negotiated a particular life transition can challenge and comfort these people about to enter it in this same mentoring way.

When Life Transition Education is carried out by people who present as role models of people who have successfully negotiated the life transition under consideration, they enrich their facilitator role by becoming mentors as well and in so doing place themselves under a strong burden to maintain the commitment to the life changes they have chosen and because of which they may have been chosen as a mentor.

Four Phases of Life Transition Education

There appear to be four major phases which are usually present in one form or another in Life Transition Education programs. These are the preparation, intervention, post transition and review. They are here treated as a temporal sequence. In practice processes from more than one phase or the same phase often continue at the same time forming as it were pedagogic overlays with one process enriching or inhibiting the other.

Preparation

Practitioners of Life Transition Education need to prepare for their work particularly if it involves to a greater or lesser extent intervening in the lives of people. They need to engage in what can be called *visioning*: becoming committed to intervene; attempting to get their motives clear so that they will be able to withstand the temptation to bully or coerce when they should persuade and dialogue. Since Life Transition Educators may also be rejected and vilified when they attempt to begin a project they may also need a clear vision of who they are and what they are endeavoring to achieve.

Intervention

Since interventionist education aims at creating a learning orientation among people who have not contracted to be part of that action, the educator needs to *arrange an appropriate introduction*. The second process is *mobilizing to learn* by which people engaged in life transitions are invited, persuaded, cajoled, into a learning/questioning reflecting stance. This includes generating a kind of contract to learn and some kind of expectations of the teacher/facilitator. The mobilizing agenda requires the facilitator to develop a range of respectful interventionist skills. John Heron's work in Intervention (1975), provides an array of skills within this agenda which will be needed in these initial stages and at various times throughout the process. The third process can be called *generating introspection*. The learner is invited to turn back on him- or herself in a direct way. It places the learner at the centre of reflection so that reflection in this case becomes reflexive. This stage is designed to heighten self awareness so that the processes and content of the program are taken to heart in terms of "what they mean to me." Techniques to achieve this include explorations of self-concept, self-esteem, future aspirations and dreams.

The fifth process is *providing information* about the character of the transition and the nature of the future chosen life. The sixth involves *skilling*: identifying and providing basic introductions to the skills required to manage the various processes which need to be carried out subsequent to the life transition choice being contemplated. The seventh concerns *reasoning and persuading*: processes designed to argue for the proposed changes and to explore reasons underpinning the life transition decisions about to be made. The eighth concerns *processes to precipitate choice* and would correspond to the confronting interventions outlined by Heron (1989, p 79). It is one of the most difficult of the stages, where the helping educator has to use what powers of discernment he or she can muster. This part of the life transition educational process is stressed since its outcome is choice. It is aimed at more than persuasion. The learner/participant has experienced a crisis whose resolution requires that he or she must choose. In the ninth process, the learner is encouraged to *let go of the past*. A phrase, "Begin by saying good-bye" quoted by David Deschler, carries the meaning well. In Life Transition Education this component needs to be directly attended to in order to facilitate the desired new orientation. The tenth process is *Healing and Rebuilding*: The overt focus on closing the past, of saying goodbye can open or reveal wounds which for effective transition to occur need to be attended to and where possible healed or at least acknowledged. *Grounding* is the final phase. It is concerned with processes to operationalize the decision through time—

to establish ways in which the choice can be put into practice at the chosen time and persevered with.

Post-Transition Education

Life Transition Education often continues long after the transition has been made and the learner has embarked on his or her new life. In this new phase the educator/mentor attempts to help the learner set out to build quality and stability into his or her life choice by working out areas requiring further learning and helping to arrange appropriate learning and training contracts as necessary.

Review

As with any purposive educational program Life Transition Education needs to develop its own review process. The learning that takes place in Life Transition Education is, in the first instance assessed by the learner at the time when he or she tests him- or herself as to the sense of achievement. Has the bullet been bitten, the dragon slain, the door opened or shut. In addition as a sponsored "helping" course, life transition educational programs will be required to provide some form of evaluation.

Reflection on the dimensions of Christian teaching and Life Transition Education leads now to a consideration of how each challenges and at the same time enriches the other.

DIALOGUE BETWEEN CHRISTIAN TEACHER AND ADULT EDUCATOR

Recent developments in the practice and theology of dialogue have generated a theology of listening and service to accompany proclamation. These are concepts which may be enriching to adult educators concerned with informing their practice with ideals of equity and democracy. The Christian theological foundations of dialogic educational action can inspire educators to greater respect for the dignity, autonomy and frailty of all people. The focus on the work of the Holy Spirit in transmission of grace has a useful symbolic message for those who work at the edge of human learning: it can highlight the mystery of the human being and the hidden character of the processes by which humans admit ideas and attitudes into their psyches. Humility before the Holy Spirit in the theology of Christian teaching can perhaps inspire in educators and trainers of adults, particularly as they encroach upon people's ideas of themselves and their place in life, a respect for the learning processes of humans and a sense of themselves as servants of that process.

Christian theology stressing the power to choose and the autonomy of each person is a useful reminder to interventionist educators to respect the autonomy of the people with which they are working. Christian teaching theology has been aware of the frailty and perfectibility of learners and teacher alike and their need for times of reflection and self critique. Such a valuable and generative notion is enriching for all adult educators.

Following these general principles, Life Transition Educators can look to gain wisdom and insight from the theology of Christian teaching generated about the various Christian educational processes especially those which seem similar to those used in Life Transition Education.

The developed Christian theology of dialogue illumines the challenge to educators to respect the perspective of the learners and to develop ways to facilitate careful and reciprocal attention to nuances of thought and feeling.

The developed Christian theology of prophetic teaching with its strong emphasis on the brother and sisterhood of all people gives a respectful foundation for loving and challenging intervention into other people's lives. Such an intervention can be illuminated by the emerging theology of dialogue described above. The approach of intervention as dialogue in the secular word has also been developed by practitioners like Paulo Freire (1972A, B, 1973) and Carl Rogers (1961, 1970, 1983). Dialogue provides an inspiring approach for respectful interventionist life transition educators wishing to reach out and share, to confront or to challenge other humans in love and equality to undertake processes leading to liberation and enrichment.

The theology of Christian teaching also takes account of the cost of discipleship. The importance of support once the commitment has been made and the act of conversion executed; the importance of healing in cases where there is suffering and pain associated with the transition and finally the importance of good works, of grounding a life transition decision in action.

The dialogue between the theology of Christian teaching and the theory and practice of adult education concerned with fostering personal and social change represents a point in the ongoing interchange between secular and sacred perspectives of the one reality. Educators and trainers of adults working to inculcate personal and social change are all challenged to ground their educational action in a coherent theory of human life and their place within it. The closeness and symbiosis of the two approaches which I experienced in my own transitions from Christian teacher to Life Transition Educator highlights the essentially symbolic nature of human meaning making and life choices which resists literalism and pure rationality. While it is true that attempts to use educational action to promote human betterment and emancipation are promoted in different ways according to the symbolic and pedagogic repertoire of the educators in question, education workers in the secular world who are enriched with ideals of equity and respect will find themselves in many ways at one with Christian teachers imbued with ideals of respectful dialogue. And it is not just religious teachers who will find themselves on sacred ground.

REFERENCES

Amaladoss, M. 1986, Dialogue and Mission: Conflict or Convergence. *Vidyajyoti, Journal of Theological Reflection*, Vol. 50, pp. 62–86.

Arum, Mary Louise, Blovin, Rose, L. Avery, Donna, M. 1981, *Experiencing Your Identity: Developmental Materials for Academic and Community Settings*. Chicago, Chicago State University, Center for Women's Identity Studies.

Aslanian, C. B. and Bricknell, H. M. 1980, *Americans in Transition: Life Changes as Reasons for Adult Learning*. New York, College Entrance Examination Board.

Baum, Steven, K. 1988, *Sources of meaning Through the Life Span*. ERIC.

Berger, P. and Luckmann, T. 1967, *The Social Construction of Reality*. Harmondsworth, Penguin.

Boud, David. 1987, *Appreciating Adults Learning: From the Learners' Perspectives*. London, Kogan Page.

Bridges, W. 1980, *Transitions*. Reading, MA, Addison-Wesley.

Brockett, R. 1983, Facilitator Roles and Skill Lifelong Learning: *The Adult Years*, Vol. 6, pp. 7–9.
Brown, G. I. 1976, The Live Classroom: *Innovation through Confluent Education and Gestalt*. New York, Penguin.
Brundage, D. H. and Mackeracher, D. 1980, *Adult learning Principles and their Application to Program Planning*. Ontario, Ministry of Education.
Burns, Robert B. 1990, *Introduction to Research Methods in Education*. Melbourne, Longman Cheshire.
Candy, P. C. 1989, Constructionism and the Study of Self-Direction in Adult Learning: *Studies in the Education of Adults*, Vol. 21, pp. 95–116.
Chin, Robert and Benne, Kenneth, D. 1975, General Strategies for Effecting change in Human System's in Bennis, Warren, G. et al. eds. *The Planning of Change*. New York, Holt Rinehart and Winston.
Clark, David. 1987, The Concept of Community Education in Garth Allen et al. eds. *Community Education*—an agenda for educational reform Milton Keynes (UK), Open University Press, pp. 50–69.
Coomb, A. 1991, Discovering Me in *The Independent* (Australian Newspaper), Dec. pp. 41 & 42.
Crittenden, Brian. 1978, *Bearings in Moral Education*. Victoria, National Press.
Crow, Edith. 1983, Shaping the Self. Using Steppingstones and Autobiography to Create and Discover Archetype in *An Illustrious Monarchy*. London, Croom Helm.
Dalmau, T. and Dick, B. 1986, *A diagnostic Model for Selecting interventions for Community and Organisational Change*. Paper delivered at Network 85, AITD, Brisbane Interchange.
Daloz, L. 1987, Effective Teaching and Mentoring: *Realizing the Transformative Power of Education*. San Francisco, Jossey-Bass.
Egan, Gerard 1975, *The Skilled Helper and Model for Systematic Helping and Interpersonal Relating*. Monterey, California, Brooks Cole.
Freire, P. 1972A, *Pedagogy of the Oppressed*. Harmondsworth, Penguin.
———1972B. *Cultural Action for Freedom*. Harmondsworth, Penguin.
———1973. Education: *The Practice of Freedom*. London, Writers and Readers.
Gilligan, C. 1981, Moral Development in A. W. Chickering and Associates: The Modern American College. *Responding to the New Realities of Diverse Students and a Changing Society*. San Francisco, Jossey-Bass.
Griffin, V. R. 1990, Holistic Learning/Teaching in Adult Education: Would you play a one string guitar? In J. Draper and T. Stein eds. *The Craft of Teaching Adults*. Toronto, Department of Adult Education, Ontario Institute for Studies in Education.
Gutierrez, G. 1973, *A Theology of Liberation*. Maryknoll, New York, Orbis Books.
Heron, J. 1975, *Six Category Intervention Analysis*. Guildford, Surrey, Human Potential Research Project.
Heron, J. 1989, *The Facilitator's Handbook*. London, Kogan Page.

Jarvis, P. 1987, *Adult Learning in the Social Context*. London, Croom Helm.

Johnson, D. 1966, When Ministers Meet: *Transaction* May/June, pp. 31–34.

Kopp, Sheldon. 1972, *If You Meet the Buddha on the Road Kill Him*. London, Sheldon Press.

Lasker, H. M. and Moore, J. F. 1980, Current Studies of Adult Development Implications for Education, in H. M. Lasker, J. F. Moore, and E. Simpson, eds. *Adult Development and Approaches to Learning*. Washington, D.C. National Institute for Community Development.

Levinson, E. 1978, *The Seasons of Man's Life*. New York, Ballantine.

Lincoln, S. Y. and Guba, E. G. 1985, *Naturalistic Inquiry*. Beverley Hills, Sage Publications.

Lovat, T. and Smith, D. 1990, Curriculum: *Action on Reflection*. Wentworth Falls (NSW), Social Science press.

Mead, G. H. 1934, *Mind, Self and Society*. Chicago, University of Chicago Press.

Merriam, S. B. 1984, *Adult Development: Implications for Adult Education*. Columbus, Ohio, ERIC Clearing house on Adult, Career and Vocational Education.

Merriam, S. B. 1991, *Learning in Adulthood: A Comprehensive Guide*. San Francisco, Jossey-Bass.

Mezirow, J. 1977, Perspective Transformation. *Studies in Adult Education*, Vol. 9, No. 2, pp. 153–164.

———1991 *Transformative Dimensions for Adult Learning*. San Francisco, Jossey-Bass.

———1985 A Critical Theory of Self Directed Learning: In S. Brookfield ed. *Self-Directed Learning. From Theory to Practice*. San Francisco, Jossey-Bass, pp. 17–30.

Motte, M. and Lang, J. R. eds. 1982, *Mission and Dialogue*. Maryknoll, Orbis.

Neugarten, B. L. and Datan, N. 1973, Sociological perspectives on the life cycle: in P. B. Baltes and K. W. Schaie eds., *Life Span Development Psychology*. New York, Academic Press.

Neville, Bernie. 1989, *Educating Psyche*. Melbourne, Australia, Collins Dove.

Pope John Paul II. 1991 *The Permanent Validity of the Church's Missionary Mandate* (translation of Redemptoris Missio). Sydney, St. Paul Publications.

Pope Paul VI 1976 *Evangelization in the Modern World* (translation of Evangelii Nuntiandi), Sydney, St. Paul Publications.

PONTIFICAL COUNCIL FOR INTERRELIGIOUS DIALOGUE (PCID) 1984, The Attitude of the Church Toward the Followers of Other Religions: Reflections and Orientations on Dialogue and Mission' Acta Apostolica Sedis, *AAS*, No. 76, pp. 816–828.

PONTIFICAL COUNCIL FOR INTERRELIGIOUS DIALOGUE (PCID) & CONGREGATION FOR THE EVANGELIZATION OF PEOPLES (CEP) 1991: Dialogue and Proclamation: Reflections and Orientations on Interreligious Dialogue and the Proclamation of the Gospel of Jesus Christ, *Origins*, Vol. 21, pp. 121–135.

Reason, P. and Rowan, J. eds. 1981, *Human Inquiry: A Sourcebook of New Paradigm Research.* Chicester, John Wiley.
Reason, P. and Marshall, Judi, 1987, Research as Personal Process in D. Boud and V. Griffin eds. Appreciating Adults Learning: *From the Learners' Perspective.* London, Kogan Page.
Reason, P. and Heron, J. 1986, *Research with people: The Paradigm of Co-operative Experiential Enquiry.* Working paper, Centre for the Study of Organisational Change and Development, University of Bath.
Rogers, C. R. 1961, *On Becoming a Person.* Boston, Houghton Mifflin.
Rogers, C. R. 1970, *Carl Rogers on Encounter Groups.* New York, Harper and Row.
Rogers, C. R. 1983, *Freedom to Learn for the 1980s.* Columbus Ohio, Charles E. Merrill.
Schutz, W. C. 1975, *Elements of Encounter*, New York, Bantam.
Skolimowski, H. 1985, *The co-creator mind as partner of the creative evolution*: Paper read at the First International Conference on Mind-Matter interaction. Universidada Estadual de Campinas, Brazil.
Schlossberg, N. K. 1984 *Counseling Adults in Transition.* New York, Springer.
Sugarman, L. 1986 *Life-Span Development: Concepts, Theories and Interventions* New York, Methuen.
Swicegood, M. L. 1980, Adult Education for Home and Family Life In E. Boone. R. W. Shearon and E. E. White and Associates, eds. *Serving Personal and Community Needs Through Adult Education.* San Francisco, Jossey-Bass.
Torbert, W. 1981, Why Educational Research has been so un-educational: the case for a new model of social science based on collaborative enquiry. P. Reason and J. Rowan, eds. *Human Inquiry, a Sourcebook of New Paradigm Research.* Chicester, Wiley, pp. 141–152.
Tough, A. 1968, Why Adults Learn: A Study of the Major Reasons for Beginning and Continuing a Learning Project. *Monographs in Adult Education, No 3.* Toronto, Ontario Institute for Studies in Education.
Tough, A. 1982, Intentional Changes: *A Fresh Approach to Helping People Change.* Chicago, Follett Publishing Company.
VII, (Second Vatican Council), 1966, *Lumen Gentium*, Rome, AAS.
VII, (Second Vatican Council), 1966, *Ad Gentes.* Rome, AAS.
Walker, Rae and Mays, Carol. 1987, *Popular Education.* Health Promotion Unit, Victoria, Australia. Health Department, pp. 1–4.
Welton, M. 1987, The History of the CAAE in Cassidy, F. and Faris, R. eds. Choosing Our Future. *Adult Education and Public Policy in Canada.* Toronto, OISE Press.
Whitelock, D. 1974, The Great Tradition: *A History of Adult Education in Australia.* St. Lucia, University of Queensland Press.
Willis, P. 1991, Community Education in Australia: Reflections on an expanding field of practice. *Australian Journal for Adult and Community Education*, Vol. 31, No. 2, July, pp. 71–87.
Willis, P. 1992, Life Transition Education: Maintenance and Transformation *Studies in Continuing Education*, Vol 14 No 2 (in Press)

PART III
LEARNING

CHAPTER 6

Meaning, Being and Learning

PETER JARVIS

Eduard Lindeman wrote one of the classic books in adult education, *The Meaning of Adult Education*, which has recently been reprinted. Here Lindeman presented his understanding of adult education—but it was his understanding! The title implies that there is a meaning to adult education but, in one sense, this is a fundamental fallacy. As will be demonstrated in this chapter, meaning is something that is given to a phenomenon by others, rather than a phenomenon having meaning in itself. Phenomena gain meaning through being given a meaning and its being used until it becomes generally accepted; only then does the meaning appear to be intrinsic, and it is transmitted as if it were objective. People either learn meanings that others have given phenomena or they impose meaning upon phenomena for themselves. In the first there is learning through the process of teaching and learning and in the second there is a sense of demonstrating an understanding of an event or phenomenon by virtue of giving it meaning.

Meaning, then, is a concept quite fundamental to learning and yet the complexity of the concept has not always been explored in learning theory. Mezirow (1988, p 223) is among the most well known in the field of the education of adults who has used the concept and he defines learning as "a process of construing or appropriating a new or revised interpretation of the meaning of one's experience as a guide to decision and action" (see also Mezirow, 1991, pp 12–13). Likewise, Dahlgren (1984, pp 23–24) suggests that to "learn is to strive for meaning, to have learned something is to have grasped its meaning" (see also McKenzie, 1991). Both of these definitions relate learning to the hermeneutical process, to interpreting and understanding an experience or communication.

It is, therefore, important to commence this chapter by discussing the different modes of experience which are related either to meaning giving or to the transmission of already given meanings. Primary experience, for instance, is meaningless until it has meaning imposed upon it either by the actors in the situation or by observers and interpreters—and then it is likely to have two sets of meaning: participative and nonparticipative ones. The meaning given to the participative experience need not assume word form until such time as it is communicated to others—people say, for instance, "it is hard to put into words but . . . " It is also in situations like this that it is possible to see the process of transforming experience into knowledge—the learning process. The nonparticipative meaning is, in fact, about mediated or secondary experience. When people give to, or are given an interpretation (meaning) of, other's experiences, they are mediating information and this is providing a secondary experience for the recipients. Meaning is then communicated linguistically between people and if there are different interpretations of events, then there often has to be a negotiation of meanings in communicative interaction, and when mutual understanding has been reached, the information experience has been transformed by reflection into knowledge.

Since meaning is clearly a complex concept, this chapter starts with a brief philosophical review relating meaning to human existence. Thereafter the meaning of the concept is explored and related to theology which is itself a meaning system, but since aspects of its transmission were discussed in the previous chapters they are not pursued here.

EXISTENCE, MEANING, AND KNOWLEDGE

Philosophy has traditionally examined a number of basic problems, two being the problem of being and the problem of knowledge. Educational philosophy has, not surprisingly, started from the epistemological problem—that of knowledge and, therefore, ideas such as rationality, forms of knowledge, and so forth have predominated. The history of rationalism in Western philosophy can be traced back to Descartes who reached the conclusion: I think, therefore I am. For him, the ability to think and, therefore, to know enabled him to conclude that he existed. Existentialism, however, starts with the problem of being (ontology) and Macquarrie (1973, p 125) has nicely turned the Cartesian statement around and suggests that "I am, therefore I think." Life's experiences, then, are the basis of thought and learning and, consequently, for the existentialist the primary questions are about exploring the meaning of being rather than that of knowledge—they are "why?" questions rather that "knowledge that" propositions. Hence, happiness and joy, sorrow and tragedy, and the affective domain generally constitute legitimate experiences upon which meaning might be imposed.

Individuals are born into the world and they exist. From the outset they have experiences and these experiences tend to be patterned and repetitive, so that young children learn to associate experiences and consequences, that is, they tend to know that something will repeat itself and they also give meanings to their experiences and their interpretations of experiences are remembered. Gradually, they construct a whole body of memories, of experiences that they have, and also memories of the outcomes of those which they initiated, but also their understanding of why those experiences occurred, that is—the meanings that they have imposed upon them. All people are born into a culture which precedes them and which will also succeed them, something which is apparently objective. As Luckmann (1967, p 51) writes:

> Empirically, human organisms do not construct "objective" and moral universes of meaning from scratch—they are born into them. This means that human organisms normally transcend their biological nature by internalizing a historically given universe of meaning, rather than constructing universes of meaning.

For Luckmann, the human organism only becomes a self when it has acquired an independent universe of meaning—when it has learned nonreflectively the encompassing configuration of meaning—and incorporated into it its own early strivings after meaning. For Luckmann the profound religious event is the time when the human organism transcends its biological nature and becomes a self. The self, then, is a universe of meaning seeking to live in harmony with the sociocultural world but when this is not achieved and disjuncture occurs, new meaning is sought in order to reestablish this harmony. New meaning is continually being unfolded with every new experience of life (Bohm, 1985), and the self gradually changes and develops with new learning experiences. But meaning, having been internalized and memorized, develops and grows independently. Individuals construct their own subjective and individual meaning systems that both relate to the social world into which they are born and which also reflect their own history and biography. As society becomes more complex, each person's biography is likely to become more unique and people become more individuated. Constructing meaning is part of the inner human experience and yet through interaction with others, meaning systems become objectified; it is objectified meaning that is transmitted across the generations and between people and learned in early socialization and throughout the remainder of the life-span.

It is clear that both modes of experience are important to this process. Primary experience is direct action experience and so the knowledge gained from these forms of experience may be practical in its application, that is "knowledge how" (Ryle, 1963) knowledge, but this differs from the meaning given to the experience, which is 'knowledge why' knowledge. People may know how to do something, it is empirical or pragmatic in character and is sometimes hard to articulate, but they can often explain what it means to them to have this knowledge or skill. This is a very personal sense of meaning that comes from participation, and different from the idea of "knowledge why." In a sense, therefore, two forms of knowledge emerge by learning from primary experience: the knowledge how and individual hermeneutical knowledge. By contrast, secondary experience is a form of communicative interaction and in this sense it comes close to Ryle's (1963) "knowledge that." This communication is linguistic information, which is transformed into knowledge through the learning process; it can be knowledge about phenomena and in this sense might also be empirical or pragmatic or it might also be logical-rational knowledge, but it might also be hermeneutic information. Individuals are not compelled to accept uncritically the information that they are given and they can question the information, whether it be empirical, pragmatic or hermeneutic. It is at this point where criticality and negotiation of meanings, and so on, come together and learning becomes reflective in character. This is a symbol of modernity.

It is significant that throughout this section the concepts of knowledge and meaning appear almost synonymous at times but there are others when they cannot be used interchangeably. It is clear that understanding or giving "meaning" is a certain kind of knowledge and different from other forms. Yet obviously there is more than one interpretation of the concept of meaning itself.

THE CONCEPT OF MEANING

But what is the meaning of meaning? Thus far the term *meaning* has been used without definition, but because it is ambiguous, it is necessary to explore some of its many meanings here. However, it is necessary to recognize that all the discussion in this section is conducted within the framework of a potentially biased culture and language, so that meaning is itself seen as socially constructed. Four aspects are discussed here. Initially, it has a metaphysical meaning—referring to the meaning of existence itself. Second, it has a sociocultural meaning, in the sense that Luckmann used it, which is to equate it with cultural knowledge that is learned during the process of socialization. Third, it is used as a noun in this objectified sense, (e.g., things appear to have meanings) which can be learned. In addition, the word is used as a verb and then it seeks to convey individual understanding or intention.

It is, therefore, difficult to provide a single definition which embraces this variety of meanings of the concept, although each of them is hermeneutical in nature, but before a definition is even attempted each of these four approaches is briefly discussed.

Metaphysical Meaning

Underlying the history of religious thought is the quest for meaning: cosmologies, theologies, and church doctrine all seek to provide answers to that fundamental question of creation and existence "Why?" but this is also the question with which all learning begins (see Chapter 1). Religious systems of meaning might be construed as humankind's answers to this fundamental quest. Theology might be regarded as institutionalized systems of meaning, and so many of the parallels in this book are attempts to show how educational theory is one interpretation of elements of humankind's behavior but there are common forms of behavior that have been given a more metaphysical interpretation.

Theological systems do not necessarily carry the authority in the modern world that they did in earlier times. The world has become more secular, more technological, and the body of humankind's knowledge has expanded beyond all recognition. Humankind is forced to trust the expert systems of contemporary technological society that the majority of people do not comprehend. The world is still a mystery to most people but not in quite the same way as previously, for now it is generally recognized that the experts understand their own part of this complex world—it is meaningful to them. But this recognition still means that humankind has a quest for meaning, although the nature of that quest might have become more complex in some ways and even the language might have changed. At the same time the metaphysical questions remain unanswered although they are less evident in the contemporary world and even are made to appear less relevant!

Within the language of contemporary philosophy, the quest for human authenticity implies that the human being still has a problem of meaning, which is nicely summarized by Fromm (1949, pp 44–45):

> Man [sic] can react to historical contradictions by annulling them through his own action; but he cannot annul existential dichotomies, although, he can react to them in different ways. He can appease his mind by soothing and harmonizing ideologies. He can try to escape from his inner restlessness by ceaseless activity in pleasure or in business. He can try to abrogate his freedom and to turn himself into an instrument of powers outside himself, submerging his self in them. But he remains dissatisfied, anxious and restless. There is only one solution to his problem: to face the truth, to acknowledge his fundamental aloneness and solitude in a universe indifferent to his fate, to recognize that there is no power transcending him which can solve his problem for him. Man must accept responsibility for himself and the fact that only by using his own powers can he give meaning to life. But meaning does not imply certainty. Uncertainty is the very condition to impel man to unfold his powers. If he faces the truth without panic he will recognize that *there is no meaning to life except the meaning that man gives his life by the unfolding of his powers, by living productively*; and that only constant vigilance, activity and effort can keep us from failing in the one task that matters—the full development of our powers within the limitations set by the laws of our existence. Man will never cease to be perplexed, to wonder, and to raise new questions. (*italics* in original)

Fromm claims here that there is no meaning to life, except that which humankind gives it. Not all people would accept this position for humankind has constructed complex theologies and idealistic ideologies that provide a meaning to existence (Hanfling, 1987a, 1987b), but they are interpretations and constructions, even social constructions! Here it would be possible to enter a debate about revelation but that lies beyond the scope of this study. The endless quest for meaning, to make sense of existence, however, is something which all people will understand.

Sociological/Cultural Meaning

Luckmann writes of a universe of meaning into which individuals are born. In his writing he (1967, p 44) combines both the metaphysical and the nontranscendental and regards them as a total system:

> ... symbolic universes are objectivated meaning systems that relate the experiences of everyday life to a "transcendental" layer of reality. Other systems of meaning do not point beyond the world of everyday life; that is, they do not contain a "transcendental" reference.

It is these universes of meaning into which individuals are born and which they learn through their socialization process. The culture of every society contains systems of meaning, some of a metaphysical nature while others are much more material (McKenzie, 1991). People make sense of the industrial, capitalist society by understanding the nature of technology and of capitalism. Part of the contemporary problem, however, is that science and technology have become extremely complex and only the experts can understand them. Hence, the meaning systems embedded in culture appear to lie beyond the understanding of many people; they cannot learn them without a greater knowledge of science and so they become apathetic or trusting, or they seek something that they can understand. The certainty of fundamentalism is one of their answers—but, perhaps, this very certainty that provides something of a psychological haven actually inhibits them learning more about the current systems of meaning. People, then, are in a position to seek meaning and yet the metaphysical systems may not provide satisfaction and they cannot understand the sociocultural ones, so that there is a void in contemporary society.

Mezirow writes about systems of meaning and while he comes close to touching upon the profound metaphysical issues in his discussion of meaning schemes he does not really do so, his approach is more individualistic, or as he calls it psychosocial when he discusses meaning perspective which he (1981, p 6; 1990, p 2) defines as "the structure of psycho-cultural assumptions within which new experience is assimilated and transformed by one's past experience" and slightly differently in another paper as "a form of consciousness involving a particular constellation of beliefs, attitudes, dispositions etc." (Mezirow, 1985, p 145) While there are slight differences in these two definitions, they are not really as significant as the fact that his real concern is with the structures of thought through which individuals make sense of their own experiences. These are the rules for interpreting experience. (Mezirow, 1990, p 2)

He defines meaning schemes as "sets of related and habitual expectations governing if-then, cause-effect and category relationships as well as event sequences, goal orientations and prototypes" (Mezirow 1988, p 223; 1990, p 2). He claims that these are mostly acquired uncritically in childhood (Mezirow, 1990, p 3) and tend to be reinforced by subsequent experiences. However, he also thinks that they change much more frequently than do meaning perspectives; the latter changes are much more momentous in the life of the learner, which Mezirow tends to regard rather like a religious conversion, empowerment or a "Eureka-experience" (see the following chapter). By contrast, meaning system transformation is more like everyday learning (1988, p 224).

Meaning as a Noun

While Luckmann was writing about systems of meaning, it is possible to use the term much more specifically: words appear to have meanings, situations also have meanings, experiences have meaning, and so on. But words do not have meaning in themselves, nor do situations. Indeed, language may be defined as an arbitrary symbol. Nothing has intrinsic meaning and things only appear self-evidently meaningful because of the frequency of use, so that individuals grow to take their universes of meaning for granted. These meaning systems reflect the subcultures into which they are born and grow up, and they are learned unreflectively and memorized. It is these early experiences that give rise to the birth of the conscious self which finds its place in a specific social structure and social situation. It is only within this specific situation, using a subculturally specific language, that individuals emerge. Meaning systems are socially constructed but they are also situation specific. Individuals have their own socially constructed and yet individualistic universes of meaning, and these are contained within their own individual biographies. Hence different people may have different interpretations of a situation and interpretations reflect something of both the interpreters and their social situation. Indeed, it follows from Bernstein's (1973) work that language might be used differently by different social groups, words carry different connotations, that is, have different meanings. A simple example is that in American English the word *elevator* means the same as the word *lift* in English English—in the latter an elevator is a mechanical hoist. People use words differently, according to their understanding. They, therefore, impose their own meaning upon them—words are arbitrary symbols. Understanding how others use language and the meaning that they are trying to convey is part of the hermeneutic exercise—it is endeavoring to interpret a word or a situation. Achieving understanding is an outcome of the learning process and this is an important relationship to make. When people have reached an understanding, it enables them to place their own meaning upon a word, a situation, and so on. Meaning is, therefore, the outcome of learning and has to be linked conceptually to understanding. People's individuality is reflected in their different understandings and the different meanings they place upon objects and events—understanding is part of human being!

To Mean

When people say that they mean something, they are trying to convey an understanding or express an opinion to other people. It is here in the verb that the subjectivity of meaning is to be found—communicating is seeking to share understanding, opinions, and attitudes with other people. Even when the word is used in the sense, "they meant to do it but they forgot" the intention conveyed is still trying to make others understand an experience.

Meaning, then, is a complex concept used in a variety of different ways and it is, therefore, difficult to provide a single definition. It contains elements of interpretation and of understanding, both aspects of the learning process, and is very closely related to knowledge. Initially, however, meaning refers to interpretations of human experience and, therefore, the study of hermeneutics lies at the heart of understanding the process of both interpretation and learning. Once these understandings are objectified, meaning tends to be treated as something beyond individuals and as objective knowledge, but they are actually objectified since there is no empirical meaning.

Hence, meaning is regarded here as an objectification of a subjective understanding of any aspect of human experience. Meaning can be placed upon a phenomenon but it can also be created as a result of reflecting upon an experience, or it can be shared through interaction, and it is primarily a linguistic exercise. It is through sharing of meaning that it sometimes appears to be objective, since there is a commonality about it which allows people to assume that they understand a situation or, perhaps, to have common knowledge about a phenomenon or an object. But meaning, as interpretation, can also be transmitted as if it were objective knowledge, or true. Herein lies the heart of communicative interaction and mediated experience.

MEANING-SEEKING AND LEARNING

Luckmann (1967, p 50) suggests that an organism becomes a "self" by constructing with others an "objective and moral universe of meaning." Prior to the construction of such a universe of meaning, many questions of meaning are posed. This process of focusing upon the "unknowns" of human experience begins in early childhood (Piaget, 1929) and appears to be fundamental to humanity—indeed, there has never been a people on earth that has not yet devised its own system of religious meaning. As the child's universe expands, so its questions of meaning change. For most people, seeking to understand the meaning of their existence is an intermittent but lifelong quest. Mezirow (1978, p 104) claimed that people move through a maturity gradient during adulthood which involves a sequential restructuring of frames of reference that enable them to construct meanings and the mechanism of change is through the adoption of the meaning perspective of others. Three points need to be highlighted here. The first suggests that there is a sequence, as if people are moving in a linear manner through time but this sequential idea of maturation is open to severe questioning, since ultimately it almost presupposes some form of predestination and certainly a form of convergence. Second, the only way people can acquire new perspectives, according to Mezirow, is through adopting those held by others, a position which, it is claimed here, occurs only in childhood and before the development of an individuated self, so that there is an implicit denial of creativity in his position. Third, this is not just a process which begins in adulthood but is a lifelong process.

It was pointed out above, however, the religious response is only one manner of understanding meaning, but this brief analysis (which is expanded in far greater depth in Jarvis, 1983) demonstrates that even though children are born into a universe of meaning, they are still faced with questions, faced with experiences for which they do not have a ready answer. They learn an answer, but paradoxically, many of the systems of religious meaning emerged many centuries ago and no longer appear to satisfy people quite so easily as they did in the past, and humankind's questions of meaning appear again to be a fundamental issue in the contemporary world. As Fromm pointed out, humankind has become aware that there seems to be no absolute meaning, although such a quest for certainty is something that most people appear to retain.

The mechanism of this quest is significant in this analysis of learning. When people are in harmony with the world, when their meaning system is sufficient to cope with the daily process of living, they are not faced with "unknowns," (see Chapter 9), but suddenly they are confronted with a situation that their meaning system cannot handle and they are forced to ask questions. Herein lies disjuncture—the need to seek meaning, to learn. It matters not whether the unknown demands a major theological exposition or merely a brief explanation from everyday experience. It is, paradoxically, a realization that the meaning system (which is a dimension of the self) cannot cope with the present experience as so recognition of ignorance is the beginning of wisdom (see Jarvis, 1992 for the paradoxes of learning). At the same time it is an aspect of an apparent spiritual void in contemporary society—those systems of meaning that have sufficed for so long seem to be dated and little or nothing has appeared to take their place—this is one of the outcomes of the modernity project.

The desire to discover meaning seems quite fundamental to humanity and where there is ignorance, then there is questioning. In answering those questions there is learning, seeking sometimes to interpret the meaning that others have placed upon those experiences and to make sense of those meanings in the present. This assertation raises some quite fundamental questions about motivation theory in education; in some studies it is almost as if human beings do not want to learn and their motivation has to be understood. But learning lies at the foundation of the human essence (I am, therefore I think) and usually when disjuncture occurs individuals will seek harmony, when they do not understand their situation they will raise questions. Perhaps the question of motivation lies in going to enroll in a course, or devoting specific time to learn certain subjects—but not in learning as such. Had the philosophy of education started from an existentialist foundation, perhaps some of the questions it raised would have been rather different!

CONCLUSIONS

Not all experiences can have meaning placed upon them: occasionally people have experiences which are meaningless to them and it is beyond the bounds of their experience to place a meaning upon them—these are anomic experiences for them (Jarvis, 1987). The apparent meaningless of existence is one of the issues of late modernity (Giddens, 1991). If existence is meaningless, then there is a profound paradox between it and the fact that humankind has always sought to place meaning upon experience and by so doing humanity itself is born, grows, and develops. Fundamentally, it appears, the human being is a meaning-seeking animal, but what of humanity if there is no meaning? Indeed, whether there is ultimate meaning or whether it is only relative remains the religious question.

There is a sense in which reference to Lindeman's (1926) book poses another set of educational questions—if meaning, of whatever type, is learned, then might there not be teachers of meaning systems? If meaning is not only metaphysical and not only the prerogative of the

churches, which other institutions in society provide opportunity for
people to explore their questions of meaning? Should adult education
actually have a role in helping meaning-seeking people to discover
systems of meaning for themselves? Should this be one of the meanings
(functions) of adult education? Perhaps this is one of the functions of
liberal adult education, for as Lindeman (1926, pp 69–70) wrote:

> And a meaning is always a fermentation which, because of its potential
> relatedness to other meanings opens the way toward successive enjoy-
> ments and enlarged meanings.

Elsewhere in the same book, he (p 110) concluded:

> Life is experiencing and intelligent living is a way of making experience
> an educational adventure. To be educated is not to be informed but to
> find illumination in informed living. Periods of intellectual awakening are
> correctly named "enlightenments" for it is then that lovers of wisdom
> focus the light of learning upon experience and thereby discover new
> meanings for life, new reasons for living.

REFERENCES

Bernstein, B. 1973, *Class, Codes and Control*. St. Albans, Paladin.
Bohm, D. 1987, *Unfolding Meaning*. London, ARK Paperbacks.
Buber, M 1959, *I and Thou*. Edinburgh, T. & T. Clark.
Dahlgren, L.-O. 1984, Outcomes of Learning in Marton *et al.* eds. *op cit.*
Dewey, J. 1938, *Experience and Education*. New York, Collier-Macmillan.
Fromm, E. 1949, *Man for Himself*. London, Routledge and Kegan Paul.
Giddens, A. 1991, *Modernity and Self-Identity*. Cambridge, Polity.
Hanfling, O. 1987a, *The Quest for Meaning*. Oxford, Basil Blackwell in asso-
ciation with Open University.
Hanfling, O. ed. 1987b, *Life and Meaning*. Oxford, Basil Blackwell in associ-
ation with Open University.
Jarvis, P. 1983, The Lifelong Religious Development of the Individual and the
Place of Adult Education in *Lifelong Learning: The Adult Years*, Vol. 6
No. 9.
Jarvis, P. 1987, Meaningful and Meaningless Experience: Towards and Analy-
sis of Learning from Life on *Adult Education Quarterly* Vol. 37 No. 3.
Jarvis, P. 1992, *Paradoxes of Human Learning: On Becoming a Person in
Society*. San Francisco, Jossey-Bass.
Lindeman, E. C. 1926, *The Meaning of Adult Education*. reprinted by Okla-

homa Research Center for Continuing Professional and Higher Education, University of Oklahoma.

Luckmann, T. 1967, *The Invisible Religion*. London, Macmillan.

Macquarrie, J. 1973, *Existentialism*. Harmondsworth, Penguin.

McKenzie, L. 1991, *Adult Education and Worldview Construction*. Malabar, FL, Krieger.

Marton, F. Hounsell, D., and Entwistle, N. eds. 1984, *The Experience of Learning*. Edinburgh, Scottish Academic Press.

Mezirow, J. 1978, Perspective Transformation in *Adult Education*. Vol. 28 No. 2 Winter.

Mezirow, J. 1981, A Critical Theory of Adult Learning and Education in *Adult Education*. Vol. 32 No. 1 Fall.

Mezirow, J. 1985, Context and Action in Adult Education in *Adult Education Quarterly* Vol. 35 No. 3 Spring.

Mezirow, J. 1988, Transformation Theory in *29th Annual Adult Education Research Conference Proceedings*. University of Calgary, pp. 223–227.

Mezirow, J. and Associates 1990, *Fostering Critical Reflection in Adulthood*. San Francisco, Jossey-Bass.

Mezirow, J. 1991, *Transformative Dimensions of Learning*. San Francisco, Jossey-Bass.

Piaget, J. 1929, *The Child's Conception of the World*. London, Routledge and Kegan Paul.

Ryle, G. 1963, *The Concept of Mind*. Harmondsworth, Penguin Books.

CHAPTER 7

Seeing the Light: Christian Conversion and Conscientization

MICHAEL WELTON

When anyone is united to Christ, there is a new world; the old order has gone, and a new order has already begun.

— II Corinthians 5:17

I send you to open their eyes and turn them from darkness to light, from the dominion of Satan to God, so that, by trust in me, they may obtain forgiveness of sins, and a place with those whom God has made his own.

— Acts 26:18

Amazing grace! How sweet the sound
That saved a wretch like me!
I once was lost, but now am found,
Was blind, but now I see.

— John Newton (1725–1807)

INTRODUCTION

In our spiritually ravaged and desperately cynical times talk of conversion is apt to raise skeptical eyebrows. Conversion conjures up images of sweaty tent meetings, sawdust trails, rampant emotionalism, melancholy, fraudulent televangelists in silk suits, once-born criminal politicians suddenly twice-born and no longer sick of soul. Certainly these images capture a slice of contemporary cultural and religious reality, whether deemed authentic or inauthentic. But any serious discussion of conversion must probe deeply beneath the surface of deformed and degraded forms of religious expression to discover the core meanings of this most human of experiences. Conversion refers to a wide range of realities—from the shift from one religion to another to the routine joining of a church, from the highly charged sense of being "born again" to the profound religious experience of St. Paul, Mary Magdalene, Augustine, Calvin, Luther, Bunyan, or Simone Weil. Indeed, conversion narratives—metaphors of journey from darkness into the light—have organized central dimensions of Western experience for thousands of years. Conversion, for our purposes, designates a "profound, self-conscious, existential change from one set of beliefs, habits, and orientation to a new structure of belief and action" (Brauer, 1978, p 227). Conversion, says Charles Cohen, "reorients one's life course, asking more of the person than lip-service to ceremony or willingness to perform moral obligations. Turning enlists the entire personality; it engages all of one's faculties" (1986, p 5). Christians affirm that Christ, the Light, mediates the transformational process.

If conversion refers to a variety of realities, it is equally true that a range of "discourses" (conceptually elaborated interpretive frames) attempt to understand the multiplex phenomenon of conversion. Biblical studies of the Old and New Testaments provide careful analyses of Hebrew (*shubh*) and Greek (*metanoia, strephein* and *epistrephein*) usages of the idea of a turning, a redirection of one's life away from sin toward God (Barclay, 1964; Barth 1967; Heikkinen, 1967; Nissiotis, 1967; Gaventa, 1986). For many contemporary theologians, the experience of radical, personal transformation has become central to contemporary theological reflection (Baum 1978; Gutierrez 1978; Kerans, 1974; Kung, 1978; Sobrino, 1984). Historical studies of Christian experience and ecclesiastical life have also contributed insights into the understanding of conversion (Krailsheimer, 1980). These sorts of studies, however, have the Christian faith as their horizon.

Those who speak from a secular vantage point attempt to grasp conversion as a "natural" human experience. Historically, the most significant secular discourse has been psychology. In his classic text, *The Varieties of Religious Experience* (1902), William James interpreted the conversion experience as a psychological process whereby the "self hitherto divided" becomes "unified" (James, 1958 [1902], p 157). This rendering has been enormously influential in conversion studies. More recently, psychologists like James Fowler (*Stages of Faith*, 1981) and theologian Walter Conn (*Christian Conversion*, 1986) have adapted stage theory frames to understanding transformational or depth learning processes. Outside psychology, contemporary literary critics and historians focus on the "structures of spiritual conversion" primarily to understand how language organizes experience. Language provides a mold into which the "pilgrim can pour his agony and thereby make sensible his chaos and seeming confusion- . . . " (King, 1983, p 58). Cultures provide narrative frames within which persons fashion their selves, and the conversion narrative, set within the meta-narrative frame of creation, fall and redemption, retains its power (in sacral and secular forms) into the present distraught moment.

The Western tradition, beginning perhaps with Plato and threading through the Judeo-Christian stories, envisioned human reality as deeply alienated though potentially salvagable (Fay, 1987). Plato's cave metaphor suggested that humankind could turn from an illusory shadow existence to the bright light of reality. The central event of Judaism, the Exodus, taught humankind that knowledge of the true source of meaning, God, could empower them to journey from oppression to a land of freedom. Moses, one could argue, was converted to do justice in the dark world when he confronted the "I am" in the burning bush. The conversion of the Apostle Paul, the persecutor of Jesus' followers, has served as a prototype for many Christians. Struck by the blinding light on the road to Damascus, Paul's life was decisively redirected from the "dominion of Satan to God" (Acts 26:18). Since the beginnings of the Christian Church to the present, the biblical conversion motif has served as template to bring order, discipline and meaning into the chaos and confusion of human life. But we should by no means assume that Christian conversion is the culminating achievement, entry into a zone of eternal comfort. Conversion is an invitation to live life on the edge of the raft. The transformative journey unsettles the comfortable, subverts the ordinary and inverts the conventional (McFague, 1978).

Even though we inhabit a religiously pluralistic, largely secular world, the belief that human beings can experience transformative, depth learning is deeply rooted in our culture. James Loder argues in *The Transformative Moment* (1989) that "no realm of human life is without its version of transformational logic" (p 64). The pervasive impact of Thomas Kuhn's conception of the transformational logic of scientific movement from one paradigm to another is but one striking illustration. Another example of a non-Christian but not quite secular version of the conversion narrative is that of Alcoholics Anonymous (Oates, 1978). The famous 12-step approach to alcoholism, recently extended to other addictions and the victims of dysfunctional families, is anchored in the ontological assumption that human beings can turn from their addiction (sin), and, depending on a "higher power" (God), radically redirect their lives in the service of sobriety and healthy functioning (kingdom of God).

Loder claims that the "logic of transformation, by a variety of other names (conscientization, dialectic process, and so on), has been the subject of study and the guiding principle in nearly every area of human experience" (1989, p 64). The field of adult education is no exception. It should not surprise us to find an essay by Paulo Freire on *conscientization* included in *Conversion: Perspectives on Personal and Social Transformation* (Conn, 1978). However, our field of study has *not* adequately traced out the complex relations between explicitly Christian assumptions and their transposition into pedagogical vocabularies and practices ("perspective transformation" or "critical pedagogy"). To what extent, for example, can Freire's concepts of oppression, liberation and conscientization be grasped apart from acknowledging his spiritual roots in Liberation Theology (Berryman, 1987) and Pauline modes of thought (Laporte, 1988)? What is the relationship between the secular pedagogical vocabularies of emancipatory learning and the theological languages of transformative learning? Placing two discourses, Christian and Critical Theory, in dialogue with each other might lead to mutual enlightenment and provocation. In this chapter, then, I am particularly interested in explicating the biblical teachings about conversion in order to learn more about the "emancipatory education" movement in adult education.

BIBLICAL PERSPECTIVES ON CONVERSION

The fiery call of John the Baptist to repent and bear fruit (Matt. 3:8) opens the portal of the New Testament and bridges the Old Testament prophetic proclamations to turn to God and oppressed neighbor simultaneously. Through this gate enters Jesus announcing that the "time has come; the kingdom of God is upon you; repent, and believe the Gospel" (Mark 1:15). Repent and believe the goodnews! Jesus' foundational call demands a "threshold commitment" (Fackre, 1974, p 175) from men and women, a total turning away from the old toward the new . . . breaking into history. The kingdom of God (the "powers of darkness" need not triumph) has broken decisively into history, and Jesus proclaims "unconditional turning to God" (Kittel 1974, p 1002). Unlike the classical Greek conception of change (*metanoia*)—which never suggested a "profound change in life's direction, a conversion which affects the whole of conduct" (ibid., p 979)—the New Testament demands a radical "about-face, re-orientation, a change of direction, a fresh tack" (Fackre, 1974, p 173).

In New Testament teachings and language, four concepts—repent, believe, be baptized and serve—capture the phases of the Christian conversion experience. These concepts have been contaminated in our consumer revivalist religious culture, their explosive power contained by ideologies of individualism. In the New Testament, the word *metanoia*, translated as "repent," emphasizes the element of turning away from; the word *epistrophein* the turning toward the new. What do we turn from? The New Testament speaks of turning from the dominion of darkness, the world of shadows where the "power of Satan" reigns. Paul speaks of how the Thessalonians "turned from idols, to be servants of the living and true God, . . . " (1 Thes. 1:10). These idols symbolize human bondage to the "powers of darkness": the powers that exercise control over human lives. We have turned our faces away from the light; we have "eyes only for the shadowside of the world" (Fackre, 1974, p 176). Donald Baillie depicts the "primal divine vision of God's intended shalom" as a "campfire of celebrative dancers," and the "fall of humanity as the turning of the figures away from the light and away from each other, facing toward the outer darkness" (Baillie, 1948, pp 205–206). The New Testament notion of "idol" encompasses both those powers that exercise control over our intimate lives (multiple forms of addiction) and the vast, world-ranging demons of political and economic oppression (sinful social structures). What gods have us in their vice-grip? "The gods are everywhere," says Fackre. "The intimate enemies and personal idolatries include bondage to drugs, racism, power, lust, sexism, sports, cars, television, and torpor. These are the private demons that have to be exorcised. And there are public powers that tyrannize over us, the modern Caesars that claim hegemony" (op. cit., p 176). The goodnews, symbolized in the

Easter Story, is that the powers of death have lost their sting. "O Death, where is your victory?" exclaims the Apostle Paul. The Light of Christ pierces into the domain of darkness, illuminating our horizon. "The Christic Dawn heralds a New Day. Therefore, repent! That is to say: shake loose! The strength has gone out of that grip upon you by the demonic private and public powers. Night is over. The powers of darkness have been defeated. Break the spell they have had upon you. You *are* free. Be what you are; be free!" (Fackre, 1974, p 177).

Contemporary North Americans, captive to the Ideology of Individualism, cannot easily comprehend the biblical teaching of repentance. Gregory Baum, the Canadian "critical theologian," has argued incisively that theological reflection must place itself in a *learning relationship* to suspicious social theories so as to be able to "discern the ideological and pathogenic trends in their own religious tradition . . . " (Baum, 1978, p 281). Critical theology has its eyes fixed on the "structural consequences of doctrine or institution, that is, the effects on consciousness and society exerted by religious language and religious forms, quite independent of the subjective intention of the believers" (ibid., p 283). Baum believes that *one* of the major distortions of Western Christianity has been the privatization of the gospel. Pat Kerans concurs: "Far from being a corrective prophetic presence in today's world, the Christian community tends only to reinforce the worst in modern culture by insisting on an individualist notion of sin" (1974, p 55). An "excessively individualistic" reading of the Christian message has actually helped maintain and reproduce an alienated and predatory economic system. Consequently, the Christian message has been reduced to a "truth about personal salvation" (Baum, 1978, p 284)—the transposition of a system-bursting message into a system-conforming one.

Baum challenges us not to forget the social dimension of sin, and provocatively reads the biblical teachings about "inherited sin" towards the assertion that evil is built into the structures of society. Social sin, he says, is often accompanied by collective blindness, and resides in a group, a community, a people, producing "evil consequences but no guilt in the ordinary sense" (ibid., p 288). He identifies three distinct levels of social sin. On the first level, social sin manifests itself in "injustices and dehumanizing trends built into the various institutions . . . " (ibid., p 288). The piercing Light of the goodnews spotlights the way institutions disable and damage (oppress) men and women. Another source of evil, Baum declares, are ideologies (cultural and religious symbols) that seduce the imagination and legitimate harmful and unjust institutions. On the third level, social sin manifests itself in an illusionary, or false, consciousness created by "institutions and ideologies through which people involve themselves in destructive action as if they were doing the right thing" (ibid., p 288). The concept of social sin permits us to grasp the full, personal and social meaning of what we as human beings are called to turn away from. Conversion cannot be pure interiorization, and our acknowledgment of guilt restricted to personal shortcomings. The oppression of human beings extends from the outer worldly realm of the ecosystem to the deepest, most inward part of the person. The disordered heart is intimately linked to the disordered world; inner worlds influence the outer; the outer the inner (Laporte, 1988, p 116–118). The moment of repentance casts a different light upon all our interconnected relations. "Conversion, therefore, can no longer be understood as the repentant recognition of one's personal sins; included in conversion are the critical recognition of, and the turning away from, the social dimension of sin, present in the various collectivities to which a person belongs. The *metanoia* to which the gospel summons us demands that we examine our own personal lives as well as the injustices and contradictions in the various institutions to which we belong,.." (Baum, 1978, p 290).

The second phase of "convictional knowing" (Loder, 1989) is that of belief. A "belief-ful turning to" follows on the "heels of a repentant turning from. It is an orientation to the God who has vanguished the gods" (Fackre, 1974, p 179). Christ has lit up the horizon, and the believer begins to "see by the light." With these new eyes the believer stumbles forward toward the "horizon rise of the Easter God who is above every dark god, the name that is above every name" (ibid., p 179). One is now to take her bearings from this Light . . . walk in it . . . see it . . . Fackre thinks that repentance is inextricably linked with belief. "In fact, some belief must precede repentance, the indicative give birth to the imperative. We catch a glimpse of the horizon glow before we turn from the darkness. Yet the full affirmation of that Dawn reality comes only we turn toward it" (ibid.). Paul's code word for this hope-full affirmation is faith (Rom. 1:6–7). Here we of secular mind are apt to be baffled. Over and over again Paul will attribute his turning to transcendent power outside himself, the grace of Christ (Eph. 2:8–9). "To believe in God," Fackre says, "is to have faith that the source of our wrongs has been dealt with, our beguilement is forgiven, our ruptures are healed, and a way back around is possible, not by our merit, but by God's grace" (1974, p 180).

But our age is icily inhospitable to hope and utopias; our time is apocalyptic, our temper pessimistic and despairing. In the face of this void, the Christian sojourner finds her hope in the cross, on which Christ "discarded the cosmic powers and authorities like a garment; he made a public spectacle of them and led them as captives in his triumphal procession" (Col. 2:15). Hope turns toward the horizon, and the Christ-Light opens out the future. The maverick German Marxist philosopher Ernst Bloch believes that we are creatures of the Not Yet, traveling to something beyond ourselves, to the Light shimmering out of reach ahead of us. We are creatures of hope capable of losing hope. "Hope is an appetite whetted for the Not Yet, one made possible by the fact that Jesus Christ has torn down the no exit sign over the door of Tomorrow. The powers of darkness, whose sovereignty over our lives and our historical future seemed so secure, have met their match" (Fackre, 1974, p 180). One recalls Karl Barth's courageous call to British Christians in the midst of World War II to remember that Christ rose from the dead. Hope mobilizes and energizes our hearts; unbelief breeds despair into our bones and spiritual sinews.

Too many, transformative journeys—the pilgrimmage of conversion—end with repentance and belief. To this I can attest personally . . . conversion of a crew-cut, sixteen-year-old walking the aisles of a Youth Crusade rally . . . struggling to live out my belief hemmed in by teachers who drove my faith into the interior. Like Baum, Fackre argues that ending with "repent and believe" flirts with the "interiorizing of conversion" (1974, p 181) and aborts the "new birth." We have now moved on to severely contested spiritual ground. Contemporary American Christianity (particularly its revivalist stream) is especially prone to privatization and pietism (the Light goes out on the horizon only to be rekindled in the inner soul). The dominant way of thinking about conversion in the late twentieth century is, as Lesslie Newbegin has observed, "the idea that one is first converted, and then looks around to see what one should do as a consequence, . . . " This view, he says, has "no basis in Scripture" (1969, pp 93–94). How is it that the "born again" North American Christian can look around and be attracted to neo-conservative agendas? The transformational logic of the New Testament challenges the culturally conventional logic that "outer re-orientation" follows from "inner change of heart" (Fackre, 1974, p 181). "The failure to understand that the threshold commitment must include turning to other human beings as well as the divine other, the love of neighbour as well as the love of God, is the constant peril of pietist evangelism" (ibid.). Conversion, then, is both "seeing the Light" and "seeing by the Light," and "what we see in new light of that dawn is both the brother and sister in Christ and the neighbour in need" (ibid., p 182).

In *Evangelism in the Early Church* (1970) Michael Green observes that New Testament references to baptism "all make it abundantly clear that baptism and conversion belong together; it is the sacrament of once-for-allness of incorporation into Christ" (pp 152–153). The Christian's threshold commitment, conversion, includes movement through the "doorway of a new household" (Fackre, 1974, p 182), membership in a new community. Now, in the third phase of the transformative journey, the pilgrim turns toward and into the new humanity—a transformative learning community. The baptismal act affirms that life is not a heroic solo-trip. Feminist theologian Rosemary Reuther speaks of "conversion to community [which] then becomes an alternative upon which we base ourselves in order to wage a cultural and social struggle" against "group egoism and passivity" (1983, p 64). Faith and hope are believing responses to seeing the Light; love the "patient, kind, and questing outreach to those brothers and sisters who are made visible by the light" (Fackre, 1974, p 183).

John the Baptist's searing words to "prove your repentance by the fruit it bears; . . . " (Luke 3:8) and Paul's militant defense before Agrippa—"I turned first to the inhabitants of Damascus, and then to Jerusalem and all the country of Judea, and to the Gentiles, and sounded the call to repent and turn to God, and to prove their repentance by deeds" (Acts 26:20) capture the essential truth that convictional knowing begins in repentance and climaxes in service. There can be no doubt whatsoever that the "act of love" cannot be consumed in the love of Christian brother and sister—a kind of inward-turned, exclusive orientation to one's community. John the Apostle writes: "And yet again it is a new command that I am giving you—new in the sense that the darkness is passing and the real light already shines. Christ has made this true, and it is true in your own experience. A man may say, "I am the light'; but if he hates his brother he is still in the dark. Only the man who loves his brother dwells in the light: There is nothing to make him stumble" (1 John 2:9–11). For the Christian, the transformed perspective leads us to see the "wretched of the earth"—the hungry, the naked, the imprisoned. The hand stretched out with the "cup of cold water" symbolizes Christian praxis. "For when I was hungry, you gave me food; when thirsty, you gave me drink; when I was a stranger you took me into your home, when naked you clothed me; when I was ill you came to my help, when in prison you visited me" (Matt. 25:35–37).

Servanthood cannot, therefore, be postioned "subsequent to conversion." This is the "perennial and fatal temptation" (Fackre, 1974, p 184) for the First World Church and its theologies of the rich. To be sure, good works flow from the warmed heart (William James speaks of the "hot place in man's consciousness" (1958, p 162)). "But more fundamentally, the very act of conversion, of doing an about face, *includes* a bending down to offer the cup of cold water to those in need. The 'fruits meet for repentance' . . . are part of the original posture" (Fackre, 1974, p 184). Paul Loffler also insists that we "cannot separate conversion to God from service to man. Both happen in one and the same act. The reality of the Kingdom expresses itself primarily in transformed relationship with God and neighbour. Conversion requires a neighbour because there exists no change of heart apart from a change of all relationships" (1967, p 260). In his monumental text, *On Being a Christian* (1978), Hans Kung argues that Jesus demanded a "revolution emerging from man's innermost and secret nature, from the personal center, from the heart of man, into society. There was to be no continuing in the old ways, but a radical change in man's thinking and a conversion (Greek, *metanoia*), away from all forms of selfishness, toward God and his fellow man [sic]. The real alien powers, from which man had to be liberated, were not the hostile world powers but the forces of evil: hatred, injustice, dissension, violence, all human selfishness, and also suffering, sickness and death. There had to be therefore a changed awareness, a new way of thinking, a new scale of values. The evil that had to be overcome lay not only in the system, in the structures, but in man. Inner freedom had to be established and this would lead to freedom from external powers" (p 191). The relation between "conversion" and "social action" is indissoluble (Loffler, 1965, p 54). Fackre says the "seer of Jericho road victims deals with the bandits as well as after effects of banditry. Servanthood must contest the social, economic and political structures that oppress. Road patrols that prevent the assaults mean just and human societary designs that assure bread for the hungry, freedom for the slave, power for the powerless, peace for the war-ravaged. Seeing the Light, and seeing by it, is the vision to see as well the encroachment of the dark principalities and power structures are longest at the Dawn" (1974, p 184).

Turning away from social sin is dialectically related to turning towards the poor. *Metanoia* in the New Testament, like *shub* in the Old Testament, requires "two inseparable elements, a change in outlook and the bearing of the fruits proper to conversion" (Tamez, 1978, p 78). It is worth recalling here that the prophetic literature distinguishes true from false conversion in terms of its manifestations. True turning to God did not manifest itself in external expressions such as sacrifices, fasting or the wearing of sackcloth. Rather, the actions that pleased God were "to loose the fetters of injustice, to untie the knots of the yoke, to snap every yoke and set free those who have been crushed? Is it not sharing your food with the hungry, taking the homeless poor into your house, clothing the naked when you meet them and never evading a duty to your kinsfolk?" (Is. 58:6–8). Only then, Isaiah says, will the "light break forth like the dawn . . . " (Is. 58:8). The biblical linking of "doing justice" and "knowing God" or the "presence of Christ" presents severe challenges to the secular humanist mindset and First World church. Gustavo Gutierrez, the Peruvian "founder" of Liberation Theology, believes that placing oneself in the "perspective of the Kingdom" means participating in the "struggle for the liberation of those oppressed by others" (1978, p 307). He believes that when Christians live before the Lord in solidarity with the immiserated working towards their "freedom from everything that hinders us from fulfilling ourselves as [human beings] . . . " (ibid., p 308), they confront the difficulty that encountering Christ in the oppressed other may seem to "make God irrelevant—a God filtered by our long time indifference to these problems- . . . " (ibid., p 309). To be sure, one of the "temptations" of Liberation Theology is that of "activism"—the dissolution of Christ's presence into history, or the identification of the kingdom of God with a particular political system or ideology. How are we to understand New Testament language that speaks of God dwelling in us if we love one another (1 John 4:12)?

Gutierrez maintains that a "spirituality of liberation" centers on a "conversion to the neighbor, the oppressed person, the exploited social class, the despised race, the dominated country" (1978, p 309). Today we would no doubt include nature as part of God's oppressed creatures. Conversion entails choice and conflict: a decisive decision on the part of those possessing standing (riches and power) in the culture to cross-over to the oppressed other. This truth, I believe, is fundamental to understanding Paulo Freire's *Pedagogy of the Oppressed* (1970). "Conversion," continues Gutierrez, "means a radical transformation of ourselves; it means thinking, feeling, and living as Christ—present in exploited and alienated man. To be converted is to commit oneself to the process of the liberation of the poor and oppressed, to commit oneself lucidly, realistically, and concretely. It means to commit oneself not only generously, but also with an analysis of the situation and a strategy of action. To be converted is to know and experience the fact that, contrary to the laws of physics, we can stand straight, according to the Gospel, only when our center of gravity is outside ourselves" (ibid.). In this interpretation conversion is a process inextricably affected by the environment within which it occurs. Those who see by Christ's Light are embodied, traditional and historical beings who are challenged to "adapt yourselves no longer to the pattern of the present world, but let your minds be remade and your whole nature [be] thus transformed. Then you will be able to discern the will of God, and to know what is good, acceptable, and perfect" (Rom. 12:2). Gutierrez challenges Christians to break with all barriers preventing solidarity within the human community. Only then "will the 'new [person]' arise form the ashes of the old" (1978, p 310). Gutierrez, who is a humble pastor with Lima's poor, speaks of experiencing the "peace of the Lord in the heart of the social struggle" and being "filled with a living sense of gratuitousness" (1978, p 310). The confessing Christian claims that it is God's grace that enables us to encounter God with and in the other. "By God's grace I am what I am" exclaims Paul in 1 Cor. 15:10. Fackre acknowledges that "our repentance, faith, baptism and service are made possible by the power of God working in, with and under our powers" (1974, p 185). This is the gift of conversion. Perhaps the image of Martin Luther King kneeling, along with black and white civil rights proponents, and praying out loud on the streets in the face of sheriffs' rifles captures both sides of the dialectic of the "piety of transcendence" and the "piety of solidarity" (Moltmann, 1978, pp 47–48) better than a thousand academic essays.

CONSCIENTIZATION AND CONVERSION

Paulo Freire speaks softly about his Christian faith, of his commitment to becoming a Christian. But the conversion motif is strongly present in Freire's praxis and reflection; indeed, one might argue that it is the ontological foundation of his pedagogical works. When he began to teach workers and peasants in Recife's slums, Freire confesses that he did so "pushed by my Christian faith" (Bell, Gaventa, Peters, 1990, p 245). There, with the workers and peasants Freire began a lifelong process of openness to the oppressed. The title of his most famous text, *Pedagogy of the Oppressed* (1970), speaks out of the passionate center of Liberation Theology. A pedagogy *of* the oppressed assumes that the "blessed poor" (Matt. 5:1–16) teach the profoundest lessons about human suffering and hope. "This, then, is the great humanistic and historical task of the oppressed: to liberate themselves and their oppressor as well. The oppressors, who oppress, exploit, and rape by virtue of their power, cannot find in this power the strength to liberate either the oppressed or themselves. Only power that springs from the weakness of the oppressed will be sufficiently strong to free both" (1970, p 28). One can hear the words of the Magnificat streaming through Freire's. "The arrogant of heart and mind he has put to rout". . . . "The humble have been lifted high" (Luke 1:51–52).

The Pauline theme of reconciliation is central to the grace event. "For through faith you are all sons [sic] of God in union with Christ Jesus. Baptised into union with him, you have all put on Christ as a garment. There is no such thing as Jew and Greek, slave and freeman, male and female; for you are all one person in Christ Jesus" (Gal. 3:26–29). Jean-Marc Laporte (1988) thinks that Freire's commitment to a process of liberation which overcomes the opposition between oppressor and oppressed dovetails with his namesake's grappling with the process whereby the peculiar distortions inherent in the opposition between Jew and Gentile, or strong and weak, are overcome in a process which leads to true community in the body of Christ. This is an important insight: implicit in Freire's notion of humanization is an openness to the divinization of humankind which, for Christians, is only completely manifest in Christ and fulfilled at the end of time. For Freire the new humanity "comes about when human beings are no longer separated from each other in terms of those who have and those who have not but are seen in their radical unity as persons and brought to reconciliation" (Laporte, 1988, p 107). Both Freire and Paul work with the have/have not dichotomy, though what distinguished "haves" from "have nots" in Paul's eyes was "status" in the eyes of God, rather than economic wealth or political power (ibid., p 111). It is tantalizing to see parallels between Paul's despised Gentiles bringing salvation to the Jews and Freire's "wretched of the earth" bringing wisdom to the elites. Both Paul and Freire believe that the birthing of the new humanity is an arduous process. "Liberation," says Freire, "is thus a childbirth, and a painful one. The man who emerges is a new man, viable only as the oppressor-oppressed contradiction is superceded by the humanization of all men. Or to put it another way, the solution of this contradiction is born in the labor which brings into the world this new man: no longer oppressor nor longer oppressed, but man in the process of achieving freedom" (1970, p 34). The Pauline category of sanctification is implicit in the conscientization process. "When anyone is united to Christ, there is a new world; the old order has gone, and a new order has already begun" (11 Cor. 5:17).

Freire speaks of the sanctification process as the "new apprenticeship" (1985, p 122). The conscientization process—the process whereby the oppressed emerge from their "culture of silence" and begin to "name their worlds" in the act of changing them—requires that some oppressors be converted to act with the oppressed. Freire asserts that the "naive" can renounce their idealistic illusions altogether, forsake their uncritical adherance to the ruling class and commit themselves to the oppressed. They can repent and have faith! They must turn away from the sin of elitism. The "*sine qua non* of the new apprenticeship demands that the oppressors really experience their own Easter, that they die as elitists so as to be resurrected on the side of the oppressed, that they be born again with the beings who were not allowed to be" (ibid., p 123). This process implies a "renunciation of myths that are dear to them: the myth of their superiority, of their purity of soul, of their virtues" (ibid.).

In a manner that often makes First World Christians nervous, Freire

links faith, authentic love and praxis. The Easter event cannot be merely intellectually apprehended; the "real Easter" propels the twice-born
into "historical involvement." "It is only in the authenticity of historical praxis that Easter becomes the death that makes life possible"
(ibid.). Again, the Pauline language of death of the old self—"But now,
having died to that which held us bound, we are discharged from the
law, to serve God in a new way, the way of the spirit, in contrast to
the old way, the way of a written code" (Rom. 7:6)—is given historical
context. Freire, drawing from insights of Erich Fromm, confronts the
middle-class church with its captivity to the bourgeois world-view: a
death-loving as opposed to Christic life-loving view. Says Freire: "The
bourgeois mentality—which is far more than just a convenient abstrac-
tion—kills the profound historical dynamism of Easter and turns it into
no more than a date on the calendar" (ibid.). Freire believes that we
can "only experience rebirth at the side of the oppressed by being born
again, with them, in the process of liberation. I cannot turn such a
rebirth into a means of owning the world, since it is essentially a means
of transforming the world" (ibid.). Consciousness is transformed by the
"action of human beings on the world" and not by "lessons, lectures
and eloquent sermons . . . " (ibid.). Freire's notion of conversion to the
oppressed is closely linked with Jesus' emptying of himself for the
suffering world (kenosis). Throughout *Pedagogy of the Oppressed*
(1970) and his other texts Freire counsels the new apprentices of liberation that the sanctification process will not be easy. The foremost
temptation to be overcome for the middle-class person who crosses
over to the oppressed is "cognitive praxis": reducing praxis to talking
liberation in scholarly theological forums and other arenas removed
from the daily suffering of people. The prophetic Church, Christians
and Educators are engaged in a permanent Exodus . . . "forever dying
and being reborn" (Freire, 1985, p 139) as we learn to live a "messianic life-style" (Moltmann, 1978) in an intellectualist and consumerist
society.

It is only in this context of heeding the call to be converted to the
oppressed that Freire's pedagogical reflections make full sense. Within
the Freirian universe, pedagogy (or theological reflection for that matter) can never be *for* the oppressed. A hierarchical relationship between
educator and educatee would perpetuate the divisions and separations
within the "body of Christ." The educational process—as dialogic encounter of humans engaged in a common task of learning and acting"

(Freire, 1970, p 78)—presupposes the "intense faith" in human ability to fulfil their "vocation to be more fully human" (ibid., p 79). Freire's method, conscientization, is shaped consciously in opposition to all ideologies of "liberation *for* the people", be they Marxist or Christian. We ought to recognize that a pedagogy *of* the oppressed affirms the people (the "least of these" [Matt. 25]) as subjects before the educators arrive. Christ is already present "*in* the people and there with the true messianic dignity of the hungry, sick, and imprisoned" (Moltmann, 1978, p 105). Freire's pedagogical turning to the poor reminds us of the prototype of all liberating pedagogy, Jesus, who "enkindled (a) movement in which the people itself becomes the subject of its own new history in the liberation movement of God" (ibid., p 107). The enclosing of a particular ideology within the achievement of critical consciousness would appear to be a violation of a pedagogy of liberation. A true learning community only emerges when we break common bread in common hope before speaking of our concrete needs and discussing the "possibilities of common action and the strategies of self-liberation" (ibid., p 111).

CONCLUSION

My explication of the Christian understanding of conversion and the transformative journey has led down several surprising pathways. For one thing, in the blazing light of the Christian gospel, much of our discussion of "perspective transformation" (Mezirow, 1978) in the field of adult education seems to be too much of a head-trip and too normatively rootless. Biblical conversion is "being opened up to the world and to God in a new way, a being-in-relation-to-God-and-the-world that is played out in one's fundamental option and action" (Haight, 1985, p 136). And, inescapably, the Christian's option is to the poor. This commitment transforms the "habitual centre" of the individual's "personal energy" (James, 1958, p 162) and hardly leads to comfortable re-integration into new societal roles. Nothing in the gospel's challenge to see and live in the Light of Christ's presence in the dark world is easily assimilated to North American Individualism and Consumerism. Nothing in the gospel's challenge allows us to separate faith, authentic love and praxis. Christian conversion is a radical depth turn from sin and darkness, historically mediated, and entry into a transformative learning community sharing a common life and attuned to the least of God's creatures. Second, Paulo Freire's pedagogical praxis and reflection can only be fully understood when we seek its spiritual roots in Liberation Theology. His ontological assumption of becoming human and the binary opposition of oppressor and oppressed, and their reconciliation partially in history and fully at the end of time presupposes the redeeming presence of Christ in history. His understanding of the conscientization process as a "conversion to the oppressed" transposes explicitly biblical themes into historic pedagogical practice. In the field of adult education we have tended to repress the Christian origins of his thought, and, subsequently, we have not grappled with those aspects of his teachings which speak of dying to the old bourgeois ways of being and being born-again in the service of the oppressed as well as those aspects which speak of radically egalitarian pedagogical communities. I also think that North American adult educators, myself included, have very little idea of what the little preposition "of" means in the title of that most famous of texts in our field, *Pedagogy of the Oppressed* (1970).

REFERENCES

Baillie, Donald. 1948, *God was in Christ*. New York, Charles Scribner's.

Baum, Gregory. 1978, "Critical Theology" in Walter Conn, ed. *Conversion: Perspectives on Personal and Social Transformation*. New York, Alba House.

Barclay, William. 1964, *Turning to God*. Grand Rapids, Baker Book House.

Barth, Christoph. 1967, "Notes on 'Return' in the Old Testament." *The Ecumenical Review*, Vol. XIX (3), July.

Bell, Brenda, Gaventa, John and Peters, John. 1990, *We Make the Road by Walking: Myles Horton and Paulo Freire*. Philadelphia, Temple University Press.

Berryman, Phillip. 1987, *Liberation Theology*. New York, Pantheon Books.

Brauer, Jerald. 1978, "Conversion: From Puritanism to Revivalism." *The Journal of Religion*, Vol. 58 (3), July.

Cohen, Charles L. 1986, *God's Caress: The Psychology of Puritan Religious Experience*. New York, Oxford University Press.

Conn, Walter. 1986, *Christian Conversion: A Developmental Interpretation of Autonomy and Surrender*. New York, Paulist Press.

Conn, Walter, ed. 1978, *Conversion: Personal and Social Perspectives*. New York, Alba House.

Fackre, Gabriel. 1974, "Conversion." *Andover Newton Quarterly*, Vol. 14(3), January.

Fay, Brian. 1987, *Critical Social Science: The Limits to Liberation*. Ithaca: Cornell University Press.

Fowler, James. 1981, *Stage of Faith: The Psychology of Human Development and the Quest for Meaning*. New York, Harper and Row.

Freire, Paulo. 1970, *Pedagogy of the Oppressed*. New York, Herder and Herder.

Freire, Paulo. 1985, "Education, Liberation and the Church" in *The Politics of Education*. Mass., Bergin and Garvey.

Gaventa, Beverly. 1986, *From Darkness to Light: Aspects of Conversion in the New Testament*. Philadelphia, Fortress Press.

Green, Michael. 1970, *Evangelism in the Early Church*. London, Hodder and Stoughton.

Gutierrez, Gustavo. "A Spirituality of Liberation" in Conn, ed. *Conversion: Perspectives on Personal and Social Transformation*.

Haight, Roger. 1985, *An Alternative Vision: An Interpretation of Liberation Theology*. New York, Paulist Press.

Heikkinen, K. 1967, "Notes on 'Epistrepho' and 'Metanoeo.' " *The Ecumenical Review*, Vol. XIX (3), July.

James, William. 1958 [1902], *The Varieties of Religious Experience*. New York, The New American Library.

Kerans, Patrick. 1974, *Sinful Social Structures*. New York, Paulist Press.

King, John. 1983, *The Iron of Melancholy: Structures of Spiritual Conversion in America from the Puritan Conscience to Victoria Neurosis*. Middletown, Wesleyan University Press.

Kittel, Gerhard, ed. 1967, *Theological Dictionary of the New Testament*, Vol. 4. Grand Rapids: William B. Eerdman's.

Krailsheimer, A. J. 1980, *Conversion*. London, SCM Press.

Kung, Hans. 1978, *On Being a Christian*. Great Britain, Collins Books.

Loder, James. 1989, *The Transformative Moment*. Colorado Springs, Helmers and Howard.

Laporte, Jean-Marc. 1988, *Patience and Power: Grace for the First World*. New York, Paulist Press.

Loffler, Paul. 1965, "The Biblical Concept of Conversion." *Study Encounter*, Vol. 1(2).

Loffler, Paul. 1967, "Conversion in an Ecumenical Context." *The Ecumenical Review*, Vol. XIX (3), July.

McFague, Sallie. 1978, "Conversion: Life on the Edge of the Raft." *Interpretation*, Vol. XXXII (3), July.

Mezirow, Jack. 1978, "Perspective Transformation." *Adult Education*. Vol. 28.

Moltmann, Jurgen. 1978, *The Open Church: Invitation to a Messianic Lifestyle*. Philadelphia, Fortress Press.

Newbigin, Lesslie. 1948, *The Finality of Christ*. New York, Charles Scribner's.

New English Bible. 1972, New York, Oxford University Press.

Nissiotis, Nikos. "Conversion and the Church." *The Ecumenical Review*, Vol. XIX (3), July 1967.

Oates, Wayne. "Conversion: Sacred and Secular" in Conn, ed. *Conversion: Perspectives on Personal and Social Transformation.*

Reuther, Rosemary. 1983, *Sexism and God-Talk: Toward a Feminist Theology.* Boston, Beacon Press.

Sobrino, Jon. 1984, *The True Church and the Poor.* Maryknoll, Orbis.

Tamez, Elsa. 1978, *Bible of the Oppressed.* Maryknoll, Orbis Books.

PART IV
THE INDIVIDUAL

CHAPTER 8

Self, Soul, and Learning
HAROLD W. STUBBLEFIELD

Genuine education is rare in a technicist society that requires for its effectiveness persons who have been socialized, indoctrinated, schooled, and trained rather than persons who have developed personal consciousness (Stanley, 1978, pp 212–213). To most professional adult educators whose task is to serve institutional purposes, the words "self" and "soul" associated with learning will appear strange indeed. Learning as an activity undertaken by a person conceived of as a self or a soul places human agency rather than institutional purpose at the forefront of educational decisions. A person regarded as a self or soul is not an object to be acted upon; they are instead subjects—agents— who act upon the world. The purpose of adult education—as opposed to socialization, indoctrination, training, or schooling—is to enhance the ability of persons to act as agents.

The world of learning enlarges considerably when learning becomes the act of persons acting as agents and not the responses of persons to conditions manipulated by an "educational agent." Exploring the relation of self, soul and learning (epistemology and ethics) takes us to a literature that encompasses theology, history, sociology, philosophy, psychology, and education. Steering clear of the technical arguments by scholars in these fields, we will explore the literature for a fuller understanding of the meaning of self and soul, examine how selected adult education theorists have treated the self/soul from the perspective of education, and conclude with a constructive statement suggested by this exploration.

THE SOCIAL SELF

A dictionary definition of self defines it as the identity, character or essential qualities of a person. In the first half of the twentieth century a new understanding of human nature began to emerge around the concept of the "social self." The key concept held that the self was an actor. George Herbert Mead, a professor at the University of Chicago and the principal theorist of the social self position, postulated a social psychology in which the individual developed in a social context in association with others and not as an isolated individual (Pufetze, 1961). In these interactions he takes note of what other persons tell him, demand of him, or judge him to be. To become a self requires that a person be known and appreciated by others.

Social consciousness develops as a natural course of putting ourselves in the place of others. From these actions the "generalized other" arises, that is, a community of meaning emerges—a community consensus—in which individuals move beyond their private experience by taking the experience of others into themselves. For the social self, moral action "is intelligent, socially directed action, guided by consequences and experiment and by all the knowledge that science can give, in which the interests of others are considered equal, indeed, identical with one's own" (Pufetze, 1961, p 99).

While Mead did not apply his theory of the social self to education, some inferences can be drawn. Learning is a dialogical process in which the self evolves through dialogue with self, with others, and with "Significant Others." Only in relation to and in opposition to others does the self evolve. The self is guided by social impulses and learning is a cooperative act in which the self draws upon information, uses scientific method, and incorporates or rejects new information about self and the world.

From the client-centered therapy of Carl Rogers (1961) came an understanding of the self and a process for facilitating personal growth. Rogers had faith in the individual's internal capacity. His goal as a therapist was to help persons "To Be the Self Which One Truly Is" (Rogers, 1961, p 163). Persons who are free to choose what they want seek to avoid facades, oughts, meeting expectations, and pleasing others; and they move toward self-direction, being a process and not a product, complexity, openness to experience, acceptance of others, and trust of self.

THE SOCIAL SOUL

The idea of the soul remains a powerful symbol in contemporary society. In Jungian psychology the soul points to the depth of human personality. In mechanistic brain science research on the physical causes of behavior, the soul points to another conception of human behavior: persons act because they are thinkers and decision makers. The Hebraic-Christian meaning of soul points to human obligation, to the responsibility of persons to God for their actions in the world. Later positions in religion and philosophy viewed the soul as distinct from the body or equated the soul with the mind. Here we explore the Hebraic-Christian meaning of soul for its implications for learning.

In Hebrew psychology, "man is a living soul who *has* a created human body" (Moody, 1981, p 181). The central biblical statement about the soul in Genesis 2:7–24 portrays persons as created, but the most important truth is theological, the I-Thou relationship between God and persons. The writer of Psalms 139:13–18 depicts this intimate relationship: because God conceived him God knows his character. Psalms 42–43 portrays the soul in dialogue with itself, God, and others. The soul of Genesis is the social soul. Made in the image of God, the soul is rational, male and female, uses language to communicate, and is given dominion over the earth. As Moody (1981, p 487) said, "the living soul of man . . . is the concrete human self in all its relations." The soul exists in the order of nature where it can be studied, and ancient writers such as Proverbs and Ecclesiastes observed and generalized about the soul in its wisdom and foolishness and in its seeking to overcome futility (Sherrill, 1955, p 8).

The knowledge that the soul seeks is neither objective knowledge as in a Great Books program nor subjective knowledge as in the pursuit of individual interests. It is knowledge of a deeper order, knowledge of one's responsibility and obligation to God and to others. That knowledge is gained developmentally, for as animal life seems propelled through certain stages of physical growth so does the soul. In a pioneering book on religious development, Sherrill (1955) traced the distinctive tasks of the soul's development from childhood through old age. To move to the next stage means to go into the unknown, each stage marked by hardships, risks, and suffering. From these the soul shrinks back, an act the Bible describes as rebellion against God.

In secular terms this crisis of shrinking back or moving forward occurs in a particular time and place, and the solution is made in secular terms. In religious terms the crisis has an universal and eternal dimension: persons confront the crisis as a source from beyond themselves, as a confrontation with God. Shrinking back is unbelief, moving forward is faith. Hebrews 11 is the classic New Testament passage that describes the heroic actions that persons take in the temporal sphere because of their faith.

In Sherrill's thought, education addresses the issue of the crisis of growth and development. In Martin Buber's thought, education addresses the issue of life beyond functions. Buber can be characterized as a Jewish philosopher, but that characterization does not do justice to his contributions to philosophical, religious, and communal thought. The key to Buber's philosophy is the I-Thou relationship, the life of dialogue. Life viewed as a dialogical relationship between an I and a Thou does not reduce persons to functions, that is, to their economic value and technical productivity (Friedman, 1960). The life of dialogue is the authentic life, a life that confirms the "thouness" of other persons, avoids appearances, and takes responsibility for its actions.

Education for the life of dialogue is essentially education of character, an education that creates persons who will take responsibility in a specific situation and time. Adult education, in Buber's theory and practice, was not just the extension of university training but "a means of creating a certain type of man demanded by a certain historical situation" (Friedman, 1960, p 182).

Considerable demands are made on the teacher in this educational encounter. It means that the teacher sees the learner in light of what he is now and what he may become. Only by developing mutuality and trust between teacher and learner is the teacher able to see the concrete situation of the learner and the learner is willing to be influenced by the teacher. For learning to occur the learner must participate, but more than participation is necessary. The learner must also "encounter something really 'other' than himself before he can learn" (Friedman, 1960, p 177). In this encounter the teacher maintains his own self. In education the teacher "discovers and nourishes in the soul of the other what one has recognized in oneself as the right" (Friedman, 1960, p 180).

For Sherrill and Buber life calls upon the soul to act responsibly in the concrete situation and time. The soul is called to responsibility, to fulfill the human obligation of responsible action. A similar theme is central to the logotherapy of Victor Frankel (1963), a psychiatrist and survivor of the Nazi concentration camps of World War II. Though Frankel did not write directly about education, his understanding of human freedom, vocation, the meaning of life, and self-transcendence identify essential elements of the human experience that constitute the core concerns of adult education as a moral enterprise.

In his concentration camp experience, Frankel discovered the irreducible truth that persons were always left with the freedom to choose their attitude toward their particular set of circumstances. In experiences of extreme deprivation or in the comfort of middle-class life, persons are questioned by life every day, and they have to answer with concrete action, not meditation. Only by being responsible to one's unique vocation or special mission in life does one find the meaning of life. Persons may see themselves as responsible to society, to their conscience, or to God. Those who consider themselves responsible to God "do not interpret their own lives merely in terms of a task assigned to them but also in terms of the taskmaster who has assigned it to them" (Frankel, 1963, p 174). However persons might interpret their life tasks, the true meaning of life is found in relation to the world, not within the person, and in self-transcendence. For Frankel in contrast to Maslow, the key is self-transcendence, not self-actualization which can only be a by-product and not an end of life.

The self as responsible and guilty permeates Reinhold Niebuhr's (1955) *The Self and the Dramas of History*. Niebuhr, an American Protestant neo-orthodox theologian and social critic, called the human self unique, a uniqueness derived from man's creation in the image of God. Reason is part of what it means for man to be created in the image of God. According to the biblical viewpoint, the self is a creature which is in constant dialogue with itself, with its neighbor, and with God. The self has an internal life that denotes its freedom. The self's dialogue with neighbors confirm its image of itself and provides spiritual security. Beyond empirical verification, dialogue with God is the self "yearning for the ultimate" (Niebuhr, 1955, p 5). Persons cannot escape the search for meaning. Every self "is religious to the degree that the self must commit itself to a system of meaning" (Niebuhr, 1955:62).

A technical age presents unique problems. Communities have expanded so that personal and communal relationships are difficult to create and justice has become more complex. The key problem of a technical age is how to bring self-interest to serve the larger social interest. To Niebuhr biblical faith is not enough. Rational discrimination—the heritage of the Enlightenment—is necessary as well as a sense of the contingency of the historical situation. But even in a technological age biblical faith cannot be set aside as irrelevant. Neither science nor philosophy has invalidated the claims of the Christian faith. A technological and rationalistic society has not prevailed "against the inner witness of the human self, that it is a real self, burdened with both responsibility and guilt" (Niebuhr, 1955, p 147). In biblical faith persons are free and responsible and they have capacity for evil. This is the Hebraic-Christian witness to modern culture.

THE PERSON AS AGENT: GROUNDING ADULT EDUCATION IN THE THEORY OF SELF AND SOUL

Vocation, crisis of faith, education for character, responsibility and guilt, and life's meaning are words not commonly found in the professional adult education literature on discussions of the adult as learner, the teaching-learning transaction, and the aims of adult education. Nonetheless, the themes elaborated by these theorists of the self and soul resonant in the work of several adult education scholars who have probed deeply into the domain of self, soul, and learning. An analysis of several of these yield surprising insights when their works are probed for answers to these questions: (1) Who is the self as knower and what is the world to be known? How does the self know and how should the self live? (2) What is adult education as education of the self?

A contemporary school of thought in adult education portrays the self as knower in such behavorial characteristics as self-directing and self-actualizing, striving to more adequately fulfill social role expectations but restrained by an oppressive pedagogy divorced from the realities of the adult world. This view is only partially true and should be expanded to incorporate a darker, less optimistic picture of the self as knower.

By the 1920s the nascent adult education field had begun to respond to the changes wrought by the emergence of an interdependent society. Lindeman's (1961 [1926]) *The Meaning of Adult Education* is a perceptive diagnosis of the interdependent society and the failure of the educational system to equip adults for life in that society. Central to

Lindeman's understanding of the nature of adult education is his understanding of the nature of the adult personality, which we will treat as his understanding of self. Many characteristics of modern society worked against the development of fully functioning adult personalities, namely, industrialization, urbanization, collectivism, and specialization.

Through adult education, as Lindeman conceived it, adults could become fully functioning personalities as individuals and exercise power in relation to specialized knowledge and large organizations. The self as knower is concerned with meaning, and persons find meaning, Lindeman noted, in the ends for which they strive. Persons want intelligence, power, self-expression, freedom, creativity, and appreciation. The meaning that results from these experiences is not determined beforehand and pre-packaged. Persons find the meanings of life in the process of adult education and not before they begin the experience: "Adult education is a process through which learners become aware of significant experiences" (Lindeman, 1961, p 109).

The self as a responsible actor emerges as the theme in images of the self in the writings of Kenneth Benne, John Walker Powell, and Paul Bergevin. The self as tragic agent is Kenneth Benne's image of the self in adult education. Of the forms of drama, tragedy best fits the response needed for the crisis created by the departmentalization of knowledge, resulting in the division of concerns into the ethical, political, or religious (Benne, 1967). In tragedy an agent acts in response to conditions, and the action taken calls forth counterassertions by those who do not accept the action. Consequences follow actions, and those consequences entail suffering. Human action in the tragic mode is always complex and the character of the agent has strengths and weaknesses. In tragedy persons act in freedom, responsibility, and dignity. As they struggle between competing principles of right they suffer, and through suffering they learn wisdom.

The self divided into multiple roles, a performer of functions, is John Walker Powell's (1949) image of the self that adult education should redress. Multiple roles result from the structure of modern society and cannot be avoided. Providers of adult education took their cue from multiple roles and organized education to equip persons for the functions they performed. In these provisions, no education, however, addressed the problem of how adults could become intelligent about their actions. For the self as intelligent actor and not role performer, Powell organized the educational task around the vocation of citizenship.

The civic self is Paul Bergevin's (1967) image of the self in adult education. Bergevin (1967, p vi) centered his adult education philosophy on the democratic social order and what the adult could contribute to the "civilizing process," which he described as the positive action of the environment on the individual. Adult education was the agency "for the development of free, creative, and responsible persons in order to advance the human maturation process" (Bergevin, 1967, p 5). A critical problem in the formation of the civic self was how to move persons from self-centeredness to socio-centeredness. An arrested social development prevented them from seeing their responsibility for the rest of society. The adult self resisted change because he had not been trained to think in experimental, developmental terms nor helped to see meaning in terms of his own abilities and interests.

The self as knower seeks a worldview. Self-creation—"the responsibility for shaping an identity out of what has been given at birth"—is Leon McKenzie's (1991, p 94) image of the self in adult education. Shaping a better self-creation requires that persons examine their worldview. McKenzie derives the term worldview from the German *Weltanschauung*, a concept originating in the eighteenth-century Enlightenment. People develop worldviews out of their life experiences. Though the worldview that persons construct exist independently of their mind, they do construct a view of the world from their personal experience and perspective. Their worldview results from the interaction of the objectivity of the world outside the person and the subjectivity of experience.

A worldview is developed through tradition. The tradition of the family and significant others in the formative years is the basis for defining who we are and how we interpret our experience in the future. The self does not experience tradition as a dead authority. Tradition is, instead, a living force that changes through time and circumstances, and in some sense we can be said to dialogue with tradition. In self-creation persons seek meaning about life's ultimate meaning and questions of daily concerns. Understanding entails a social dimension. A person's understanding is social, that is, it arises in communication with other persons.

The self as knower seeking release from a prison of expectations imposed by self and by others informs the images of self in Brookfield and Daloz. The self enmeshed in its own self-history is Stephen Brookfield's (1986) image of the self in adult education: the norms and beliefs of others have been so internalized that the self acts in accordance with them without question. The knowledge the self needs is self-knowledge.

The self in transformation is Laurent Daloz's image of the self in adult education. Daloz (1986) described education as a transformational journey in which the driving motive for learning is the search for meaning. Working with adult students studying various curricula in an nontraditional college degree program, Daloz saw their experience as a sense-making, meaning-generating search that was far more encompassing than the study of a subject matter. In the study of subject matter they confronted themselves. Learning entailed development and growth in which occurs a transformation in how they created meaning. Persons experienced growth when they began to look at life through their own eyes and not the eyes of others.

Each of these metaphors of the self as knower points to an educational process that transcends the transmission of knowledge addressed toward greater role efficiency. They point instead to an education of the self becoming and doing. Again, Lindeman was the first to point the way to this new adult education, and for him adult education became a process for discovering meaning.

The adult personality could not become fully functioning nor find meaning through conventional pedagogy. Lindeman's conception of adult education—of what it was and what it was not—appeared then and now as an idiosyncrasy. The meaning of life could not be found in further study of vocations, that is, in specializations that prepared one to perform a narrow function, no matter how intellectually demanding that study might be. Nor could it be found in the study of subjects, that is, in knowledge ordered into disciplines. Such education had to be nonspecialized and nondiscipline based, drawing upon the life experiences that persons brought to the learning experience and centering on the situations they were confronting in their daily life.

Adult education seeks to "give meaning to the categories of experience, not classifications of knowledge" (Lindeman, 1961, p 123). In words similar to those of Frankel, Lindeman (1961, p 115) wrote: "Life is confronted in the form of situations, occasions which necessitate action." Adult education is the method for learning how to analyze situations and plan action. This kind of education takes place through communication, for freedom and intelligence are learned only through interaction with others. The self learning in the situation-experience approach looks inward at what it wants and outward toward the circumstances it confronts. In an educative approach, problems cannot be found solely in ourselves nor in our circumstances. Adults have to examine their interests and wishes as part of the educational equation. The consideration of situation and action becomes an educational experience through discussion with others.

For Benne, Powell, and Bergevin adult education as an education of the self becoming and doing centered around assisting adults to become responsible social actors. Beginning with Benne (1967), the most distinctive human function is the function of choice. Confronted with choosing between different rights, the tragic self searches for wisdom but finds none because in contemporary society knowledge is fragmented. Education is the discipline of choice, and in adult education laboratory education is the form that it takes.

Laboratory education itself is both a form of tragedy and an education for tragedy, Benne claims. In tragedy as well as laboratory education, a person's assertions are met with counterassertions. In the T-Group experience, persons learn through confrontation with others as group members create a new culture. Behaviors appropriate in other circumstances and daily role functions are challenged. This experience requires persons to act as whole persons, make choices, recognize the complexity of human motivation, and overcome barriers to communication. From this experience emerges a self who through the testing of values, beliefs, and behaviors has reoriented its relationships with others.

For Powell (1949) as for Benne, education took the form of an action in which persons confronted themselves and modified their behaviors in more desirable directions. Through the method of group reading as they interacted with others, persons would acquire a common understanding and standards for their actions as citizens. The goal was rational intelligence. Drawing upon psychiatry to interpret his observations, Powell regarded most adult thinking as more emotional than rational.

Rational intelligence—a social product produced by a social process—could be formed in group reading and discussion as adults examined their private beliefs in relation to a common culture represented by the group. Group reading provided the setting in which persons could be reoriented in their relationships. The group provided opportunity to test beliefs by using standards emerging out of the group process. As the group became a society in a microcosm, group members moved first toward norms acceptable to the group, then to norms acceptable to society.

A form of group-based learning, known first as the Indiana Plan and later as Participation Training, was developed by Paul Bergevin and John McKinley (1958) to move adults to social responsibility. In Participation Training adults learned group discussion and program planning skills in a design governed by norms of shared planning, shared appraisal, effective listening, voluntary participation, and mutual acceptance. Through structured discussion group members entered into a learning process that led to personal change. Bergevin and McKinley drew upon the personality defense mechanisms in psychiatry theory for theoretical conceptions of learning. Free to experience and express their resistance, group members learned to express themselves appropriately, accept personal responsibility, cooperate in a common task, and guide their own behavior. Understanding their responsibility for corporate life through the group experience, persons then took responsibility for the larger activities of the organization and community.

For McKenzie (1991), adult education as a process of becoming and doing requires a process for constructing a worldview. A student of Bergevin and McKinley and an adult educator with considerable philosophical acumen, McKenzie regarded Participation Training as a model of how discussion facilitates the construction of a worldview in adults. Continuous self-creation—the construction of a worldview—occurs through conversation, and in some instances these conversations are formally structured in learning activities.

To free a self constrained because it acts unknowingly on the internalized expectations of others requires an educational process that permits the self to examine and challenge these expectations. Adults experience growth in understanding themselves and the meaning of their life when they begin to look at life through their own eyes and not the eyes of others. For Brookfield (1986, p 17) this occurs through a process of reinterpretation of "the culturally constructed nature of knowledge, beliefs, values, and behaviors." In this process the teacher does not hide his "self" in deference to the learner's expressed needs and interests. Rather the teacher inserts his "self" fully into every phase through dialogue with the learner so that the learner can examine the origin and constraints of his values and behaviors. From this transactional dialogue, learners gain ability to engage in self-direction, that is, to act in full awareness of their previously unexamined assumptions, norms, and belief systems.

Growth for Daloz (1986) occurs through dialectic when one moves through the contradictions of knowledge rather than choosing one or the other. Truth emerges as new assertions are derived from the previous assertion and as one understands the opposing position. In this process the teacher offers "the tools of methodology; we can model for them new ways of making meaning" (Daloz, 1986, p 151). As adult students move through the contradictions of their knowing, the teacher holds different frames of reference before them. As students dismantle the old meanings and explore the new, the teacher becomes the "Other" with whom they dialogue, who provides legitimacy to their positions, and who helps them develop meanings that are broadly based.

THE ADULT EDUCATOR AS AN EDUCATOR OF THE SELF

This brief and partial examination of selected adult education theorists in the context of self, soul, and learning shows unmistakingly that theological and moral concerns are embedded in adult education philosophy and practice. Education for becoming and doing takes the form of moral education, for an explicit normative system informs the diagnostic and prescriptive process and addresses the central question of how to create educative processes that would empower adults to live responsibly and in freedom.

Interpretations of the internal and societal constraints that prevent adults from living responsibly and in freedom differ among the theorists, but their interpretations share common elements. In the education of the self, the most important kind of knowledge is neither objective nor subjective but intersubjective. Intersubjective knowledge emerges from a dialogical learning process in which the values, beliefs, and behaviors of the self are challenged by an encounter with other selves. In dialogical learning the teacher or trainer plays an active role. As an educator of the self, the adult educator's expertise lies not in a subject matter or in design skills but in the method of helping persons test knowledge intersubjectively. The epistemology contained in the method embodies ethics as well, for the dialogical learning process is both a way of knowing and a way of acting (Palmer, 1983, p 21).

REFERENCES

Benne, K. D. 1967, *Education for Tragedy*. Lexington, University of Kentucky Press.

Bergevin, P. 1967, *A Philosophy for Adult Education*. New York, Seabury Press.

Bergevin, P. and McKinley, J. 1958, *Design for Adult Education in the Church*. New York, Seabury Press.

Brookfield, S. D. 1986, *Understanding and Facilitating Adult Learning*. San Francisco, Jossey-Bass.

Daloz, L. A. 1986. *Effective Teaching and Mentoring: Realizing the Transformational Power of Adult Learning Experiences*. San Francisco, Jossey-Bass.

Frankel. V. E. 1963, *Man's Search for Meaning*. New York, Pocket Books.

Friedman, M. S. 1960, *Martin Buber: The Life of Dialogue*. New York, Harper Torchbooks.

McKenzie, L. 1991, *Adult Education and Worldview Construction*. Malabar, Florida, Krieger Publishing Company.

Moody, D. 1981, *The Word of Truth*. Grand Rapids, Michigan, Eerdmans Publishing Company.

Niebuhr, R. 1955, *The Self and the Dramas of History*. New York, Charles Scribner's Sons.

Palmer, P. J. 1983, *To Know As We Are Known: A Spirituality of Education*. San Francisco, Harper & Row.

Powell, J. W. 1949, *Education for Maturity*. New York, Hermitage House.

Pufetze, P. E. 1961, *Self, Society, Existence*. New York, Harper Torchbooks.

Rogers, C. R. 1961, *On Becoming a Person*. Boston, Houghton Mifflin.

Sherrill, L. J. 1955, *The Struggle of the Soul*. New York, Macmillan.

Stanley, M. 1978, *The Technological Conscience: Survival and Dignity in an Age of Expertise*. Chicago, University of Chicago Press.

CHAPTER 9

The Fall and the Tree of Knowledge
PETER JARVIS

Humankind has always endeavored to make sense of existence and many of its answers to the problems of meaning are encapsulated in beautiful philosophical tales—this is so not only for the Judeo-Christian faith but for other religions as well. It is a function of myth to embody philosophical responses to questions of meaning in simple, easy-to-remember stories that can be related in a variety of settings. These stories contain a number of different answers to the questions being posed, reflecting the state of knowledge and understanding of the culture from which they emerge. There is evidence to suggest that in nonliterate societies' myths are adapted and changed as the knowledge base and the experience of a society develop; the stories in the second and third chapters of the book of Genesis are no exception to this. These stories are, of course, among the most well known of all of those of the Old Testament and yet they tell a philosophical story that is both profound and relevant to the human condition in all ages. This is their truth, not that they are historically true but then they were not meant to be understood that way; they are responses to problems of meaning. This chapter, then, is an exercise in hermeneutics, seeking to understand the meaning that the writers of these stories gave to experiences which are common to all humankind (Gadamer, 1976, p 7) and fusing their response with more modern interpretations in order to reach a fresh understanding of the problems implicit in the questions that are being posed.

These stories do provide interpretations to questions that are quite central to the philosophy of adult education, especially to the philosophy of learning, and in this chapter some of them are explored. First of all the stories in these two chapters will be examined briefly and from this analysis a number of pertinent points will be drawn which will form the basis of the ensuing discussion. However, it must be recognized from the outset that this analysis will not necessarily reflect the generally held views of the churches. Gerhard von Rad (1961, p 72) wrote about these chapters:

> The results of . . . research, recorded in many monographs and articles are complex, to be sure, and often mutually contradictory; but they are agreed, nevertheless, on one point: that they vigorously contradicted the traditional exposition of the churches.

No attempt, therefore, is made to reconcile any of the points made here with any of the traditional ecclesiastical interpretations or theological orthodoxies of these stories.

CREATION AND FALL

There are two stories of creation in the first three chapters of Genesis, the first story is probably the later one and is contained in the first chapter of Genesis and the first three and a half verses of the second. The second account, the earlier one, is contained in the stories of the remainder of the next two chapters—they are different on many accounts, with the first being cosmological and the second being more concerned with the creation of the world. But even the second story is not a single story—there are two or three strands interwoven which Old Testament scholars have sought to disentangle (see von Rad 1961, for example). However, it is not the purpose of this chapter to enter a debate about biblical scholarship; suffice to note that parts of the story are about rivers and add little to the narrative and there are two trees mentioned in the Garden of trees, those of life and knowledge of good and evil are both specified, with the latter being the more central to the story. Many creation myths contain a tree of life, but in this one it is only mentioned twice—at the beginning and the end—the focus here is on the tree of knowledge of good and evil which is, surprisingly enough, mentioned nowhere else in the Old Testament. According to von Rad, the tree of knowledge of good and evil may actually have been called initially only "the tree of knowledge," for the latter words appear to be a later addition but, in any case, the phrase "good and evil" actually means "of everything," although it could be argued that the possession of knowledge has ethical overtones and that learning is itself a moral activity. However, the topic here is about eating from the tree of knowledge.

Briefly, then, the story goes like this: God created a male human being and he then planted a garden into which he placed the man. Unlike the interpretation given by Fromm (1984, p 27) who suggests that the man was not expected to work in paradise, the man was expected to work in the garden, but not to eat of the fruit of the trees of knowledge and life. Thereafter, all the animals were created whom the man named and, finally, a woman was formed. It was the woman who was tempted by a serpent who spoke to her and enticed her to eat from the fruits of the tree of knowledge. When she and the man did so, they immediately knew that they were naked and, when they revealed their discovery to God, he realized what they had done and, therefore, he punished them by putting enmity between them and between peoples generally, and then he drove them from the Garden and insured that they could not return by placing guards on the gates. He also made them toil in the fields for the remainder of their lives.

This story, then, needs to be seen as a philosophical response to questions of meaning, written within the conceptual framework of the people of the time and transmitted to them in a manner which they could understand and which could easily be remembered. It uses the historical perspective of creation to convey, and almost to legitimate, a philosophical response to a question. This story contains answers to the questions of meaning that some of the ancient peoples must have posed. But what were the questions? Since the story does not specify what they were, it is only possible to surmise that they revolved around the nature of humankind in the world: why was it that human beings appear to have a different relationship with the natural world to that of the animals, why was it that the world was not perfect, why are people not perfect, and so on. For educators, it also raises some nice points about freewill, language and learning.

LIVING IN HARMONY WITH THE NATURAL WORLD

Humankind was created, according to the myth, and lived in harmony with nature in the Garden. In the beginning, then, humankind was an intrinsic part of the animal world and could live in harmony with it in paradise. This is the picture drawn in the first part of the story. It points to human beings who responded to the demands of nature in an instinctive manner, who fitted into the scheme of things without apparently creating any form of disharmony. Like the animals, humankind could respond to the commands of the Creator and could, therefore, be taught and could imitate. This appears, according to the storyteller, to have been the divine plan, with humankind at the apex of creation. After all, the man named all the animals. This is a rather difficult passage to understand and von Rad (1961, p 81) suggests that:

> This naming is thus both an act of copying and an act of appropiative ordering, by which man intellectually objictifies the creatures for himself. Thus one may say something is said here about the origin of language, so long as one does not emphasize the discovery of external words but rather that inner appropriation of recognizing and interpreting, which happens in language.

In a sense the ancient authors had highlighted, without commenting upon it, one of the major differences between humankind and the natural world—humankind is linguistic—a point drawn out by Aristotle in his discussion about the differences between human beings and the animal world. Gadamer (1976, p 59) summarizes Aristotle's position thus:

> Aristotle once developed the difference between man and animal in the following way: animals can understand each other by indicating to each other what excites their desire so that they can seek it, so that they can flee from it. To men alone is the *logos* given as well, so that they can make more manifest to each other what is useful and harmful, and therefore what is right and wrong. (*Italics* in original)

However, no emphasis is placed upon linguisticality in this story, although it is a significant feature throughout this chapter. Gadamer, for instance, points out that further advance about the nature of language had to be sought outside of this biblical story, and then it became necessary to recognize that it was impossible to inquire into the nature of humankind without reference to language. Language is essentially human, or humankind is essentially linguistic. Perhaps, even more significant to this discussion, the Greek word *logos* carries with it not only the connotations of *word*, and *language*, but also those of *reason*, *thought*, *concept* and *law*. Hence, language is a complex phenomenon which reveals some of the problems in any investigation about the nature of humanity. Gadamer (1976, p 63) suggests that learning "to speak does not mean learning to use a pre-existent tool for designating a world already somehow familiar to us; it means acquiring a familiarity and acquaintance with the world itself and how it confronts us." That the storyteller did not include a notion of learning to use language is not surprising, for the use of language assumed the humanity of the man, for humanity is fundamentally linguistic—but this is a problem, since thought and reason are potentially disruptive to a world which is controlled by nature and instinct, and this is part of the purpose of the story.

A WORD OF TEMPTATION

And so to the serpent! Perhaps it matters little about what the snake represents, although curiously enough it could even represent thought itself! For this is the nature of temptation—thoughts are put into words! The snake engaged the woman in dialogue, first of all in an innocuous manner and then in a quite specific tempting way. Here the temptation is phrased in knowing "good and evil"—the words of the temptation are significant:

> . . . . For God knows that when you eat of it your eyes will be opened, and you will be like God, knowing good and evil. (Genesis 3:5)

Von Rad (1961, pp 86f) writes about this significant phrase:

> "Good and evil" is therefore a formal way of saying what we mean by colorless "everything"; and here too one must take its meaning as far as possible. The fascination of this statement is in its lack of restriction, its intangibleness; it is intentionally mysterious, and after it has brought its throughts of man in a definite direction, it is again open on all sides and gives room to all whispering secret fantasies. What the serpent's insinuation means is the possibility of an extension of human existence beyond the limits set by God at creation, an increase of life not only in the sense of pure intellectual enrichment but also of familiarity with, and power over, mysteries that lie beyond man.

In a sense the temptation might be seen as a question being posed—why? Why should humankind not know more, if there is more to be known? Why should individuals not develop beyond limits imposed externally? Why should not humankind reach out and become as gods? There is a disjuncture between the thought processes of the thinker and the thinker's understanding of the wider world. Herein lies the possibility of making a choice and knowing, or between being obedient to the command and being safe—but learning nothing more. The biblical story, significantly, equates the issue of freedom with the act of disobedience. The choice was made and, as Fromm (1984, pp 27f) writes:

> From the standpoint of the Church which represented authority, this is essentially sin. From the standpoint of man, however, this is the beginning of human freedom. Acting against God's orders means freeing himself from coercion, emerging from the unconscious existence of prehuman life to the level of man. Acting against the command of authority, committing a sin, is in its positive human aspect the first act of freedom, that is, the first *human* act. In the myth the sin in its formal aspect is the acting against God's command; in its material aspect it is the eating of the tree of knowledge. The act of disobedience as an act of freedom is the beginning of reason. (*Italics* in original)

The ability to think and reason means that humankind cannot be constrained by the instinctive behavior of the natural world. Humankind transcends that world and can decide to act, can make decisions to act in ways that appear contrary to the demands of nature. But more, there is an inquisitiveness about humankind, always seeking to resolve those questions that keep being raised by the very process of existing. It is part of the nature of humankind to inquire, or as Kelly (1963) argued: humankind is like a scientist living in the world, experimenting and trying to make sense of it all.

THE PROCESS OF LEARNING

"And they knew that they were naked"—or that they had learned as a result of eating the fruits of the tree of knowledge. The process of learning is described only in the temptation: they saw, they thought about the possibilities and then they acted. And here is the outcome! Part of the essence of humanity is the ability to learn and, like obedience, it is paradoxical that it should be associated with the first sin. But how can it be a fall when the process being described is one in which the human being begins the process of growing and developing? It can only be a sin if obedience is the only good, whatever the circumstances. It is also paradoxical that the first chapter of this book should argue that learning is a religious phenomenon—and here it is associated with sinfulness. This then is a paradox of learning: for some it is good and for others it might be seen as an act of disobedience. But it is this break with nature, this ability to learn and transcend nature which is of the essence of humanity; it is the ability to be free to learn and grow and develop which is fundamental to the human being. It is this which is the religious process.

Learning, then, lies at the very essence of humanity; learning is at the heart of growth. Here humankind is different from the animal kingdom—animals can be taught, as the behaviorists have shown—but can they inquire and learn without being taught? Can they adapt to great changes and learn from new situations. In the natural world many species and creatures have become extinct because they have been unable to adapt to change, because their instincts controlled their behavior so that they were unable to learn and to change as climatic, and other, conditions on earth changed. It is by having the ability to learn that has enabled humankind to survive. Learning lies beyond education and at the center of human experience itself. Learning is the process of transforming that experience into knowledge, skills, attitudes and so on (See Jarvis, 1987 for an early discussion of this and Jarvis, 1992, for a fuller philosophical discussion of learning). Learning occurs at the intersection of individual human experience and the wider world. It is, however, not merely a matter of internalizing perceptions of that outside world, it is a matter of experiencing it—either through direct action or through language—and then reasoning and thinking about it and thereafter reaching an understanding of it. This is the process of knowing—not that there is fruit on the tree that are merely eaten; it is not just a process of taking and having, but of being and knowing. This is a significantly different process: people have knowledge which, as Marcel (1976, p 145), is essentially communicable but "knowledge is (also) within being, enfolded by it . . . We can only arrive at it by a reflection at one remove, which depends upon an experience of presence" (Marcel, 1976, p 115), which is linguistic reflection upon actual experience of the world.

Some educators have rather tried to reduce learning and contain it within the classroom, and the extent to which they have succeeded in producing a social definition of learning that relates it primarily to education, they have succeeded in their unconscious quest of reducing it to a managable phenomenon! But to seek to control learning itself is perhaps a more difficult thing—whether it be the educator, or the church, or the state, as this story suggests, is a problematic, even immoral, phenomenon. It was John Stuart Mill (1962, p 239) who wrote:

> The objections which are urged with reason against State education do not apply to the enforcement of education by the State, but to the State's taking upon itself to direct education; which is a totally different thing. That the whole or any part of education of the people should be in the State's hands I go as far as any one in deprecating. All that has been said of the importance of individuality of character, and the diversity of opinions and modes of conduct, involves, as of the same unspeakable importance, diversity of education.

Individuals are prone to be disobedient when others seek to control their learning, since they seek to be free! But to control the people's learning is something that states, dictators and, even, teachers have tried to do for many centuries. People need to know, need to be free to learn, for learning is at the heart of their humanity and emanates from their experience of living; to locate it elsewhere is to artificialize it.

Through this process people are going to grow, but they will also individuate and so the possibility of disagreement and, even, conflict between peoples becomes even more possible.

THE OUTCOMES OF LEARNING

The story suggests that the man and the woman were driven from paradise, never to return, and they were to know conflict and work the land. That was the perceived punishment for disobedience! Perhaps, it was also the outcome of learning as well, and this will become apparent in the ensuing discussion. One of the first outcomes of learning is to gain knowledge and to become more individual and free. Descartes started his quest to understand existence from the idea of knowing—I think, therefore, I am. Macquarrie (1973, p 125) has nicely turned this around the other way: I am, therefore, I think! Humankind, by the very fact of existence, thinks and questions: knowing comes first and stems from being which is always becoming as more opportunities to learn present themselves to individuals. At the heart of this quest is the knowing, developing person in the world rather that confronting objective knowledge that has to be internalized. This then places a different emphasis upon education for now it is possible to see truth in subjectivity and help individuals grow rather than merely to transmit and receive knowledge. This is different from what is frequently regarded as learning, when students are expected to learn objective knowledge from the teachers and from those who control the learning process.

In a sense Rogers (1983) captures this idea in a number of his case studies about education where he contrasts education and learning. It is a contrast of control and direction with humanity and growth. Perhaps this is an over-simplification and yet it is the type of dilemma that lose some people from education (Rogers, 1983, p 11) and cause others to become a threat to their colleagues. While not all that Rogers claims about being free to learn is necessarily acceptable, he has highlighted one quite essential element of this story—control of the knowledge for whatever reason, good or evil, does not always prevent the learning occurring and, indeed, some seek to facilitate this process to the chagrin of others.

Some try to control learning because the control of knowledge is power—this is one of the lessons of this story, and those who act freely and learn, run the risk of punishment from those who exercise power. It is part of the paradox of contemporary society that the control of knowledge is power and while learning is regarded as a good thing, it is only that learning which is controlled that is really acceptable. Here is a necessary tension in human living: there needs to be trust and relationship, but there is often power and endeavors to produce conformity, even harmony with the world. Some people seek this, in any case, for they fear freedom (Fromm, 1984) and prefer peace and harmony. Perhaps in this idea there is a desire for that harmony lost in the Garden, but to which the people cannot return since there were guards set at its gate.

The myth promised enmity between the man and the women, however. This, in itself, is significant since all the outcomes of learning are not necessarily good for everybody. Learning leads to individuation and part of the process of becoming and individual involves breaking the ties that bind people together. One of the problems of learning and growing, one which has become prevalent in contemporary society, can be easily illustrated by the following example: two people who are close friends have different experiences of work and life—the one has exciting experiences that encourage growth and development, but the other has less exciting opportunities and a life that is rather repetitive so that what growth occurs is more gradual. The two friends might easily develop different interests and totally different understandings about the world; they grow apart! Their friendship changes and then declines because they have grown at different speeds and have developed differing interests and concerns; perhaps not enmity comes between them, although this is sometimes the case, but at least disaffection occurs. Learning, then, is a paradoxical phenomenon—it leads to growth and to individuation, to development and, possibly, to detachment from others. It puts disharmony where there was harmony, but then, paradoxically, this disjuncture itself provides the conditions for yet more learning!

CONCLUSIONS

Learning is a human process that is infrequently discussed but often present in the literature. Indeed, the philosophy of learning is a neglected topic in educational literature, but here in a beautiful philosophical myth lie some profound ideas about human learning and, indeed, about human being itself. This story is: about the fact that the human needs to be free but somehow longs for the situation where there is harmony and security; about the fact that freedom is both associated with the nature of humanity and with disobedience; that human learning is both about human growth and development, yet the differentiation and individuation that can result might lead to disaffection and conflict. This story then looks back for its legitimation, back to prehistory, in order to answer questions about the present and, yet humankind exists in time but often looks forward to a period beyond

time when that paradise can be discovered and, perhaps, even learning
will be no more! But then, would it be paradise?

> For it began with a tale of a garden
> And ends with a city of gold

REFERENCES

Fromm, E. 1984, *The Fear of Freedom*. London, ARK Paperbacks.
Gadamer, H.-G. 1976, *Philosophical Hermeneutics*, trans D. Elinge Berkeley,
    University of California Press.
Jarvis, P. 1987, *Adult Learning in the Social Context*. London, Croom Helm.
Jarvis, P. 1992, *Paradoxes of Learning*. San Francisco, Jossey-Bass.
Kelly, G. 1963, *A Theory of Personality*. New York, W. W. Norton.
Macquarrie, J. 1973, *Utilitrianism*. Harmondsworth, Penguin.
Marcel, G. 1965, *Being and Having*. Gloucester, Peter Smith.
Mill, J. S. 1962, *Utilitarianism* and Other Essays. London, Fontana.
Rogers, C. 1983, *Freedom to Learn for the 80s*. New York, Merrill.
Von Rad, G. 1961, *Genesis*. London, SCM Press.

CHAPTER 10

Personhood—Personal and Faith Development
BRADLEY COURTENAY

For well over half a century, adult educators have maintained the importance of personal development as a factor in planning and conducting educational experiences for adults. Growth in individuals is assumed and is judged to be positive. Lindeman (1926) advocated that the responsibility of adult education is to assist adults with change: "Changing individuals in continuous adjustment to changing social functions—this is the bilateral though unified purpose of adult learning" (p 166). More recent adult education scholars hold similar views, acknowledging that adult education's role is to help people grow (Tennant, 1990); to promote movement beyond the familiar and unquestioned (Daloz, 1988a); to help individuals improve self-development and institutions enhance employees, members, and clients (Knowles, 1980; Cross, 1981).

It is no surprise then that textbooks on adult learning and adult program planning consistently emphasize the importance of adult development with particular attention to personal social roles and the need for growth (Cross, 1981; Long, 1983; Merriam and Caffarella, 1991; Knowles, 1980; Caffarella, 1988). Social roles are frequently presented within a developmental scheme of tasks that adults must fulfill throughout life. For example, in early adulthood, the individual faces the tasks of selecting a mate, learning to live with a spouse, starting a family, rearing children, managing a home, getting started in an occupation, taking on civic responsibility, and finding a congenial social group (Havighurst, 1972). Almost no attention is given to the tasks associated with an individual's faith. No doubt a major contributor to this absence in the adult education literature is the concern not to proselytize or to give the appearance of supporting one religious point of view over another. Yet, as we shall see in this chapter, faith development and personal development have distinct similarities in their origins, characteristics, and implications for adult education.

The purpose of this chapter is to identify and explain the linkages and distinctions between personal and faith development and to discuss the implications of those development models for adult education. The first section of the chapter is an overview of the origins and characteristics of personal development models. The second section of the chapter provides a similar portrayal of a faith development model. Commonalities and dissimilarities of the two sets of models are presented in the third section. The final section of the chapter identifies and critiques the implications of both sets of models for adult education.

OVERVIEW OF PERSONAL
DEVELOPMENT MODELS

In their comprehensive text on adult learning, Merriam and Caffarella (1991) identify physical aging, psychological changes, and sociocultural factors as the three major contributors to models of adult development. Within the physical aging category are such changes as declines in vision and hearing, losses in reaction time due to changes in the central nervous system, and onset of chronic diseases such as cardiovascular complications, cancer, and arthritis. In one way or another these physical changes affect all adults as they age and these changes may impact learning, for example, timed exercises in the learning opportunity have the potential to discourage older adults who respond more slowly than younger adults. Physical changes may also be the stimulus for alterations in the psychological category, such as perceptions of self, examination of the ego, and inquiry over the meaning of life in the presence of a debilitating physical condition.

It is within the psychological category that Merriam and Caffarella (1991) identify the roots of personal development models. They conclude that

a number of diverse concepts have been placed in . . . personal development, including the theories of ego development (Erikson, 1963; Loevinger, 1976), general personality development (Levinson and others, 1978;
Gould, 1978; Vaillant, 1977), moral development (Kohlberg, 1973;
Gilligan, 1982), and faith development (Fowler, 1981). The common
theme in this vast array of work is the changing nature of the internal
self as we develop. (p 103)

Two groups of models emerge from the psychological literature according to Peck (1986). The first, the age or stage model, is dependent
mostly on Erikson (1963). Basically, this model reflects that life-span
is a linear progression through various age-related stages of development. In each stage, the individual must address developmental tasks,
and as these tasks are mastered, the individual moves on to the next
stage. Biological and social pressures provide awareness that new tasks
need to be addressed. Havighurst's (1972) developmental tasks, which
outline the critical challenges for adults at different ages, is a long-
standing example of the age/stage model. Of particular significance to
adult education is Havighurst's *teachable moment* proposition, that
point in individuals' lives when they are ready to learn the knowledge
and skills to complete one of life's tasks.

Merriam and Caffarella (1991) observe that later researchers, such
as Kohlberg (1973), Loevinger (1976), and Kegan (1982) describe
stages of development, but not in relation to specific ages or age periods. A major characteristic of these models is that they are hierarchial
in nature with each stage qualitatively different from the others. Individuals move from simple to complex ways of viewing self and the
world and into more comprehensive, flexible stages. But while all individuals can make the transition from stage to stage, the researchers
acknowledge that not everyone will. It is possible, and likely, that some
people will accommodate so readily to a particular stage or feel constrained by external factors such as family pressure that they will settle
for a less complicated stage. Daloz (1988b) identifies and analyzes the
factors that prevented "Gladys," a returning student, from transcending
to higher stages of development.

The second group of models is based on life events. A major pro-
ponent of the life events model is Neugarten (1976). For her, chronological time and age should not be indicators for measuring
development. Individuals are too complicated for such a simple solution. Rather, development is to be evaluated by the individual's "sub-

jective reaction to the aging process that determines how she responds to the passage of chronological time. The person is therefore strongly influenced by a socio-historical context that shapes both the stereotypes of aging and these stereotypes' effects upon the experience of aging" (Peck, 1986, p 275). Thus, in planning programs for adults, the successful adult educator will give consideration to the effects of such life events as births, deaths, divorces.

Lately, increasing interest is being given to the importance of sociocultural factors and adult development. Merriam and Caffarella (1991) cite several researchers who advocate the assumption that contexts defined by social and cultural variables are the critical factors in development. These researchers are less interested in identifying generalizable predictions that will hold over time. Social class is an example of the concerns of this perspective, that is, the effects of the differences of working-class and middle-class people. In particular, social class is likely to have an effect on the choices adults will make and the opportunities they will have. Jarvis (1987) captures the challenge of this perspective, namely, the importance of recognizing that individuals, through socialization, take on to some extent, the values, beliefs, and knowledge of the society at large.

Models of personal development have emerged from consideration of physical changes with age, psychological perspectives of development and the effects of sociocultural factors. Within the psychological perspective is the view that development is linear and sequential. Individuals move from one stage to another, in some cases by age, in other cases because a crisis or new task presents itself. Each stage is qualitatively different from others, hierarchically ordered, and increasingly complex, comprehensive, and flexible. While all individuals have the potential to pass through the stages, not everyone will choose to do so. Movement from stage to stage is preferred because it promotes growth.

OVERVIEW OF FAITH DEVELOPMENT MODELS

The most outstanding model of faith development is found in the research of Fowler (1981) and includes six stages. The model's origins are eclectic, but traceable to the cognitive stages of Piaget (1967), the moral stages of Kohlberg (1974), and the personality stages of Erikson (1963). Additionally, the model incorporates the consistent points of exchange between individuals and the world as advocated by Levinson, Darrow, Klein, Levinson, and McKee (1978) and the influence of socialization on people found in Westerhoff's *Values for Tomorrow's Children* (Fowler, 1976a).

Despite the variety of the roots of Fowler's model, the cognitive, personality, and moral models of development appear to have had the greatest impact on faith development. In fact, to demonstrate the connections between faith development and the age/stage personal development models, reflected by the cognitive/personality/moral proponents, Fowler (1981) devotes six chapters of his book describing the stages to a fictional conversation with Erikson, Piaget, and Kohlberg. The intent of the dialogue is to reflect the linkages and gaps among the precursors and Fowler's thinking. In an earlier work, Fowler (1976b, p 190) claimed that the six stages are in the Piagetian and Kohlbergian genre; "they do constitute *integrated structural wholes*, which are *hierarchically related* (each successive stage incorporating the capacities of all the previous ones)." To Fowler (1976b, p 190) the order of the stages "is sequential and invariant."

Faith development is unique in its differences, particularly with Piaget and Kohlberg models. Fowler claims that both Piaget and Kohlberg conceptually distinguish between the cognitive and affective dimensions of development. According to Fowler (1976a), Piaget and Kohlberg claim that cognitive structures tend to dominate over affective dynamics and only cognitive structures can serve as the basis for describing stages. For faith development both cognitive and affective dimensions are important. In addition to the psychological processes embedded in Piaget, Kohlberg, and Erikson, Fowler also incorporates theological and philosophical traditions which emphasize will and reason, knowing and valuing.

There are several characteristics of the stages of faith development. As discussed in the next section of this chapter, many parallel the personal development models. Because the characteristics of the model emerge from the stages, a brief description of each stage is provided below:

Stage 1: Intuitive-Projective Faith (Early Childhood, Ages 2–6)—fantasy filled, uninhibited imagination that may be challenged later by more reflective thinking. The emergence of concrete thinking is the stimulus for moving to stage 2.

Stage 2: Mythic-Literal Faith (School Years)—beliefs are expressed as literal interpretations, very controlling. The stimulus to move to the next stage is contradictions in beliefs that lead to reflection on meanings; literalism breaks down.

Stage 3: Synthetic-Conventional Faith (Adolescence)—conformity best describes this stage. Here, individuals are not strong enough to establish independent, autonomous identity. Many adults never move from this stage. Sources that help individuals move to stage 4 are clashes and contradictions between valued authorities; changes by leaders that are considered unshakable; and critical reflection that recognizes that beliefs are relative.

Stage 4: Individuative-Reflective Faith (Young Adulthood)—Unavoidable tensions highlight this stage: individuality vs. group identity; subjectivity vs. critical objectivity; and commitment to the relative vs. possibility of an absolute. The individual moves to stage 5 out of dissatisfaction with existing perceptions and meanings or disillusionment with one's compromises.

Stage 5: Conjunctive Faith (Midlife and Beyond)—this stage is characterized by the ability to see both sides of an issue simultaneously. Persons in this stage are open to paradox and contradictions. The impetus to move to stage 6 is the awareness of an untransformed world and a vision to be a transformer.

Stage 6: Universalizing Faith (no age range)—Individuals in this stage are outside the criteria for normalcy. Lack of concern for self and a passion for transcending characterize this stage. People in this stage are brought to it by the providence of God and the forces in history, e.g., Gandhi, Martin Luther King, Jr., and Dietrich Bonhoeffer.

A major characteristic and certainly a key factor in understanding Fowler's stages of faith development is his definition of faith. A cursory review of faith development is likely to result in the conclusion that it describes the progression of one's religious beliefs. It does, but as used by Fowler (1981, p 9), faith transcends religion: "faith, at once deeper and more personal than religion, is the person's or group's way of responding to transcendent value and power as perceived and grasped through the forms of the cumulative tradition." Fowler would have us see faith as a verb, "faithing" for example, a dynamic, active concept. Thus, if one's faith is not static, then it can develop; it can evolve through stages. Faith, then, is to be seen as

> people's evolved and enhancing ways of experiencing self, others and world (as they construct them) as related to and affected by the ultimate conditions of existence (as they construct them) and of shaping their lives' purposes and meanings, trusts and loyalties, in light of the character of being, value and power determining the ultimate conditions of existence (as grasped in their operative images—conscious and unconscious—of them). (Fowler, 1981, p 92–93)

To those who would see the faith stages as associated with the spiritual disciplines, Fowler (1976b) counters that mystical spirituality is prescriptive, while faith stages are descriptive. Moreover, faith stages do not make claims to "religious sufficiency." Yet, despite the disclaimers of strong ties to religion, Fowler (1976a, p 204) admits " . . . that there is likely no way toward Stages 5 or 6 except through the powerful and particular *contents* of specific religious traditions."

A second characteristic of the faith stages is the relationship to distinct age ranges of life. While specific ages are not attached to the stages, periods of life are quite evident. According to Fowler (1976a), the ages are averages, minimal ages below which no given stage emerged in his research. While the stages are dependent on age and maturation for some of the necessary conditions for stage transition, they are not sufficient conditions. Other factors include the richness and stimulation of the environment, the availability of models of the next "place," and the individual's encounter with crises or dilemmas which shake up his or her faith outlook (Fowler, 1979).

The hierarchial nature of the faith development stages is the third characteristic of Fowler's model. Earlier stages are simpler, with undifferentiated structures. Later stages increase in complexity, flexibility, and comprehensiveness. Later stages also carry forward the operations of earlier stages, thus each stage builds upon the other. Stages are invariant and cannot be skipped, and stage sequences are irreversible unless there is mental or emotional deterioration (Fowler, 1976a).

Also inherent in Fowler's stages is the perception that faith development is life-span, an ongoing process of forming and reforming one's ways of being in and seeing the world. With respect to the general effects on the individual, " . . . a person cannot comprehend reasoning more than one stage higher than the stage he occupies," and " . . . if individuals remain in a stage over too long a period of time, if they are not forced out of that stage, they may become *incapable* of moving to a higher level" (Duska and Whelan, 1975, p 86–87).

The origins and characteristics of faith development suggest direct linkages but also unique qualities to those of the personal development models. Faith development evolved from the personal development models, especially from the psychological and moral perspectives (Erikson, Piaget, Levinson, and Kohlberg). Fowler is quick to point out that he also relied on that aspect of socialization theory that emphasizes the interdependence of individuals and on philosophical and theological perspectives to support the importance of knowledge and value. The characteristics of faith development include a dynamic and global definition of faith, the importance of age ranges to stage transition, a hierarchial ordering of the stages (which emphasizes growth in faith, which views the stages as sequenced, which sees the stages as progressing from simpler to more complex ways of viewing self and the world, and which asserts that a person cannot move to the next stage without acquiring the basic competencies of the present stage), and a life-span perspective to faith development. Reflection back to the characteristics of the personal development models reveals similarities and differences with these faith development stages and that is the subject of the next section of this chapter.

COMPARATIVE ANALYSIS OF PERSONAL AND FAITH DEVELOPMENT

One of the obvious connections between personal and faith development is origin. Both types of adult development emerge from the same psychosocial models of such phenomena as cognition, personality, morality, and age stages/life tasks. The important difference in origin is that faith development emerged later than personal development models and thus drew from a larger body of research and theory regarding human development. Fowler (1981) claims to have produced a model with a broader theoretical base that incorporates both cognitive and affective aspects of development. He views the personal development models as limited primarily to cognitive dimensions.

A second and readily evident link between personal and faith development is the emphasis on self-identity and growth. For example, Knowles (1980, p 28) asserts that an ultimate need of individuals " . . . is to achieve complete self-identity through the development of their full potentialities." Claiming faith is learned life-style, Lang (1976, p 72) concludes that people's " . . . faith identity is inseparably bound up with their psychological identity . . . the same dynamics that are operative in the establishment of a self-identity also participate in the faith-forming process." Self-identity is often matched with growth and scholars from both types of human development advocate that growth through developmental stages is absolutely necessary. Havighurst (1972, p 7), for example, saw a direct relationship between life task accomplishment and happiness: " . . . successful achievement of which (a life task) leads to (an individual's) happiness and to success with later tasks, while failure leads to unhappiness in the individual, disapproval by the society, and difficulty with later tasks." Fowler (1986, p 39) also gives considerable attention to the growth theme in human development, concluding that " . . . we stand under an imperative toward ongoing growth."

The criticality of growth is a reflection of a third linkage between personal and faith development—hierarchial stages that range from the simple to the complex, from rigidity to flexibility, and from narrow to comprehensive perspectives. As pointed out in the two preceding sections of this chapter, scholars representing both types of adult development models not only propose hierarchial stages, but also labels for each stage, and in many cases, age ranges for each stage. Both sets of scholars advocate that competencies in one stage must be acquired before an individual can move to the next stage, implying that earlier competencies are necessities for success in the next stage and that each stage builds upon the other. Another commonality of the stages is that while individuals can, they may not choose to move through all the stages of development.

The fourth similarity between personal and faith development is the perspective that human development is life-span. The age ranges and the level of increasing complexity of competencies in each stage reflect the difficulty of mastering the requirements of even one stage at a single point in the life of an individual. Thus, whether in the personal or faith dimension, individuals can and should evolve throughout their lives.

The foregoing discussion of the links between personal and faith development highlight the areas of similarity with faith defined in the general or universal sense and religion viewed as one aspect of faith development. There are connections between both types of development where faith development is defined strictly in the religious context. Gooden (1983), as an example, identifies four ways in which "adult" and faith development merge. First, both are characterized by commitments. Adults have commitments to family, a job, the community. Faith by its basic meaning requires commitment also. To Gooden the basic commitments of adulthood are paradigmatic of a religious faith situation.

Second, adults' concerns throughout life extend beyond the major responsibilities they undertake; they result in reflection over a sense of worth, importance, and well-being. Meaning is the one word that would characterize such concerns. According to Gooden (1983, p 86–87),

> this overarching sense of meaning, which is necessary to sustain a sense of well-being and which makes it possible to sustain even difficult commitments, is again an act of faith both because one lives within the frame of meaning in a trustful, committed way and because its verity is accepted without proof.

Third, adults must relate to both the past and the future. This relationship causes constant reflection over self-understanding and insight, which may lead to reimaging the self. These possible new configurations of the self may be cause for disruptions or even crises. For Gooden, faith is a critical aid in such times. Faith can be the source of security for successful self-transformation and reimaging.

Fourth, adults usually realize their own personal immortality. Awareness of the death of significant others, as well as one's own impending death is held in tension with the goodness of life and one's contribution to life. Faith is important in these times of awareness to help the adult transcend the bodily self "to feel that the pain of present life and the injustice of human society are not all there is, and that life is ultimately significant . . . " (Gooden, 1983, p 88).

Bruning and Stokes (1983) also describe particular associations between personal and faith development (religious meaning), noting first that life cycles are related to ceremonial events. For example, the baptism of a baby focuses on the nurturing role of grandparents and the commitments of parents and the baby. Faith and change are correlated according to Bruning and Stokes and represent a second linkage between personal and faith development. On the one hand, conversion and development are interrelated. While conversion precedes development, the latter is vital for maintaining the significance of the former. On the other hand, sin and maturity reflect counterpoints between the negative and positive aspects of life: sin referring to the frailties in life and maturity to the acceptance of faults.

Another link between personal and faith development for Bruning and Stokes (1983) is what they refer to as the developmental tasks of faith. For example, they ask:

Are there not specific challenges which relate to our faith growth that must be dealt with successfully in adulthood if one's faith is to have its fullest meaning? To what extent are the experiences of establishing a family or dealing with one's singleness important elements of one's Faith Development in young adulthood? . . . Is it not the re-establishing of a marital relationship when 'family' means 'just the two of us again' a central expression of faith? (Bruning and Stokes, 1983, p 51)

Finally, while they have no tested evidence, Bruning and Stokes (1983) turn to descriptive and opinion-based literature to raise the possibility of a relationship between crises and faith. They propose the suggestion that faith development appears to correlate with the crises in individual's lives.

The comparative analysis of personal and faith development has yielded several linkages. However, there are at least three ways in which the two types of human development differ. First, as noted in the first part of this section, the origins of faith development extend beyond the personal development models. Fowler's stages of development incorporate psychosocial factors of the preceding personal development models, as well as factors from theology and philosophy, particularly the notion of the important balance of knowledge and value, cognition and affection.

Second, the use of the word faith provides an inherent distinction between the two types of models. Even though Fowler defines faith in the universal mode, as a general commitment in life, the stages describe human development in a circumscribed way. The concept of commitment, even without any religious connotations, reflects a focus on one aspect of an individual's life.

Yet, the importance of religion in faith development cannot be overlooked and is the third difference between the two types of human development. On the one hand, Fowler would have the reader divorce religion from faith development in order to make the point that faith transcends religion. But on the other hand, Fowler uses religious illustrations to explain the stages, although not exclusively, and he even asserts that religious content is probably the only source for moving from stages 5 to 6.

Similarities and differences between personal and faith development clarify the distinctive nature of the relationship. For the adult education researcher and practitioner, the implications of the relationship are important for expanding knowledge and improving practice. The final section of this chapter addresses those concerns.

IMPLICATIONS OF DEVELOPMENT MODELS FOR ADULT EDUCATION

This chapter began with an acknowledgment of the long-standing attention given to adult development by adult education scholars. The case could easily be made that consideration of adult development models is an assumption made by most adult education practitioners and researchers. However, some adult education scholars are beginning to question the importance of adult development models. Tennant (1990, p 13), for example, argues that " . . . the differences between individuals so dominate any hypothesized regularity in the life course that, for practical educational purposes, developmental phenomena can largely be ignored." After an extensive review of adult development literature, Merriam and Caffarella (1991, p 105) conclude that development models should be viewed as alternative ways of how adults can develop and that, for some adults, development is inappropriate: "This best fits our stance—that there is no right or best way of developing as we age."

This general line of questioning is bolstered by specific ambiguity or critiques of personal and faith development models. One area of uncertainty emerges out of the emphasis on growth. Based on his experiences as a counselor of returning adult students, Daloz (1988b, p 7) observes that not all adults want to grow:

> It is finally clear to me that not all students grow from their education. Some people find a point of equilibrium and remain there, resting. And, despite the best efforts of their teacher, may stay there the rest of their lives. . . . Yet in their refusal they have much to teach us. . . . Most adults are richly enmeshed in a fabric of relationships which hold them as they are, and many of their friends and relations do not wish them to change. . . . Sometimes it is just plain simpler to stay right where they are, or at least to appear that way.

Similar behavior is noted in the faith development context. Fowler (1981) reports that Stage 3 (Synthetic-Conventional Faith) becomes the point of equilibrium for the faith journey of many adults. This stage is the "conformist" level where independence and autonomy never seem to break through to help the individual move to Stage 4.

Daloz even questions his right to intrude into the life of individuals who appear to be frozen at a particular developmental level. Yet, in the same year (Daloz, 1988a), he concludes that the role of adult education is to help people move from simpler to more complex stages in life. In fact, he defines teaching as inherently moral and connected to ultimate value, thus, "our students' growth, finally, is a matter of life and death for us all" (Daloz, 1988a, p 241). And, as expressed in the preceding section of this chapter, growth is the theme of the faith development model.

The ambiguity over the presumption of adults progressing through developmental levels not only brings adult development models into question, it reflects an ethical dilemma in the learning experience (Merriam and Caffarella, 1991). How far should the teacher push a student? Should the teacher even attempt to motivate a student to develop? Does a teacher have the right to intrude into the lives of students to stimulate their development? These questions are not easily answered, and they won't be answered the same way for every adult educator. But, at the very least, they suggest that the assumption of growth, which is a pivotal element in models of adult development, is not to be taken without reflection over ultimate implications.

The hierarchial nature of personal and faith development models is related to the growth theme and has also come under criticism. The fact that most models are built with stages that are presented in a linear pattern implies that higher stages are "better" or, certainly, more desirable than preceding ones. Consequently, an individual would be considered a more worthy person in a higher stage.

Such a conclusion is ironic within the faith development model, particularly in the religious context where many religious traditions acknowledge the value and importance of all individuals regardless of their stage in life. Fowler (1976a) countered this criticism early in the preparation of his model by noting that each stage is the important stage for an individual or group at that time. He further asserted that each stage is potentially worthy. Yet, the presentation of his stages and the personal development models in a hierarchial fashion inherently imply distinctions and subsequent judgments of the value of each level. The danger of stage models for adult educators is the tendency to assume that all adults must develop in learning experiences to be better.

In addition to the critiques directed at adult development models in general, specific concern has been raised over the stages of faith development and their relationship to adult education. In response to a presentation of a series of hypotheses about faith development, Knowles (1983) simply concludes that where faith development involves adults in learning situations, adult education could make a contribution. In a further general remark, he explains his principles of andragogy and points out how they are useful in helping adults learn more effectively. But later in his response, Knowles argues that education could not help faith development unless behaviors are identified with tasks within the stages. He encourages the proponents of faith development to operationally define faith development, to determine the faithing competencies that need to be learned and how they are learned. To some extent Knowles is advocating a task development scheme within the six stages similar to Havighurst's model of adult development.

Knowles concern over the relationship between adult education and faith development is heightened by Fowler's admission that competencies within a stage cannot be directly taught. Rather, they accrue as a person interacts with the world:

> The development of faith competencies and the movement from one stage to another cannot be the *direct* results of education or schooling. Rather, in precisely the fashion described by the religious socialization theorists, faith development occurs as a person wrestles with the givenness and crises of his/her life, and draws adaptively upon the models of meaning provided by a nurturing community (or communities) in constructing a world which is given coherence by his/her centering trusts and loyalties. (Fowler, 1976a, p 200–201)

While Fowler is right to point to the importance of one's interrelationships in shaping faith stage competencies, Tulloch (1985) found that education can have a direct impact on faith development. Using a case study method, Tulloch interviewed six adults in a sixteen-week Bible study program before and after the learning experience to determine the effect of education on faith development. Measurable and positive changes were detected within a faith stage for all respondents. Tulloch concluded that positive intervention through education in an individual's faith development is possible and is measurable. These findings respond to Knowles's recommendations and also suggest the relationship between adult education and faith development.

Questions have also been raised about two other aspects of faith development. The first relates to Stage 6. Broughton (1986) observes that out of 359 individuals studied, only one case of Stage 6 is reported by Fowler. Why is this so? Are the criteria for Stage 6 so complex (rigid?) that only the few attain it? Fowler (1981) refers to such individuals as Martin Luther King, Jr., Gandhi, and Dag Hammarskjold as persons who have arrived at Stage 6. Yet, as Broughton notes, these are people whom Fowler never interviewed, making his claims intuitive. Might adult educators simply ignore preparation for this stage as a possible learning opportunity because it is virtually unattainable?

A second additional concern over the faith development model, the gender of the sample, also relates to adult development models generally. Unquestionably, males are the dominant gender in the samples of almost all the models. For that reason, Bruning and Stokes (1983) and Peck (1986) caution that making generalizations to the adult population must be qualified. A different aspect of the gender concern emerges in Fowler's model. He concludes that males derive scores that are superior to females, but he does not account for this discrepancy. The percentages of males and females in Fowler's sample were virtually identical. These observations provide further evidence for a tentative approach in using adult development models in planning and conducting adult education learning experiences.

The identification of ambiguity within and critiques of personal and faith development models obviously reflect the need for additional research in adult development. The concerns and issues with current models are ample evidence for a cautious approach in extensive application of the models. Perhaps new models, based on more comprehensive criteria are appropriate. Merriam and Caffarella (1991) suggest that recent models developed by Baltes (1982), Peck (1986), and Peters (1989) are representative of more interactionist, multicausal, and inclusive criteria called for in recent criticisms of existing models.

SUMMARY

Although they are not identical, personal and faith development models have strong ties in origins and respective components. A comparison of the two types of models can easily lead one to conclude that there is a universal framework for human development. Yet, there are distinctions between the two types of models that make them unique and conducive to individual analysis and usefulness.

Personal development models are acknowledged by adult educators as primary elements of consideration in understanding the needs and motivations of adults. However, careful reflection over the characteristics of personal and faith models indicates areas of weakness that call into question the seemingly blind acceptance of their importance. Flaws in assumptions (that growth is for everyone or that higher stages are better), in research methodology (gender biased samples), and in questionable criteria for higher stage attainment (only the "chosen" appear to reach Stage 6 in faith development) suggest the need for reexamination of the usefulness of human development models. More recent, though untested adult development models have the potential to overcome these flaws. Adult educators are encouraged to use personal and faith development models as general explanations of adult differentiation, rather that prescriptive formulas for planning and conducting adult learning experiences.

REFERENCES

Baltes, P. B. 1982, Life-span development psychology: Some conveying observations on history and theory. In K. W. Schaie and J. Gerwitz, eds., *Readings in Adult Development and Aging*. Boston, Little Brown.

Bruning, C. and Stokes, K. 1983, The hypotheses paper. In K. Stokes, ed., *Faith Development in the Adult Life Cycle*. Minneapolis, MN., Adult Faith Resources.

Broughton, J. M. 1986, The political psychology of faith development theory. In C. Dykstra and S. Parks (eds.), *Faith Development and Fowler*. Birmingham, AL., Religious Education Press.

Caffarella, R. S. 1988, *Program Development and Evaluation Resource Book for Trainers*. New York, Wiley.

Cross, K. P. 1981, *Adults as Learners: Increasing Participation and Facilitating Learning*. San Francisco, Jossey-Bass.

Daloz, L. A. 1988a, Beyond tribalism: Renaming the good, the true, and the beautiful. *Adult Education Quarterly*, Vol.38, No.4, pp. 234–241.

Daloz, L. A. 1988b, The story of Gladys who refused to grow: A morality tale for mentors. *Lifelong Learning*, Vol.11, No.4, pp. 4–7.

Duska, R. and Whelan, M. 1975, *Moral Development: A Guide to Piaget and Kohlberg*. New York, Paulist Press.

Erikson, E. H. 1963, *Childhood and Society*. Second edition, revised. New York, Norton.

Fowler, J. W. 1976a, Faith development theory and the aims of religious socialization. In G. Durka and J. Smith, eds., *Emerging Issues in Religious Education*. New York, Paulist Press.

Fowler, J. W. 1976b, Stages in faith: The structural-developmental approach. In T. C. Hennesy, SJ, ed., *Values and Moral Development*. New York, Paulist Press.

Fowler, J. W. 1979, Perspectives on the family from the standpoint of faith development theory. *Perkins Journal*, Vol.33, No.1, pp. 1–19.

Fowler, J. W. 1981, *Stages of Faith: The Psychology of Human Development and the Quest for Meaning*. Philadelphia, Harper and Row Publishers.

Fowler, J. W. 1986, Faith and the structuring of meaning. In C. Dykstra and S. Parks, eds., *Faith Development and Fowler*. Birmingham, AL., Religious Education Press.

Gilligan, C. 1982, *In a Different Voice: Psychological Theory and Women's Development*. Cambridge, Mass., Harvard University Press.

Gooden, W. 1983, Responses and comments from an adult development perspective. In K. Stokes, ed., *Faith Development in the Adult Life Cycle*. Revised edition. Minneapolis, MN., Adult Faith Resources.

Gould, R. 1978, *Transformations: Growth and Change in Adult Life*. New York, Simon & Schuster.

Havighurst, R. J. 1972, *Developmental Tasks and Education*. Third edition. New York, David MacKay Company, Inc.

Jarvis, P. 1987, *Adult Learning in the Social Context*. London, Croom Helm.

Kegan, R. 1982, *The Evolving Self: Problem and Processes in Human Development*. Cambridge, Mass., Harvard University Press.

Knowles, M. S. 1980. *The Modern Practice of Adult Education: From Pedagogy to Andragogy*. Revised and updated. New York, Cambridge.

Knowles, M. S. 1983, An adult educator's reflections on faith development in the adult life cycle. In K. Stokes, ed., *Faith Development in the Adult Life Cycle*. Revised edition. Minneapolis, MN., Adult Faith Resources.

Kohlberg, L. 1973, Continuities in childhood and adult moral development. In P. Baltes and K. Schaie, eds., *Life-span Developmental Psychology: Personality and Socialization*. New York, Academic Press.

Kohlberg, L. 1974, Education, moral development, and faith. *Journal of Moral Education*, Vol.4, No.1, pp. 5–16.

Lang, M. A. 1976, Faith as a learned life-style. In G. Durka and J. Smith, eds., *Emerging Issues in Religious Education*. New York, Paulist Press.

Levinson, D., Darrow, C., Klein, E., Levinson, M., and McKee, B. 1978, *The Seasons of a Man's Life*. New York, Alfred A. Knopf.

Lindeman, E. C. 1926, *The Meaning of Adult Education*. New York, New Republic, Inc.

Loevinger, J. 1976. *Ego Development: Conceptions and Theories*. San Francisco, Jossey-Bass.

Long, H. B. 1983, *Adult Learning: Research and Practice*. New York, Cambridge.

Merriam, S. B. and Caffarella, R. S. 1991, *Learning in Adulthood: A Comprehensive Guide*. San Francisco, Jossey-Bass.

Neugarten, B. 1976, Adaptation and the life cycle. *Counseling Psychologist*, Vol.6, pp. 16–20.

Peck, T. A. 1986, Women's self-definition in adulthood: From a different model? *Psychology of Women Quarterly*, Vol.10, pp. 274–284.

Peters, J. M. 1989, Programming through the client's lifespan. In D. J. Blackburn, ed., *Foundations and Changing Practices in Extension*. Guelph, Ontario, University of Guelph.

Piaget, J. 1967, *Six Psychological Studies*. New York, Random House, Vintage Books.

Tennant, M. 1990, Life-span developmental psychology and adult learning. *International Journal of Lifelong Education*, Vol.9, No.3, pp. 223–236.

Tulloch, E. F. 1985, *A Study of Faith Stage Transition in Adults*. Unpublished doctoral dissertation. Commerce, TX., East Texas State University.

Vaillant, G. 1977, *Adaptation to Life*. Boston, Little, Brown.

Westerhoff, J. H., III. 1970, *Values for Tomorrow's Children*. Philadelphia, Pilgrim Press (United Church Press).

CHAPTER 11

The Autonomous Person And Self-Directed Learning

DAVID WALKER

INTRODUCTION

We live in an age in which the importance of freedom, and the right to be autonomous in determining one's life is given paramount importance. Freedom has always been an important issue for humanity, and is a consequence of the recognition that individuals are responsible for their acts, and indeed for their whole destiny. Human experience over many cultures and many centuries has prized freedom, and recognized personal responsibility as an important pillar of human existence. Religiously, this freedom and responsibility has been focused on one's relationship with God. However, today, in a much broader context, there has been, and is increasingly, an emphasis on human responsibility, and a concerted effort to educate the person to a greater responsibility, autonomy, and freedom. To reflect on autonomy is inevitably to be drawn into an appreciation of responsibility and freedom which are its essential constituents. It is interesting to see how these same issues are approached from the different perspectives of theology and education.

THE THEOLOGICAL PERSPECTIVE

The religious debate within the Christian tradition about grace and freedom was not the first to consider how the individual could be autonomous or free. The Greek philosophers explored this areas and have influenced our own searchings. They often saw freedom in terms of liberation, and linked freedom to the concept of virtue. The only person who is truly free is the virtuous one. Longergan sees this emphasis on the virtuous person in Aristotle as embodying the more fundamental freedom of the individual which is important for understanding freedom (Lonergan, 1972, p 41). The Aristotelian virtuous man is, in Lonergan's language, "the self-transcending subject" in whom ultimate freedom rests. It is interesting to note the influence of Aristotle in the ideas relative to this chapter. Kemmis points to the influence of Aristotle on the three primary cognitive interests of Habermas, which have influenced the development of self-directed learning (Kemmis, 1985, p 144). There was already present in Greek thought the tension of how to reconcile human freedom with divine action; a question that was to be the particular focus of the Christian debate on grace and freedom.

The focus of freedom in the Jewish-Christian tradition was the free, gratuitous approach of God. This divine initiative is the whole foundation of biblical revelation, and the designation given to it in the Christian tradition, "grace," emphasis the freedom and autonomy of the divinity in reaching out to humanity. The concept of freedom finds particular attention in the writings of Paul. He stresses that in Jesus the believer has been liberated from the power of sin, and achieves the liberty of the children of God (Romans 8:21). The freedom here is not just the freedom to choose this or that action, but an underlying orientation of the person which lies behind the individual action. It is a state of freedom to which one is drawn by God and comes about through conversion. This conversion, this being caught up in the divine love, pertains to the fundamental freedom of the person (Lonergan, 1972, pp 237–238).

The Early Church Fathers proclaimed the new freedom that had come in Jesus, and they considered that human freedom was really a participation in the divine freedom. This led them to the position that it is in its freedom that the human person is the image of God. In his debate with Pelagius, Augustine introduced the distinction between freedom (*libertas*) and free will (*liberum arbitrium*). The former referred to the total, all embracing reaching out in love to God, seen as the final goal of the person. The latter refers to the freedom of choice that the person has. It is freedom, rather than free will, that is the principal focus of Augustine's teaching. In the later theory of freedom of St. Thomas, an act was free when four elements were present: the availability of a variety of courses of action; an intellect capable of working out more than one course of action; a will that was not predetermined to any one course of action; and a will that could move itself (Lonergan, 1970, p 95). However, behind this act lies a deeper reality, in which the real nature of the act is revealed. It is here that the more fundamental dialogue with God takes place, and it is here that grace and freedom are the real issues (Lonergan, 1970, p 115).

To draw together the issues of the tradition and the discussion of the moderns, I would like to draw on the writings of Karl Rahner and Bernard Lonergan. Rahner begins with the belief that the hearer of God's word is a person and subject, of whom responsibility and freedom are essential characteristics (Rahner, 1978, p 35). Freedom is the presupposition of responsibility: the two "are mutually clarifying concepts" (Rahner, 1974, p 199) both relating to the experience of the subject in its actions, but being of the subject, not of the actions. While expressed in concrete acts, responsibility and freedom are not primarily characteristics of the act, but of the subject which acts. Freedom is a transcendental characteristic of the very being of the human person: something that the person experiences of itself; its "authentically original" element. He can even say that the person is freedom (Rahner, 1963, p 239). Freedom is never just choosing the object, this or that, it is always the self-achievement, self-actualization of the subject who chooses. It is a freedom of self-understanding, the possibility of saying yes or no to oneself, the possibility of deciding for or against oneself, the "capacity for wholeness" (Rahner 1974, p 203). "Ultimately he does not do *something*, but does *himself*" (Rahner, 1978:94).

This self-realization is always in relationship to God. Freedom is "an autonomous self-possession of man before or even against God . . . Man disposes over the totality of his being and existence before God and this either toward him or away from him" (Rahner, 1974, p 200). This core freedom is linked always to the finality of the person and reflects individuals responsibility for their eternal salvation. Individuals temporal decisions determine the eternal finality of their existence. Rahner believes that this experience of freedom and responsibility can be known independently of Christian revelation, and it is in this fundamental choice made at this core level of freedom that the person comes to salvation. This is his teaching on "fundamental option." The fundamental option and individual acts together create the concrete existence of the individual (Rahner, 1974, p 204).

In the Christian tradition the freedom-grace debate was often seen in terms of an opposition of the mastery of divine grace to the responsibility of the human person. This was often contrasted in terms that suggested the more one became dominant the less the other was active or needed. However, the divine mastery is the possibility of human responsibility, and is able to be this without limiting the latter (Romans, 1974, p 204). The interplay between the divine initiative and human freedom is one which is enriching for human freedom and brings it to fulfillment rather than undermines it. They both grow in equal and not inverse proportion (Rahner, 1978, p 22).

Central to Rahner's theology is the distinction between freedom predicated of acts, and freedom predicated of the person. The former can be verified by showing that the act was, or was not, free. Freedom of the person is attributed to the whole subject, and is concerned with the finality of its whole existence, not just that of a particular act. Individual actions of which we predicate the concept "free" always need to be seen within the larger framework of core freedom. Every particular act of freedom is an expression of this fundamental human freedom. It is a personal self-actualization, because it takes place within the framework of the whole existence of the person, and receives its weight or proportion from this framework. For this reason not every individual act of freedom has the same degree of freedom and responsibility nor the same degree of self-disposition (Rahner, 1974, p 203).

Individual moral acts do not tell the whole story. True freedom is at the deepest level of human existence, where one is constituted by God and related to God. While core freedom is realized in, and can only be expressed through, particular human acts, it is not just to be identified with these acts; to be seen as their sum total; or something deduced from them. It is something that exists at a deeper level. It is primarily "a freedom of being" (Rahner, 1974, p 203). One of the great contributions of Rahner has been to show the complexity and depth of the moral act (McCormick, 1989, p 8; Modras, 1985). No individual act can bring us fully into contact with this core freedom.

This core freedom is something that can never be really objectified (Rahner, 1974, pp 204–5). The person is never able to actually confront it in its entirety and be totally in touch with it. This is expressed in the traditional teaching that no one can be sure of their salvation.

Only God knows the real disposition of the person. However, while this fundamental freedom can never be completely objectified, there is still a need for serious self reflection. The person is a reflective subject, whose destiny is linked to its core freedom. It is important that it come to some awareness of that core freedom and the quality of its exercise. Rahner places great emphasis on this reflective activity and sees the self-knowledge that flows from it as an important characteristic of human existence (Rahner, 1974, p 205).

Like Rahner, Lonergan is aware of the deeper foundation of freedom and responsibility within the person, and explores it more fully. He makes use of the distinction of Joseph de Finance between horizontal and vertical liberty (Lonergan, 1970, p 40). The former is the simple exercise of liberty within a given horizon or world view. The latter is more fundamental being the liberty involved in selecting the horizon or world view. This liberty is basically self-determination, a thrust of the person to act in a way that achieves moral self-transcendence, authentic existence, and real self-value (Lonergan, 1970, p 50). He develops this more fully in his own distinction between essential and effective freedom (Lonergan, 1978, pp 619–620). Lonergan offers a deeper insight into this liberty in his exposition of realms of meaning, which explore the person's relationship to the world, people, itself, and God.

He distinguishes four realms of meaning: common sense, theory, interiority, and transcendence (Lonergan, 1970, pp 81–85, 257). The first two regard the same real objects from different points of view. The realm of common sense is the realm of the universe, of persons and things seen in relationship to self. However, when we begin to define these things, to systematize, they need a context in which to be expressed. This context is theory, and it considers things of the world, not in the experiential way of human experience, but in the realm of theory. The realm of common sense expresses its meaning in ordinary, everyday language. The realm of theory expresses its meaning in language which is technical and tends to refer to the subject and its operations as objects.

The third realm is that of interiority, to which the person comes through critical reflection (Lonergan, 1970, pp 106–107, 121–122). This is the realm of one's subjectivity and its operations. He describes interiority in terms of intentional and conscious acts on the four levels of experiencing, understanding, judging and deciding. These constitute the individual's capacity for self-transcendence. Understanding and judging are concerned with marshalling and weighing evidence and making judgments of fact or possibility. They can lead to a cognitive self-transcendence. Deciding is the arena of judgments of value, decision, and from which the person acts responsibly and freely. This level of deliberation "is the level of freedom and responsibility, of moral self-transcendence, and in that sense of existence, of self-direction and self-control" (Lonergan, 1970, p 121). It is here that true authenticity and freedom lie. This level of deliberation is responsible for the functioning of the first three levels. Failure to function here can lead to feelings that we associate with conscience.

The activities of this third realm reach out for fulfillment in the fourth realm, transcendence (Lonergan, 1970, pp 83–84). It is important to see this realm in its relationship to the activities of the previous realm. This is the realm in which the person moves beyond the previous three realms to reach fulfilment, peace and joy in the realm in which God is known and loved. In this realm, the person reaches out in love, is related to the divinity in the language of prayer and of prayerful silence, and comes to an awareness of new values which become the basis of new life. Notice that it is the level of deliberation in the third realm that is the level of freedom and responsibility, but the direction such responsibility and freedom point to is the experience of God in the fourth realm.

THE EDUCATIONAL PERSPECTIVE: SELF-DIRECTED LEARNING

The recognition of the responsibility and autonomy of the person has found particular expression in this century in the movement for self-directed learning. Its origins lay in diverse strands in our philosophical and educational history, but they found particular focus in the writings of Tough (1979) and Knowles (1970). The latter preformed a particularly significant role in dispersing the ideas associated with self-directed learning, particularly with his emphasis on andragogy.

It is clear that in this movement there is a definite move from an understanding of education as the acquisition of knowledge to a perception of it as the development of the individual. Knowles make use of Maslow's hierarchy of needs, and sees in their peak, self-actualisation, a goal that they share with his concept of adult learning. He defines self directed learning as "a process in which individuals take the initiative without the help of others in diagnosing their learning needs, formulating goals, identifying human and material resources, and evaluating learning outcomes" (Knowles, 1975, p 18).

He presents learning as a process of maturation, and the outline of this maturation clearly shows that it goes beyond just the acquiring of learning to a real development of the individual. It is described as a movement from dependence to autonomy; passivity to activity; subjectivity to objectivity; ignorance to enlightenment; small abilities to large abilities; few responsibilities to many responsibilities; narrow interests to broad interests; selfishness to altruism; self-rejection to self-acceptance; amorphous self-identity to integrated self-identity; focus on particulars to focus on principles; superficial concerns to deep concerns; imitation to originality; need for certainty to tolerance for ambiguity; impulsiveness to rationality (Knowles, 1970 pp 24–25). These movements indicate that the person is taking responsibility for learning, is able to act creatively, and has the corresponding freedom that is necessary for the exercise of such responsibility and creative action.

Andragogy has brought to the fore two important elements: the importance of experience in learning, and of applying learning to life. The valuing of experience and the use of experiential techniques together with the immediate application of learning to life brings the learner as subject into clearer focus. It is not just the actions done, but the one who is doing them that becomes the focus. Learning is not independent of life, but is the very heart of it. Mezirow suggest that "the purpose of learning is to enable us to understand the meaning of our experiences and to realize values in our lives" (Mezirow, 1985, p 17). He sees andragogy as having an important role in this process and defines it "as an organized and sustained effort to assist adults to learn in a way that enhances their capability to function as self-directed learners" (Mezirow, 1981, p 79).

Brookfield (1985) examines the various characteristics that have been attributed to self-directed learning, and finds many of them inadequate. It is not enough to define it in terms of control of planning and execution, independence in regard to purpose and intent, command over methods and self-instructional techniques. These leave out the element of "autonomous critical thought" which he considers to be an essential characteristic of self-directed learning. This presupposes that learners are aware of their separateness and conscious of their personal power, and thus possess a personal autonomy in what they do. They can interact with, and transform, the environment in which they live.

Critical reflection and the search for meaning are the elements that transform the use of self-directed processes into true self-directed learning. Brookfield offers the following statement:

> As the mode of learning characteristic of adults who are in the process of realizing their adulthood, self-directed learning is concerned much more with an internal change of consciousness than with the external management of instructional events. This consciousness involves an appreciation of the contextuality of knowledge and an awareness of the culturally constructed form of value frameworks, belief systems, and moral codes that influence behaviour and the creation of social structures. The most complete form of self-directed learning occurs when process and reflection are married in the adult's pursuit of meaning. (Brookfield, 1985, p 15)

In seeing self-directed learning as the realization of adulthood, Brookfield is continuing a line of thought mentioned above: that of Knowles when he attributes to self-directed learning the goal of self-actualization, as described by Mazlow. There seems to be in this tradition of self-directed learning a real awareness of the depth at which it needs to take place: a depth that is sometimes overshadowed or clouded by an emphasis on particular self-directed techniques and strategies. The external, which is meant to be the instrument and the expression of the internal, can take over from it with an apparent life of its own, which keeps learners on a superficial level, often trapped within parameters of which they may not even be aware.

This deeper understanding of the nature of self-directed learning was brought about by the application to self-directed learning of the categories of interest of Jurgen Habermas (Habermas, 1971). The application was made by Mezirow (1981). It unveiled the complexity of the learning process and revealed how the proposals of earlier writers in this area could not meet the complex demands of the learning process. Indeed, as the picture became more explicit, it showed that some of the earlier attempts had grave limitation (Mezirow, 1985, p 26). To appreciate these developments we need to explore briefly the teaching of Habermas.

Habermas related knowledge to the interests of the learner and distinguished three general types of interest which related to the older Aristotelian forms of reason: technical, practical, emancipatory (Kemmis, 1985, p 144). These interests reflect different aspects of social organizations: work, communication or language, and power. They involve different approaches to knowledge and require different methodologies. The technical interest refers to the control of nature or one's environment. The knowledge it gives arises from empirical and analytical observation of the environment, points to relationships within it, and shows how we can control it. A common fault in adult education is to approach all adult education from this point of view (Mezirow, 1985, p 18).

The practical interest is concerned with intersubjectivity: interaction and communication between people. It explores the consensual norms which exist between them, and is concerned with such things as values and ideals. It explains how communication takes place and what hinders or enhances it. The important thing here is not observation, but understanding of meaning: what is it that people are communicating. Its method is interpretative and its goal is meaning. It is the third interest, the emancipatory interest, that has become a particular focus for self-directed learning. It is directed to freeing the person from the bonds of their assumptions. to liberating them from those forces in their past which have enslaved them into particular ways of experiencing and acting. It is in this emancipatory interest that self-directed reaches its fullest expression.

Habermas's whole approach centers round "self-reflection" (Ottman, 1982, p 79), a concept deeply rooted in the history of philosophy (Habermas, 1982, p 229). It is directed to self-understanding. Identification of and transformation of inhibiting presupposition are its goal. Action here is emancipatory. It is directed to "providing the learner with an accurate, in-depth understanding of his or her historical situation" (Mezirow, 1981, p). It results in a new way of interpreting one's experience, a framework within which ones' values are appreciated anew; a new insight into the meaning of life; a new interpretation of reality. Responsibility and freedom are integral to this process. "in self-reflection, knowledge for the sake of knowledge comes to coincide with the interest in autonomy and responsibility. For the pursuit of reflection knows itself as a movement of emancipation" (Habermas, 1971, pp 197–197).

Mezirow (1981 p 65) groups this category with conscientization, the process whereby a false consciousness is transcended by adult education (Friere, 1970), and his own concept of perspective transformation (Mezirow, 1975, 1978). He describes the latter as

> the process of becoming critically aware of how and why the structure of our psychocultural assumptions has come to constrain the way in which we perceive our world, of reconstituting that structure in a way that allows us to be more inclusive and discriminating in our integration of experience and to act on these new understandings. (Mezirow, 1985, p 22)

There are three elements within this statement. The first is the raising of an awareness of these assumptions, not only of their existence but why and how they have come to enslave the learner. The second element is to restructure them, so that the foundation of experience has been altered with a consequent transformation of experience itself. The assumptions are not only raised, they are critiqued and reshaped. The third element is action. The learner is able to act in new ways. The looking back to the past is an investment in the future, for it is the future experience of the learner that will be enhanced by it (Mezirow, 1985, p 26).

Critical reflectivity plays an important role in this process. Reflection has been present throughout the development of self-directed learning, but it is this emphasis on critical reflection that has enabled it to break through to focus on the learner as subject, and to become aware of and work with the deeper foundations of experience. The freedom and responsibility that flow from it are not just concerned with the various acts that are performed, but rather belong to the learner as a self-reflective subject. It is important that educators do not become preoccupied with particular techniques or strategies in self-directed learning at the expense of the more fundamental emphasis on the self-actualization of the learner. To do so is to return to the starting point of self-directed learning movement and to make education again simply the acquiring of knowledge.

The approach that I have taken to self-directed learning has been to focus on what I believe to be the most powerful force within it: the need to see learning and education in terms of the self-actualization of the learner. It is in this process that real autonomy lies. One can profitably explore practical strategies and methods which can develop independence from the teacher (Boud, 1988), or one can emphasis the need for the learner to be aware of alternative possibilities of action (Strong, 1977) and Cheyne (1983). However, the most basic autonomy, the most fundamental freedom and responsibility, is that which stems from critical reflectivity and the search for meaning. It is in this that the final autonomy of the learner lies (Dearden, 1972, 1975; Gibbs, 1979).

CONCLUDING REMARKS

The reason for reflecting on the theological and educational approaches to human experience was to examine the values and insights that are found there. Certain common directions emerge which reflect common insights. In mentioning some of these common insights, I do not wish to suggest that the way they have been taken up is exactly the same. However, at the most fundamental level, they do have remarkably common assumptions.

The first of these is to place great emphasis on the individual as subject. Both traditions have, at times, been preoccupied with the external, individual actions of the person. Both have currently moved to look beyond these, and to recognise that true autonomy, true responsibility and freedom, lie at a deeper level of human existence. The ability to choose this or that action, to choose goals, to plan and carry out these plans can exist within a framework in which the more fundamental autonomy of the person does not exist. People can exist within very limited world-views which they cannot escape, and still be free with the instruments of learning. A real concern to approach the individual as subject, and to be aware of what is taking place at that level, will continue to be important for both these traditions in the immediate future.

Another important common insight is the essential role of reflection, and in particular critical reflection. What has emerged in this brief study is that the reflection taken up in both groups is rooted in a long history of philosophical opinion. While it has become a particular focus of attention in more recent times, it has been very central to philosophical traditions for some time. While some research into reflection has been done (Boud, Keogh, Walker, 1985), it needs to be taken further, particularly with regards to its critical function. The reflection that brings people to an awareness of their own freedom and responsibility and the quality of their exercise of them is important to human life.

Another common point was the analysis of human action in the search for meaning. This was particularly true in the writings of Habermas and Lonergan. Both traditions have come to realize the complexity and intricacy of human activity. They reveal a depth to human action which needs to be understood by those who are involved in the formation and education of people. To continue to act in a manner, which did not take into account the different cognitive interests, the different language in which these were expressed, and the different methodologies that each of them require, would be to do more harm than good. The complexity of these analyses may mean that they take some time to be absorbed by those who are not involved in research. However, the importance of them is such that those responsible for forming educators need to make them available to all.

The urge to bring the person to self-actualization is another common insight of these two traditions. The theological tradition sees the exercise of core freedom as a fundamental option in which the individual's destiny is determined. It is a major underlying force in human actions. Mezirow sums up the essential purpose of education when he says it is concerned with enabling people to "understand the meaning of our experiences and to realize values in our lives" (Mezirow, 1985, p 17). The outcome here is clearly action, but I have wondered as I reflected on these two traditions whether the emphasis on critical reflectivity has been exploited more in terms of understanding the assumptions out of which people act than in looking at the type of self-actualization that flows from it. Is the theological emphasis on transcendence an aspect of human existence that is adequately explored in the present research into self-directed learning, and what place does it have within it?

This leads me to a final comment on the relationship between religion and learning. The influence of religion on learning is an issue that has preoccupied me for some time. It is obvious that at times particular religious cultures have created an obstacle for learning, and it has been the task of critical reflectivity to show up this situation. However, the human forces involved in religion are powerful and can exert a tremendous influence on learning. Critical reflectivity does bring us into contact with the assumptions and presuppositions that influence out perception and experience. However, when we speak of religious assumptions and presuppositions, we say that they are a framework within which a personal reaching out to God takes place. It is possible for some religious people to live within the framework of the assumptions, but not to have the basic commitment that is associated with them. There are others, however, who do have that more basic commitment to God; a commitment that would endure even if, through critical reflection, the framework of assumptions and presuppositions were drastically changed. Both of these situations are shown up in recent religious changes. The issue I am raising is how that commitment to God, that fundamental option, that self-actualization before God, or whatever expression it finds in a non theistic explanation, really affects the learning process. Such a powerful and influential force within the person really needs to be considered if we are to reflect on the autonomy of the person. The bringing together of the two traditions of theology and education is a step in this direction.

REFERENCES

Boud, D. Keogh, R. Walker, D. 1985, *Reflection, Turning Experience into Learning*. London, Kogan Page.

Boud, D. 1988, *Developing Student Autonomy*, 2nd ed. London, Kogan Page.

Brookfield, S. 1985, Self-Directed Learning: A Critical Review of Research in *Self-Directed Learning: from Theory to Practice*. London, Jossey-Bass Inc. pp. 5–16.

Dearden, R. F. 1972, Autonomy and Education, *Education and the Development of Reason*. London; Routledge and Kegan Paul, pp. 448–465

Dearden, R. F. 1975, Autonomy as an Educational Ideal, Philosophers Discuss Education. London, Macmillan, pp. 3–18.

Gibbs, B. 1979, Autonomy and Authority in Education, *Journal of Philosophy of Education, Vol 13, pp. 119–132.*

Habermas, J. 1971, *Knowledge and Human Interests*. Boston, Beacon Press.

Habermas, J. 1982, A Reply to My Critics in *Habermas Critical Debates*. Massachussets, The MIT Press pp. 219–283.

Kemmis, S. 1985, Action Research and the Politics of Reflection, In *Reflection, Turning Experience into Learning*. London, Kogan Page, pp. 139—163.

Knowles, M. S. 1975, Self-Directed Learning. Chicago, Follett.

Knowles, M. S. 1980, *The Modern Practice of Adult Education: from Pedagogy to Andragogy*. Chicago, Follett.

Lonergan, B. 1970, *Grace and Freedom, Operative Grace in the Thought of St. Thomas Aquinas*. London, Darton, Longman & Todd.

Lonergan, B. 1972, *Method in Theology*. London, Darton, Longman & Todd.

Lonergan, B. 1978, *Insight: A Study of Understanding*. San Francisco, Harper and Row.

McCormick, Richard, 1989, Moral Theology 1940—1989. *Theological Studies*, Vol. 50 pp. 3–24.

Mezirow, J. 1975, *Education for perspective Transformation: Women's Reentry Programs in Community Colleges*. New York, Center for Adult Education.

Mezirow, J. 1978, Perspective Transformation, *Adult Education*, Vol. 28, No 2, pp. 100–110.

Mezirow, J. 1981, A critical Theory of Adult Learning and Education, *Adult Education*, Vol. 32, pp. 3–24.

Mezirow, J. 1985, A Critical Theory of Self-Directed Learning in *Self-Directed Learning: from Theory to Practice*. London, Jossey-Bass Inc, pp. 17–30

Modras, R. 1985, "The Implications of Rahner's Anthropology for Fundamental Moral Theology." *Horizons* 12, pp. 70–90

Ottman, H. 1982, Cognitive Interests and Self Reflection in *Habermas Critical Debates*. Massachussets, The MIT Press pp. 79–97

Rahner, Karl, 1963, The Dignity and Freedom of Man, *Theological Investigations*, Vol. 2, London, Darton, Longman and Todd, pp. 235—263

Rahner, Karl, 1974, Theology of Freedom, *Theological Investigations*, Vol. 6, London, Darton, Longman and Todd, pp. 178–196

Rahner Karl, 1978, *Foundations of Christian Faith, An Introduction to the Idea of Christianity*. London, Darton Longman and Todd.

PART V
COMMUNITAS

CHAPTER 12

Foundations of Community Education and the Danger of "Aestheticism"

RUUD VAN DER VEEN

In our quest for the origin of this planet, scientific evidence seems to have overruled theological explanations. In our search for "the cause" of this world, in our efforts to create a better society, however, theology cannot be ignored. One important question remains: what is the unique role for theology, religion, church? How does this role differ from other academic disciplines, ideological movements or social institutions? I will discuss this question with respect to a very specific but crucial subject: the role of theology and religion in the processes of community building. What could the "Imitation of Christ" still mean in this context?

In this paper I will first of all deal with the concept of community. I will treat "community" as the "cement," the binding agent between society and societal institutions on the one hand and the individual on the other. I will compare in more detail two central and at the same time partly contradictory interpretations of the concept of community. Second I will briefly discuss some common characteristics in the various uses of the concept of "community education." The major part of this chapter is an analysis of possible foundations of community education. In this analysis I will compare community education based on Christian principles to alternative foundations.

TWO RIVAL CONCEPTS OF "COMMUNITY"

Community is a concept that does not very well fit in with the conceptual schemes of modern sociology. These schemes are dominated

188 ADULT EDUCATION AND THEOLOGICAL INTERPRETATIONS

by dialectical relations which exist between society and the individual, between structure and culture and between intended actions and unintended consequences. The concept of community only seems to have a significant place in a historical context. A generally accepted thesis formulated by Toennies (see, e.g., Timasheff, 1957, pp 97–99) states that, during the last centuries, Western society has developed from a traditional community (*Gemeinschaft*) to a modern society (*Gesellschaft*).

Nevertheless, the word "community" emerges again and again outside the context of sociological theory. This apparently incidental use of the term "community" seems to express values related to cooperation (as criticism of competitiveness in society), solidarity (as criticism of individualism), personal relationships (as criticism of functional relations) and so on. I take this to be more than just a nostalgic reverie. In fact, it points to values that are still important or even crucial in modern society. In this section I will therefore attempt to defend the concept of community and redefine it for our modern society. As I will illustrate below, there are two types of community still very much alive in our society, both of them prerequisite for the functioning of our society. Moreover I will argue that it makes sense to join these two types in order to understand the underlying problem in social criticism of authors like Habermas (1981) with respect to the "colonization of the life world" and Sennett (1977) with respect to "the fall of public man."

The first type of community I would like to call *the community of people of goodwill*. It refers to the assumption that in an effective society there is always a delicate balance between consensus and conflict. For example, people accept the ultimate power of the national state but within the political system they fight for their own interests; people accept the rules of the market and try to make as much profit as possible. In the history of political thinking, this necessity of a basic consensus is expressed in several ways. Aristotle built his idea of a "polis" on the value of "friendship" between citizens. In the ideals of the French Revolution, "brotherhood" had a similar function. In our century, we are more familiar with the concept of "solidarity," which Durkheim explains as "organic solidarity" (see, e.g., Timasheff, 1957, pp 15–29). "Citizenship" has been an important concept in modern democracy after the Second World War. With a view to the present-day dominant market ideology, an equally modern term could also be the "honest entrepreneur."

The "community of people of goodwill" which I deal with in this chapter is sometimes described as a group of people who share a common culture. In this sense, culture specifically implies shared symbols, heroes, rituals and so on, all of them expressing the values and central principles of a group of people. This group of people (i.e., community) may still be very large (cf. "Western democracies" or "German society"), but it can also be used more specifically to refer to the culture of a particular religion/church or even a particular organization or enterprise (cf. Schein, 1985).

I have chosen the phrase "community of people of goodwill" to express the fragile nature of this community. On the one hand, this consensus on basic values is essential for an effective community; on the other hand it is a brittle relation. Consensus is an indispensable basis for what Habermas calls "communicative rationality," a prerequisite to criticize certain behavior as irrational, not justified, not in agreement with common values. For example, on the basis of these shared values, community activists may argue that the well-to-do should show more consideration for the poor living conditions of some other groups in the community. Community is at the same time fragile: it is, after all, tempting to break the rules when people's individual, short-term interests are at stake. And because this temptation is always present, there are people who place themselves outside this community of goodwill and solidarity in order to acquire more power and profit than the community would allow them to do.

The second type of community in present-day society I would like to call *the community of the personal life world*. The growing importance of this type of community is characteristic of our modern society. Industrialization and urbanization have enhanced its development into one of the main carriers of a change from a traditional instrumental culture to a modern expressive culture. In pre-modern society, culture was *instrumental* in the sense that "survival" was indispensable (food, shelter, protection against aggression). In present-day society (especially as a result of industrialization) food, shelter and protection are still important, but there are more opportunities. Life means more than just survival; it also gives people the opportunity to *express* themselves as individuals. We are more aware of the growing importance of a personal life world. For example, the family has gradually developed from a basic economic unit to a set of relations of affection and friendship. The first phase was the transition from an extended family into a nuclear family, based on the ideal of romantic love. The second phase was characterized by a strong emphasis on the "privacy" of the nuclear family. At present, we seem to be in the middle of the third phase in which formal marriage itself is gradually dissolving. Values such as "fidelity" become subordinate to values such as affection.

The social criticism of authors like Sennett and Habermas can best be understood in the light of the tension between the community of the people of goodwill and the community of the life world. Note, however, that both authors stress different causes for this tension. Sennett signals "the fall of public man," expressing his concern about a lack of attention to support and renew the community of the people of goodwill. Habermas puts more emphasis on the fact that the life world seems to be the last set of values on which communicative rationality can be built.

They both display a rather pessimistic view of the vitality of the community of people of goodwill. I disagree with them. Social critics like Sennett and Habermas confuse the *expansion* of a "community of the personal life world" with a *retreat* into this personal life world. As a matter of fact, if our culture develops from a more instrumental into a more expressive culture, this affects both types of community in a positive way. People become more active in the community of people of goodwill. They are also prepared to invest more in the community of the personal life world. In a more expressive culture like ours, there is a tendency to humanize both communities. Nowadays "human rights" are considered more important in the bigger community. Similarly, "affection" is more important in the private world. The past decades have shown an increase in community participation with growing attention for the public world (i.e., the community of the people of goodwill). The rise of new social movements such as the environmental movement provides the evidence for this development as does the growing number of volunteers in all types of social activity.

In other words: social critics like Sennett and Habermas look upon themselves as part of an intellectual minority rejecting a dominant trend which neglects the community of goodwill. At the same time they express a very broad concern in that community itself by stimulating solidarity, active citizenship, human rights and honest entrepeneurship. Critics like Sennett and Habermas have the same function as Marx in his time: by being pessimistic and prophesying pauperization (*Verelendung*) they become prominent exponents of a "self-defying prophecy" that will lead to new solidarity.

A DEFINITION OF COMMUNITY EDUCATION

However, this is not the right place to discuss the correctness of my optimism or, for that matter, of Habermas's pessimism. Maybe we should even leave this question completely to sociologists. Even if you agree with Sennett and Habermas, our engagement as educationalists remains the same: (1) how can we, by organizing "community education," improve the the community of goodwill, and (2) for what reasons should this be done? It is not very easy to disconnect the two questions of "how" and "why." I will therefore first of all attempt to provide an answer to the question of "how" to do this. Next I will analyze some reasons for engaging in community education. In that context I will also pay special attention to the Christian tradition in community education. In fact, any answer to the question why community education should be developed, is the basis for a further refinement of the type of community education that is to be organized. In the final section I will formulate and defend my own point of view.

The definition of "community education" in the literature is rather confusing. Jarvis (1983, pp 44–51) for example concludes that there are at least three different types of education labelled community education:

• *education for community action and/or community development.* Paulo Freire is the most well-known exponent of this definition;

• *education in the community* with Henry Morris as the founder of the community colleges, and

• *adult education beyond the walls.* The extramural university service is the major exponent of this type of community education.

In order to make the discussion not too complex, I will limit myself to the first type of community education mentioned above, that is, *education to support community practice.* I will use the term community practice as an overall concept for community action, community organization, community development, citizen participation, social action, neighborhood clubs and all other initiatives of citizens to improve the quality of the community. Note, however, that in this context I use the first type of community, "the community of people of goodwill."

In this section I will take up the challenge to define the concept of education. As I have stated earlier, I will only present a provisional description, mainly describing what can be observed at first glance. In the final section of this paper I will extend this description with what I regard as the essence of that activity.

First of all, education seems to be some sort of deliberate mediation between the existing culture (knowledge, experiences, values) and individual persons. I use the broader term "mediation" to stress the fact that education does not only involve the teaching of cultural issues to individuals. It also implies an evaluation and selection of these issues by individuals involved in it. Obviously, this mediation can be related to a whole range of subjects. For example, some environmentalists want an introduction into specific chemical subjects in order to understand what is going on in the processing industry in their region. A neighborhood organization wants to be informed about specific legal questions with respect to the renovation of houses. The board of a church organization wants to be trained in effective discussion techniques. Mediation of this knowledge and these skills would entail a repetitive process of selecting and discussing with each group what they specifically want to know and understand.

In the second place, an important aspect of this mediation process is to raise societal consciousness, or, to quote Wright Mills (1959), to stimulate the participants' "sociological imagination." This implies the stimulation of their capacity to understand their personal lives as part of historical and societal changes. (See also Negt, 1971 for an interesting elaboration of this principle in the field of adult education.) In other words: education, as mediating between culture and individuals, generally involves the stimulation of "imagination" in order to understand a particular fact in a broader context. In the context of community education, sociological imagination is especially fundamental.

In the third place, and this is a somewhat polemical issue, I agree with Giesecke (1971) that community practice and community education are in many respects "antinomic" ways of social behavior. Acting and learning are so contradictory that it is difficult to organize them at the same time and the same place. A prerequisite for an optimal educational process is the presumption that people are reflective/critical with respect to community practice. To achieve this reflective and critical attitude, some distance from daily practice has to be created. This is why community education is more effective when organized in special training sessions or when organized as an activity of special discussion groups or study groups. Organized at a certain distance from practice, community education might as well be a sensitization for practice (learning before action) or an evaluation (learning after action).

As I said earlier, this emphasis on the antinomical character of action and learning is a somewhat polemical issue. It means that I disagree with the thesis often expressed in the literature on community development that being active in the community itself is already an educational process. This disagreement is related to my stricter definition of education as developed above. *I defined community education as supporting community practice by stimulating a reflective/critical attitude, by stimulating (sociological) imagination, by mediation with culture at large.* In this light, it is rather naive to state that being active in community practice is already an educational process in its own right. After all, being active is mostly education in a minimal sense, for example, learning-by-doing certain skills, changing certain attitudes during discussions. If evaluation and training sessions, and/or discussion and study groups are not properly organized, the opportunity for "further" education is missed.

THREE ARGUMENTS FOR COMMUNITY EDUCATION

But why should community education as described above exist at all? In the remaining part of this paper I will discuss three arguments to validate this form of education: the utilitarian argument, the ethic or ideological argument and the aesthetic argument.

To Make Community Practice More Effective

I will call the first argument a utilitarian or, alternatively, an "instrumental" argument. It means that community education makes community practice more effective. This argument is so clear and dominant in our culture that I will not deal with it in more detail here.

The reason why community education can generate a more effective practice is not only because more knowledge is made available to participants and specific skills are trained. In the long run, it may become increasingly important for participants in community education to step back from the short-term practice for a while in order to consider underlying societal trends instead. Community education may help to formulate more fundamental problems beyond everyday issues, which is a first step towards developing mid-term strategies for a more systematic solution. For example, in addition to community action against the closure of a particular plant, there is also the need for general strategies to cope with unemployment in the neighborhood. In addition to the issue of preventing the demolition of a particular housing block, there is also the need for general strategies to fight the detoriation of the neighborhood. The issue of increasing burglary also involves the need for a general strategy for improving safety in the neighborhood.

To Introduce Participants To Normative Traditions

The second argument for facilitating community education is the "ethical" or "ideological" argument. It largely builds on the utilitarian argument but takes us one step further. The most crucial point of this argument is the fact that in teaching and discussing new knowledge we will inevitably be confronted with underlying normative, ethical, political and ideological questions. The answer to questions such as "what is?" and "what to do?" does not only depend on factual knowledge but is also determined by normative principles. As a result, community education has to facilitate discussions about underlying normative options.

In the ethical, ideological argument, the answer to this normative question is to familiarize the participants with one or more normative traditions, to help them to understand the character of a particular dilemma and to supply them with arguments for one or more acceptable solutions. MacIntyre (1985) argues at length that this manner of helping people to handle ethical questions is not very common nowadays. I am afraid this is also true for community education. Yet some conventions remain. In the first place, traditions to introduce people to Marxist, Catholic or Islamic views still crop up now and again. In the second place, in community education people are almost implicitly introduced to some very broad normative traditions, despite the fact that there is often no specific ideology at stake. I will illustrate this below for two traditions that play a prominent role in Western civilization.

The most important of these traditions seems to be the *democratic tradition* in community practice. When reading the literature on community practice—and also when participating in or observing community groups—democracy seems to be a final principle for the foundation of community practice for two reasons. First of all, democracy is regarded as a process, the standard of which is the extent to which people should have a say in decision processes. Eventually, however, democracy can be seen as a product: the standard for this is the extent to which a fair distribution can be achieved. Because of these two principles, people are confronted with dilemmas and arguments connected to the questions of what "fair participation" is and how far "human rights" reach. The democratic tradition focuses on the community at large, the community of the people of goodwill. To be more precise, it has focussed, since its origin in the Greek tradition, on the improvement of relations in the public realm (state, city). Its central concepts (democracy, rights, conflict) have rational overtones that do not very well fit into the community of the personal life world in which affection, harmony and authenticity are dominant values.

A second, in earlier centuries dominant but nowadays less important tradition seems to be the *Christian tradition*. This is obvious where community practice is initiated by the church, but more hidden aspects will also be found elsewhere. Just because this tradition often remains concealed, my characterization here will be somewhat speculative. In general I would say, following Arendt (1958), that deep down in the Christian philosophy, there is an aversion to classical (Greek and Roman) political thinking. This can be traced back to the Essene influence on Christ (see, e.g., Flusser, 1968) as well as to the factual resistance to the dominant Roman ideology in the early centuries of its development. In the tradition of Christ, the classic virtues, important for public life, are suspect. Instead of this, attention is paid to virtues important for private life. To give an example, togetherness and mercy are put central rather than courage in conflicts and strictness. Or, using the dichotomy of two types of community mentioned above, Christians have a troubled relation with the bigger "community of people of goodwill" as their whole tradition is more equipped to handle problems at the level of their individual life world. All in all, there is an innate inclination to understand and cope with problems of this bigger community as if they were problems encountered in the more restricted life world. From this it follows that, for example:

- In the Christian tradition, as opposed to the (radical) democratic tradition, values like "integration" and "harmony" are more important than "segregation" and "conflict." This tendency can easily be proved for most of the official statements made by Christian churches with respect to social conflicts; churches tend to play the role of broker rather than of accuser.

- In the Christian tradition, as opposed to the (radical) democratic tradition, there is a tendency to avoid "political" solutions, with a strong involvement of the state, and to stress the independence and responsibility of private institutions and the civil society. Often social problems are not formulated in terms of social justice but in terms of charity.

To Facilitate Personal Choices

The third argument, also called the aesthetic argument, is a reaction to the same problem that there are questions with respect to values connected with factual knowledge and questions of effectiveness. Within the context of the third argument, however, these questions are not regarded as ideological problems but as matters of authentic, personal choice. Whereas in the context of the ideological argument societal developments are tested against established ethical and ideological traditions, in the context of the aesthetic argument these societal developments are tested against personal (mainly arbitrary) preferences. Quoting the famous Dutch poet Kloos, society seems to be regarded as the individual's most personal expression of its most personal emotions. MacIntyre (1985, pp 11–12) uses the concept of Stevenson's "emotivism": "all evaluative judgments and more specifically all moral judgments are *nothing but* expressions of preference, expressions of attitude or feeling."

In the last decades we have witnessed a rapid change within community education; the ideological argument has lost its influence and the aesthetic argument has become dominant. Neither Christian theologians nor Marxist thinkers have been able to prevent the deterioration of group discussion from a substantial debate to a group dynamic exercise. In the seventies there were a number of popular methods, some of which were an interesting compromise between substantial ideological input and open group discussion, for example, those developed by Negt (1971) and Freire (1971). Negt's methods, initially very popular in especially German-speaking countries, lost their popularity in the beginning of the eighties because of their neo-Marxist foundation. The method developed by Freire became "Americanized"; during this process the ideological input was minimalized and the group dynamic aspect became dominant.

This aesthetic, emotivist approach to value questions also has a Christian counterpart. It builds on a mystic tradition and is, so to speak, a modern expression of that tradition. Central in this modern approach is the notion that God is not somewhere outside this world, but that God-is-in-me. Therefore I can be in touch with him, by trying to be as "authentic" as possible. Curiously enough, in this modern mystic tradition the methods and techniques of learning to become (more) authentic are usually not derived from the long mystic tradition within the Catholic church, but more often originate from Eastern and especially Buddhist traditions. Most of this is practiced within what I called earlier the "community of the personal life world" (expressing once again the Christian preoccupation with improving direct personal relations instead of improving societal structures). But it is also manifest as, what could be called, "Christian anarchism." Within a broader community practice such as the peace movement, it is prominent as a radical pacifist strategy or within social work as a radical servitude to the poor.

CONCLUSION I: THE DANGER OF "AESTHETICISM"

In this paper I have described community education as the backbone of community practice because it stimulates a reflective/critical attitude. I have explored some arguments for such a type of community education. It will be clear that each of these arguments will lead to a different interpretation of what community education in fact should be. On the basis of this argument, an educationalist who prefers one of these arguments will develop a type of community education with a special identity, different from community education based on other arguments. There is no final test, no standard measure to judge the best approach to community education. It is only for the sake of discussion, without any further pretentions, that I will present my personal point of view on the subject to conclude this paper. I will summarize it in three points and in a final paragraph I will compare them with the initial question: What can be the role of theology, religion, church in community education?

1. The utilitarian or instrumental argument is the basis of all other arguments. The primary function of community education is to improve the effectivitness of community practice. There is no reason why we should speak in a condescending way about the transfer of knowledge and skills (as indeed some educationalists do). Effectivitness is important, therefore knowledge and skills are important and thus instrumental education is worthwhile.

2. Obviously I am not defending "instrumentalism." There is a value dimension in community education. From time to time educationalists will be confronted with such value questions. The best way to handle this is to shed light on these questions from various normative/ideological traditions: not only to learn to formulate alternative solutions more precisely but also to learn to use the arguments for alternative solutions.

3. The biggest mistake of community education in Western society in the past two decades has been its tendency to overestimate the aesthetic argument. In other words, educationalists failed to grasp the right balance between introduction to normative traditions and the ultimate personal choice. They overemphasized the necessity of the ultimate personal choice to such an extent that they failed to introduce the participants to the rich tradition of analyses and arguments with respect to the normative problems at stake. At this point dogmatic forms of "experiential learning" were very harmful. These forms of experiential learning in particular were no more than group dynamic techniques to exchange uneducated opinions and feelings.

CONCLUSION II: THE ROLE OF CHRISTIAN CHURCHES IN COMMUNITY EDUCATION

My conclusion with respect to the role of the Christian churches in community education is even more personal. Moreover, it is also based on my rather speculative thesis about the core of Christian tradition. For centuries, community education was facilitated by the churches. This was certainly not just instrumental. Churches were very much aware of normative traditions and played an active role in all types of normative controversies. In the process of modernization of Western society, the Christian normative tradition lost its ideological dominance. If there is still a dominant normative tradition in which community education is embedded, then it is what I called the democratic tradition, emphasizing, for example, human rights and citizen participation. I see no harm in that. I consider the democratic tradition in general as more adequately equipped to understand and solve political struggles in the community at large. This does not mean, however, that the Christian tradition has lost its function. On the contrary, this tradition is still valid in our society.

The Christian tradition can have and indeed often does have an important mitigating function when political thinking in the democratic tradition comes to a deadlock by putting too much emphasis on competition, power and struggle. Let me conclude by illustrating this statement. Obviously, these examples have not been chosen arbitrarily. They are "models" that can easily be clarified by numerous stories of church community practice in the workers' neighborhoods, not only at the beginning of this century but also in the inner-city slums of today.

- The virtue of the democratic tradition "to stand up for your rights," "to fight for it" is eventually a poor mechanism to solve conflicts. The virtue to defend your rights can turn out to be the vice of being unable to find a compromise. In community action, local Christian church groups very often functioned as brokers: knowing when to fight and when to compromise, knowing how to fight without passing the point of irretrievable mutual hate and discrimination on the basis of class and ethnicity.

- The democratic tradition tends to stress material interests and is often clearly materialistic where the Christian tradition stresses moral values. What is more, because of its tendency to focus on material interests, the democratic tradition is more preoccupied with the labor movement, whereas the Christian churches engaged in organizing the local community because of their interest in moral values.

• The Christian tradition is somehow more "constructive," even to the point of what I called "Christian anarchism." Whereas the democratic tradition has a tendency to reform the world by fighting existing state structures, the Christian tradition tends to change the world by starting with the individual itself. Therefore it attempts to create and participate in self-organized alternatives for the existing structure. This is true for the various Christian labor and farmer corporations in the past as well as for the modern self-organized community development corporations which stimulate neighborhood economy, improve housing, etc.

• Finally, the Christian tradition is more aware of the fact that democracy itself does not lead to a happier or even a more meaningful life. Democracy facilitates equal opportunities, but opportunities for what? Unlike the democratic tradition in community education, the Christian tradition does not fail to provide the answer to this question, although it is obviously only one type of answer within the pluralistic nature of our society.

REFERENCES

Arendt, H. 1958, *The human condition*. Chicago, Chicago Press.
Flusser, D. 1968, *Jesus in Selbstzeugnissen und Bilddokumenten*. Reinbek b/Hamburg, Rowohlt.
Freire, P. 1971, *Pedagogy of the Oppressed*. New York, Herder and Herder.
Giesecke, H., 1970, Didaktische Probleme des Lernens im Rahmen von politischen Aktionen. Giesecke u.a., *Politische Aktion und politisches Lernen*. Munich, Juventa.
Habermas, J. 1981, *Theorie des kommunikativen Handelns*. 2 vols., Frankfurt a/M, Suhrkamp.
Jarvis, P. 1983, *Adult and Continuing Education*. London, Croom Helm.
MacIntyre, A. 1985, *After virtue*. London, Duckworth.

Mills, Wright, C. 1959, *The Sociological Imagination.* New York, Oxford University Press.

Negt, O. 1971, *Soziologische Phantasie und exemplarisches Lernen.* Frankfurt a/M, Europäische Verlangsanstalt.

Schein, E. H. 1985, *Organizational Culture and Leadership.* San Francisco, Jossey-Bass.

Sennett, R. 1977, *The Fall of Public Man.* New York, Knopf.

Timasheff, N. S. 1957, *Sociological Theory.* New York, Random House.

Veen, Van Der, R. 1982, *Aktivering in opbouw—en vormingswerk.* Baarn, Nelissen.

CHAPTER 13

Contract Learning and the Covenant

R. E. Y. WICKETT

The learning contract, as developed and popularized by Malcolm Knowles in the mid-1970s, has become a most widespread method for the implementation of self-directed learning. This method involves the adaptation of a concept with a long and varied history in human experience to the education of adults.

Malcolm Knowles (1986, p xi) developed the popular approach to the utilization of learning contracts and began to use it in his graduate courses at Boston University in the 1960s. We are fortunate to have an author as prolific as Knowles to study this method for his many writings, including the two books specifically devoted to this topic, give us much of relevance to consider.

Knowles uses the two books, *Self-Directed Learning: A Guide for Learners and Teachers* and *Using Learning Contracts*, to provide clear directions for the implementation of learning contracts in a writing style which is readily understood by many practitioners. In my opinion, the greatest strength in the majority of his writings lies in his ability to communicate with practitioners. This chapter will examine his writings from a more theoretical perspective.

It should be noted at this time that learning contracts can be used with both individuals and groups. The major difference between individual and group situations is that a support group exists in the latter as several individual contracts are being developed and implemented simultaneously. The group provides more support than that which is normally provided by the facilitator alone for the contracting process and the subsequent implementation process. A group contract situation does not involve a facilitator contracting with the collective, but a series of individual contracts in proximity and simultaneous development and implementation.

The reader can see clearly that the learning contract is based in large part on Knowles's assumptions of andragogy which is "the art and science of helping adults learn" (1970, pp 38). As we shall see in this chapter, andragogy and learning contracts have a direct link through the concept of self-directed learning.

There is a sense in which the andragogical approach of Knowles and its subsequent adaptation to the learning contract does not represent a radical departure from the pedagogical approach. Knowles takes the pedagogical structure with its needs, objectives, and evaluation of the learning based upon objectives and makes this structure more appropriate for the adult learner. This is true of the andragogical approach outlined in *The Modern Practice of Adult Education*, (1980, pp 6–7) and of learning contracts as outlined in *Self-Directed Learning: A Guide for Learners and Teachers* (1975, pp 60–61) and *Using Learning Contracts*, (1986, p 38).

Knowles notes the contributions of both Ralph Tyler (1950) and Robert Mager (1960) in the chapter on "Designing and Managing Learning Activities" to his ideas (1980, pp 222–249). These authors' works have been read widely by North American educators in school systems and elsewhere. Their influence can be seen clearly in the outline of the contract as envisaged by Knowles.

The roots of contracts are far deeper than those which may be found in adult education. The essential nature of the contract may be seen in the early writings of authors in philosophy, politics, and religion, particularly in the Christian tradition. *The Interpreter's Dictionary of the Bible* states that covenants were used in antiquity to establish a base for human relationships which did not involve kinship (1962, p 716). Shalom Paul (1970, p 5) traces the concept to the Mesopotamian civilization.

This chapter will refer to both terms, contract and covenant, which have different meanings in different contexts but considerable similarities. Although it would be impossible to examine every context in which the contract or covenant has developed, the political and biblical areas will be reviewed in this chapter along with the learning contracts of adult and continuing education. The political area should provide useful ideas for our perusal as it has had much to say over the years about the nature of people and their relationships with authority. The biblical area contains much for comment in a chapter which has theological concerns.

The central issues in this chapter will be the various forms of contracts and covenants and of the parties to those contracts and covenants. Are there important similarities or differences between these various forms of contracts in the political, biblical, and educational areas? The identification of important aspects will occur in the latter stages of the chapter.

POLITICAL CONTRACTS AND COVENANTS

Society is founded upon the ability of people to live and function in relationship to each other. This assumes the relationship to some form of authority which enables the society to function appropriately. Contracts and covenants contributed either explicitly or implicitly to the governance of society throughout history.

We see the origins of contracts in the theories of social relationships as well as those more correctly referred to as covenants which involve the relationship between God and his people. This chapter will explore both aspects of these origins in the following paragraphs prior to an exploration of its adult education dimensions.

The prominent political theorist, George Sabine (1961, p 31), traces the contracts' earliest origins in political theories to the writings of Plato. Another well-known theorist, John Plamenatz (1963a: 125), is describing what is essentially a social contract when he uses the term, covenant, in describing Thomas Hobbes's view of the relationship between the ruler or conqueror and his subjects. Hobbes (1962: 199) was specific about the way in which the "Common-wealth" was a Christian phenomenon with its roots in the "Will of God." Other authors such as Richard Hooker draw a direct link between the Church and State, the role of the monarch with both its political and religious senses (Sabine, 1961, p 439).

Plamenatz (1963a: 132) indicates that the laws of nature are not equated with the commands of God in Hobbes's writing. For Hobbes, there is no moral obligation to keep the laws of nature. Rather these laws are to be kept because it is in the interests of people to do so.

Hobbes and other early theorists supplied the base for the thinking of later authors such as Althusius, Locke, Grotius, and Putendorf (Sabine, 1961, p 431). Yet there is no denying that the theorist most closely associated with the concept of the "social contract" is Jean Jacques Rousseau.

Although many other theorists have commented on the concept, it was the central component of Rousseau's view of the nature of the state. Essentially it describes the base upon which the relationship between those who govern and those who are governed is founded.

It is important to remember that no theory of a contract can be presented unless certain assumptions about human nature are made. Rousseau's view of humanity includes the idea that society has an important impact on the shape of reasoning and morality (Plamenatz, 1963a, p 371). The ability to lead the good life means men must either live in a good society or be "made by education immune from the corruptions of corrupt society" (Plamenatz, 1963, p 385). Numerous other theorists also share this perspective.

Plamenatz (1963b, p 236) sees the relationship between the concept of property and the contract in the work of Hegel. The purpose of the acquisition of property is to enable man to lead a "rational life." This equates with Hegel's view that man acquires self-knowledge, self-mastery, and a sense of himself as a person within the community.

There is an element of the contract within the earliest thinking of Marxism. Plamenatz (1963b, p 353) indicates that Engels's perception of the more complex society with many groups would have meant the evolution of different forms of contracts from those previously identified by theorists.

Our political (and legal) theories on contracts and covenants clearly have distant roots, some of which invite direct comparison to their biblical counterparts. The next section will explore a number of biblical perspectives on the concept of the covenant.

BIBLICAL COVENANTS

In certain respects Western views of the contract owe much to the Bible and its concept of the covenant. There is no doubt that the prevailing influence of Christianity in Western society for many centuries was a critical factor in philosophical thinking. We shall examine certain biblical views about the covenant before commenting on the adult education context of the concept.

There are numerous uses of the word, covenant, in both the Old and New Testaments. Undoubtedly this word was used with a particular connotation of relationship in both parts of the Bible. The fact that the word describes different types of relationships in different passages provides an ample foundation for our discussion.

The Interpreter's Dictionary of the Bible describes both Old and New Testament covenants, covenants between people, and covenants between God and people (1962, pp 714–723). The covenants that involve God tend to be most frequently noted, but we should also be aware of the other types. According to McCarthy (1972, p 3), all forms of covenants contain conditions which must be defined.

Covenants between equals were frequently used to maintain peaceful relationships. The nature of these covenants is not always described in great detail in the Bible, but we do see their implications for peace and prosperity among nations and stable relationships between important persons. An example of this latter situation may be seen in the covenant between David and Jonathan (1 Sam. 18:3).

The most important covenants in the view of many readers would be those covenants that involve God and the collective, sometimes referred to as "the people of God," with various interpretations of the meaning of that phrase. We see a series of these covenants in both the Old and New Testaments. These covenants concern certain responsibilities for both parties as do other biblical covenants.

Old Testament Covenants involve those which bind God and also those which bind the people of Israel. An example of the former emphasis would be the Abrahamic covenant which is described in Genesis 15 and 17:1–14. An example of the latter would be the Mosaic covenant which features the Ten Commandments.

The evidence is that the early Christians saw the covenant differently from the way it was seen in the Judaic tradition (*Interpreter's Dictionary of the Bible*, 1962, p 722). Although the New Testament concept is different, it is not without linkage to the Old Testament. For example, there is a connection which can be seen between the comments on Christ's blood made at the Last Supper (Matt. 26:28, Mark 14:24, Luke 22:20, and 1 Cor. 11:25) and the "blood of the covenant" as seen in Exodus 24:8.

We have evidence that the earliest Christians quite readily used the term without its Old Testament connotations. Paul clearly indicates that this new covenant is a "covenant of the spirit" (2 Cor. 3:6) in contrast to the Mosaic law which was in written form. The Letter to the Hebrews also shows the changes from the old forms of covenant to the new (Heb. 7:1–22, 8:6, 12:24, and 13:20).

The nature of the covenant clearly changed as the "people of God" changed. As their experience molded their views of God, the nature of the covenant which exemplified the relationship also changed. There is a sense of maturation about the process.

One might suggest that this new form of covenant as developed in the New Testament is a more appropriate model in several respects. It is a covenant which emphasizes the spiritual rather than literal dimension. It is a free commitment and involvement of the Christian based on the central act of the Last Supper. There is much to learn from this to assist us in the establishment of other forms of contracts.

One might consider why and how the covenant could change. Paul (1979) has an interesting statement on the way in which the Law (seen in the Mosaic covenant) has an educational function. He sees the Law, as it is shared with the people, as having an educational function. In his words, it "constitutes, moreover, a body of teaching for this community" (Paul, 1970, pp 100).

Another interesting view of the covenant is found in the writing of Robert Sevensky (1982, pp 254–263). He describes the relationship between the physician in his or her vocation as healer and God as a form of covenant. There is a sense in which our calling by God or our vocation as educators is acted out in a covenant type of process also.

Rodney Vandoerploeg reveals another interesting dimension of the vocational aspect when he discusses the psychotherapist's relationship with the individual client (1981, p 301). The Christian therapist affirms the value of the individual within relation to God but also society. We need to remember this social dimension of the individual in the contract.

Perhaps the most interesting example of covenants with God may be seen in Dennis Kenny's work in Clinical Pastoral Education. This author sees the clinical pastoral relationship as enhancing what he considers the "personal covenants with God that influence a significant part of our behaviour and life decisions" (1980, p 109). If this is true, then we should be aware of this dimension of the person's covenant with God as we consider any form of human contract or covenant.

There is no clear example of a biblical covenant which parallels the educational setting to assist us in our formulation of the learning contract. As there is no such example, we need to create our own template while continuing to learn as much as possible about relationships and roles from the biblical examples.

ADULT EDUCATION AND THE CONTRACT

The primary exponent of the contract in adult and continuing education is Malcolm Knowles, the renowned American adult educator. His two books on the subject are widely used and quoted by those who study and follow the contract approach to support learning.

Malcolm Knowles (1980, pp 41–59) incorporates his views of the nature of adulthood in the concept of andragogy. His assumptions about andragogy are presented in his book about programming and teaching for adult education, *The Modern Practice of Adult Education*. These assumptions underlie his development of ideas for practice done in the area of learning contracts. Knowles clearly equates the self-directed approach with the assumptions of andragogy in his first work on contracts:

> The body of theory and practice on which self-directed learning is based is coming to be labelled "andragogy," from the greek word "aner" (meaning "adult")—thus being defined as the art and science of helping adults (or even better, maturing human beings) learn. (Knowles, 1975, p 60)

Andragogy had its origins in Europe (Knowles, 1970, p 38), but Patricia Cross (1986, p 222) believes that it was popularized in North America by Knowles. The impact of his attempt to describe a theoretical base for the field of adult education was considerable, although Stephen Brookfield (1986, pp 95–101) provides an overview of the concerns about the adequacy of this theory as an acceptable framework for the field of adult education. Brookfield cites the criticisms of such notable authors as Cyril Houle (1972) and John Elias (1979) to support his concerns about this "orthodoxy" (1986, p 96).

The essence of Knowles's view of adults is that they are self-directing, value life experiences in the past and present, are life and problem-centered in general, and are performance-centered in their approach to learning (1980, pp 43–44). Knowles portrays the adult as a mature, responsible person with a sense of his or her own needs and a desire to function accordingly.

The first andragogical assumption, self-direction, is essential to learning contracts. Learning contracts would simply not exist if it were not for this component. Knowles (1980, p 42) found considerable support for this assumption in the research of Allen Tough and his associates (Tough, 1967, pp 85–103; Tough, 1979, pp 85–103).

Stephen Brookfield regards the learning contract as "the chief mechanism used as an enhancement of self-direction" (1986, p 81). There can be no doubt that its utilization implies a belief on the part of the facilitator in the learner's commitment and ability to include self-direction as a key element in the learning process.

Knowles makes certain additional assumptions beyond, but partially related to, andragogy about the learner who will participate in a learning contract. The first involves an individual's self-concept which will enable the learner, with assistance, to plan and manage the learning process. The second assumes that each person has a different set of experiences to bring to any learning situation, thereby enriching it for him- or herself and for any other participants in a group contract situation (Knowles, 1986, p 9).

His list of the "conditions of learning" can be combined with the "principles of teaching" to provide considerable insight into both sides of the equation:

1. The first condition of learning is that the learner feels the need to learn. In response to this, the facilitator should assist the learner to see the possibilities, to diagnose, and to clarify the felt needs.

2. The second condition of learning is that a comfortable, supportive environment should be provided to aid the learning. In response to this, the facilitator offers support, acceptance, and an appropriate relationship for the learner.

3. The third condition of learning is that the learner perceive the goals of the learning activity as his or her own. The facilitator must engage the learner in a process whereby mutual formulation results in this sense of ownership.

4. The fourth condition of learning involves the learner's shared responsibility for planning and implementation of the contract. The facilitator needs to propose options and engage the learner in mutual decision making.

5. The fifth condition is that the learner participates "actively in the learning process." The facilitator needs to assist the learner to become organized to do so.

6. The sixth condition of learning is that the learning process is interrelated with the learner's own experiences. In a group situation, this includes having the learners support each other through the sharing of experience. In both group and individual situations, the facilitator should relate his or her own experiences to the learner(s) in an appropriate manner and assist in the integration of all new experience.

7. The seventh condition is that learner should have a "sense of progress" toward any goals. This can be supported through the support of progress toward goals and of realistic self-evaluation of progress. (Knowles, 1986, pp 7–8)

Knowles (1980, p 45) provides a vehicle for the learner to assume responsibility which had been relegated formerly to the educator. The traditional, pedagogical approach involves the reinforcement of the child's dependence on the teacher, while the contract model is a means to implement the andragogical model which wishes to reduce that dependency.

The accumulation of life experience is a critical factor in andragogy and in the learning contract (Knowles, 1980, pp 49–51; 1986, p 41). We have considerable prior life experience as adults and we can use experiential techniques to learn more effectively than those with less experience.

Learning contracts add to the life experiences of the learner in an organized, directed manner. They ensure that those experiences will be guided and appropriate. The end result of those experiences and their addition to the totality of personal experience will be somewhat predictable.

The strength of Knowles's books on contracts lies within their description of the theoretical base and the developmental process of the contract. There is less information about the actual conduct of any contracts, even in the second book where he makes a considerable effort to show the many contexts within which contracts have been utilized. This may be because the variety of settings where contracts have occurred makes it difficult to generalize about their implementation.

My own experience has shown that learners have a strong commitment to the "letter" of the contract, while my view as a facilitator is that the spirit of the contract is more important. The commitment of many students who become involved with the model is considerable. This high level of commitment may cloud their ability to be flexible as circumstances change in the process of implementation of their contract.

There is also a sense in which the learner who has experienced more than one contract changes his or her approach to the experience. Lou Lewis, a graduate student at the Ontario Institute for Studies in Education, speaks about her contract experience in the videotaped interview on adult education entitled, *The Design of Self-Directed Learning*. She indicates that there was an ease with which she was able to develop and implement new contracts after her first experience with the model.

One might regard the ability to develop contracts as a facilitative skill. Those persons who work with learners who have developed the skills of contracting will find their role quite different from what it is with those involved for the first time. It might also be said that the development of these skills will assist the learner in the process of continuous learning. This may be particularly true of those who would learn without the assistance of a facilitator in the future.

THE NATURE OF THE PERSONS INVOLVED IN COVENANTS OR CONTRACTS

Several assumptions are made about people in relation to contracts and the contracting process in whatever setting those contracts may occur. The first and most important assumption is that people are capable of participating in the contract. This is true of the political, educational, and biblical contracts. The nature of the participation may vary from situation to situation, but the fact of the person's ability to participate does not.

Another common assumption is that there are at least two parties to the contract. Whether a party to a contract is an individual or a group of people with something in common may vary from one situation to another. Biblical contracts often involve the "people of God," however that term may be defined, as a party to the contract, while political contracts frequently refer to those who rule and those who are ruled.

Learning contracts are usually highly individualized with a facilitator and a learner. When contracting does occur in a larger group situation, it is actually a series of individual contracts which merely occur in proximity in place and time with the same facilitator.

Adult education contracts altered the role of the teacher, generally a person with considerable power in the educational setting, to that of facilitator, which is generally seen as a less powerful role. As we have seen earlier in this chapter, Knowles felt that the maturity, experience, and need for self-direction of the adult learner made this approach more suitable for certain learning situations.

Unlike the adult education situation, there is normally an implied hierarchical relationship involved in most political or biblical contracts or covenants. Rulers are more powerful in reality through the exercise of power than the people from whom the authority may be derived. God is, by various definitions, most powerful in all nature.

Educational contracts do assume that the learner will work with a facilitator because that person does have something to contribute to the learning situation. Whether the skills lie in process, content, or both, the facilitator does enhance the learning beyond what is otherwise possible for the individual. If this were not true, the learner would not require the facilitator to participate and there would be no contract.

What may be critical about all three of these contractual relationships is that, although they may involve more powerful or able parties, considerable power exists in the people or learners. The withdrawal of the people or learner from the situation may have negative consequences but it remains an option which can be chosen.

One feature of contracts is that there are responsibilities to be met by the parties. This is a common component of political, biblical, and educational contracts. The political contract implies the existence of the responsibilities of both the governor and the governed. The educational contract implies the existence of the responsibilities of the facilitator and learner. The biblical covenant implies the existence of the responsibilities of God and the people of God.

There is a sense in which all parties to contracts are responding to a form of call. There is a vocational aspect to education which is identified by the educator, but there is also a sense in which the learner responds to something which might be described as "vocational."

It is also clear that sanctions in some form or another exist in contracts and covenants. These sanctions may be as mild as the simple breakdown of the relationship so that parties no longer have a relationship or they may be more punitive. The assumption behind sanctions is that not everyone will fulfil their responsibilities under the contract.

Another common feature is that contracts imply the transfer of something from one party to another in return for some other thing. A clear implication of political contracts is the transfer of power from the governed to those who would govern in order that the governed may live in a particular manner, while learning contracts transfer the power in what might be termed the opposite direction. Adult education based upon the self-directed learning model transfers power from the traditional holder of power, the teacher, to the learner so the learner may learn more effectively.

In the learning contract, the transfer of power is based on a critical assumption "that learning is an internal process with the locus of control residing in the learner." This concept of "locus of control" is of considerable interest in a contract because the location of the decision making and other responsible activities passes from its "normal" location, the teacher, to another, the learner. One might draw a slightly similar analogy with the creative, all powerful God who delegates an element of responsibility to his people through the covenant.

Contracts are enabling instruments. Political contracts enable people to live as they should. Biblical contracts enable the people of God to live in a relationship with God or each other, in order that they may live as they should. Learning contracts enable learning which should improve the quality of life of the learner.

Contracts are based upon the experience of the people who are involved in life. They cannot occur in isolation from our life experiences nor the way in which we understand those experiences. They will be conducted contextually in our experiences. As we grow and change, the nature of the contract will change, whether it be in the educational context, political context, or in the context of our relationship with God.

SUMMARY COMMENTS

Covenants and contracts have their roots in ancient history. They both vary tremendously but all have an impact upon relationships with people. They enable people to function in relationships which enhance and enable the experience of life.

The theoretical base for the learning contract is found in Malcolm Knowles's assumptions of andragogy. This approach involves taking the pedagogical model and adapting it to the situation of adult learners. The next step concerns the addition of individualization and self-direction to the process of learning. This is not a radically new approach but the results have proven effective in certain learning situations.

Covenants and contracts normally feature both preconditions and responsibilities. The preconditions should exist in order that people may participate appropriately in the contract, perhaps one should add, of their own free will. Responsibilities are basic parts of a contract in order that it may be fulfilled to the mutual benefit of the parties.

A critical issue in contracts is the nature of the "power" relationship between parties. Political contracts often have a ruler who is more powerful but in fact retains power with the expressed or unexpressed will of the people. Biblical covenants did occur between equals, but those covenants which involved God could never been seen in any light but between a more powerful party and those with less power.

Adult education introduces us to contracts where the person who normally has the most power willingly diminishes this power base to a level comparable to the less powerful. Learners must assume new power in order to become self-directed.

We have seen that contracts have an important experiential base. They develop through personal experience and are enhanced by the continued experience which they foster. There is a sense in which subsequent contracts by an individual may be seen as more mature than their predecessors.

Contracts and covenants have proven to be successful in their ability to facilitate human relationships. They also occur in the context of the relationship, perhaps one might add the personal covenant, with God. This aspect should not be forgotten when we strive to develop and implement learning contracts.

Perhaps the "spirit" of the contract needs to be considered more carefully in all contexts. Certainly the New Testament approach gives a clear message which adult educators and learners would be wise to remember. If we find ourselves unable to recall the reasons why contracts were formulated, we are likely to enjoy less success in their conduct.

Although we may regard the educational theory as weaker than the practice, there can be no denying the value of the learning contract to those who have used it, whether this is seen from the perspective of learners or facilitators. Although certain differences between the various types of covenants and contracts are obvious, the roots of the biblical covenant provide us with ample exemplars for appropriate relationships.

REFERENCES

Brookfield, S. D. 1986, *Understanding and Facilitating Adult Learning*. San Francisco, Jossey-Bass.
Cross, K. P. 1986, *Adults as Learners*. San Francisco, Jossey-Bass.
Elias, J. M. 1979, Andragogy Revisited. *Adult Education*, Vol. 29, No. 4, pp. 252–255.
Hobbes, T. 1962, *Leviathan*. London, J. M. Dent.
Holy Bible. Authorized Version, London, Oxford University Press.
Holy Bible. Revised Standard Version, London, Nelson.
Houle, C. O. 1972, *The Design of Education*, San Francisco, Jossey-Bass.
Interpreter's Dictionary of the Bible. New York: Abingdon, 1962.
Kenny, D. K. 1980, Clinical Pastoral Education—Exploring Covenants with God. *The Journal of Pastoral Care*, Vol. 34, No. 2, pp. 109–113.
Knowles, M. S. 1970, *The Modern Practice of Adult Education: Andragogy versus Pedagogy*. New York, Association Press.
Knowles, M. S. 1973, *The Adult Learner: A Neglected Species*. Houston, Gulf Publishing.
Knowles, M. S. 1975, *Self-Directed Learning: A Guide for Learners and Teachers*. Chicago, Follett.
Knowles, M. S. 1980, *The Modern Practice of Adult Education: from Pedagogy to Andragogy*. Chicago, Follett.
Knowles, M. S. 1986, *Using Learning Contracts*. San Francisco, Jossey-Bass.

Mager, R. F. 1962, *Preparing Instructional Objectives*. Palo Alto, California, Fearon Publishers.

McCarthy, D. J. 1972, *Old Testament Covenant: A Survey of Current Opinions*. Oxford, Basil Blackwell.

Paul, S. M. 1970, "Studies in the Book of the Covenant in the light of Cuneiform and Biblical Law" in *Supplements to Vetus Testamentum*, Volume 18. Leiden, E. J. Brill.

Plamenatz, J. 1963a, *Man and Society: A Critical Examination of Some Important Social and Political Theories from Machiavelli to Marx*, Volume 1. London, Longmans.

Plamenatz, J. 1963b, *Man and Society: A Critical Examination of Some Important Social and Political Theories from Machiavelli to Marx*, Volume 2. London, Longmans.

Sabine, G. H. 1961, *A History of Political Theory*, Third Edition. New York, Holt, Rinehart, and Winston.

Sevensky, R. L. 1982, The Religious Physician. *Journal of Religion and Health*, Vol. 21, No. 3, pp. 254–263.

"The Tip of the Iceberg" (Videotape) 1980, In R. Herman ed., *The Design of Self-Directed Learning with Allen Tough, Ginny Griffin, Bill Barnard, and Don Brundage*. Toronto, The Ontario Institute for Studies in Education and Ryerson Polytechnic Institute.

Tough, A. M. 1967, *Learning Without a Teacher*. Toronto, The Ontario Institute for Studies in Education.

Tough, A. M. 1979, *The Adult's Learning Projects: A Fresh Approach to Theory and Practice in Adult Learning*. Toronto, The Ontario Institute for Studies in Education.

Tyler, R. W. 1969, *Basic Principals of Learning and Instruction*. Chicago, University of Chicago Press.

Vanderploeg, R. D. 1981, *Imago Dei* as Foundational to Psychotherapy: Integration versus Segregation. *Journal of Psychology and Theology*, Vol. 9, No. 4, pp. 299–304.

PART VI
SOCIETY

CHAPTER 14

Open Multicultural Society—Access and Election

NICHOLAS WALTERS

PLURALISM OR DILEMMA

The underlying issue behind this chapter is a dilemma. How far can pluralism be sustained before a situation of contradiction and even chaos emerges? The aim of this chapter is to explore the dilemma by posing some illuminative questions. To begin, it is worth questioning how we come to a systematic understanding of the significance of experience, and what kind of processes do we employ to arrive at a conceptual awareness. Both experience which is called learning and experience which is called religious may be described as fundamental to the human condition. However, the study of theologies as a systematic conceptualization and rational reflection on religious experience is far more developed than on the study of adult learning. Yet both the practitioners of religion and adult education tend to be hostile to theoretical reflection, which leads to protectiveness, and unthinking practice to the point where theory becomes unrelated to practice. This produces a serious tension as both religious and adult education practice claims to have an ideological base, and these bases are then easily influenced by pressures and philosophical fashions of the day. For both theologians and educators, ideology rests on claimed universal views of the human condition—a desire to relieve the end of man from ruin and damnation or from ignorance. What is shared is that both religion and adult education are attempting to change the human condition by engaging in the world at large, but to do this they depend on a critique of that world.

THE NATURE OF DIVERSITY

Let us listen to what the English philosophic theologian, J. R. Illingworth had to say about the diversity of thought in the early years of the century. A really complete survey of contemporary opinion would disclose variety rather than unity—a multitude of incoherent and often incompatible points of view, all of which may in a sense be called modern, but none of which can claim to be typically representative of the age, views which approximate and interlace, and then diverge—currents and cross currents and rapids and backwaters of thought. (MacQuarrie, 1963)

This was true in the 1960s, as it is in the 1990s. Variety rather than unity is a key feature. It has been observed that awareness of the multiracial nature of society was promoted from black communities while the development of the notion of a multicultural curriculum is primarily a white response from a dominant culture. Adult education has spent considerable investment in addressing the issue that black communities tend not to "succeed" in a Western culture of enterprise education. How plural then are our plural societies? The Swann Report describes multicultural education as "fundamentally honest," perhaps better to describe it as an attempt to be fundamentally "fair" or at least "fairer." It is easy to stereotype marginalised communities from many points of view—ethically, economically, as well as from the point of view of class and qualifications. Yet, as Illingworth observes, the variety is far more subtle in reality. Ethnic minorities are far from easy to identify and increasingly so as second and third generation expectations are rapidly changing. A romantic view of pure cultural identity can quickly become stereotyped and so become at odds with real educational needs as cross cultural influences are potent. A "pure" pluralism is then unrealistic and unhelpful. There are "successful" black communities in the enterprise culture, just as other marginalized groups such as the Long-Term Unemployed can be taken up into mainstream culture. Pure pluralism, then, is a myth, but variety is a reality. Can the idea of a plural society be maintained where ideological exclusiveness is an integral part of minority culture? If one ideological system is "right" are all others "wrong," by definition, and can the diversity be maintained? Does the claim of such an ideology to be "right," then entitle the right to proselytise, or educate?

A further issue for consideration is that of cultural dominance in a multicultural society. If we are to try to be realistically "fair" we are faced with a hierarchy of different dominance. Talking to a group of young Palestinian Arabs in what was East Jerusalem, their overriding desire was to emigrate to the United States.

With some reservations, systems of ethnic monitoring are being introduced in the United Kingdom, but how does the adult curriculum reflect the nature of the society in which it is working, and in this context what is adult education concerned with in practice? It is argued that the adult educator is never sure whether he or she is engaged in a movement, a service or an institution and this leads to particular confusion when presented with the kind of variety we have been exploring. Does the actual taught curriculum reflect the real nature of a society that it purports to serve or is it repeating what it has always done, perhaps by making the mainstream provision "colored," then targeted and marketed for minority groups. If adult education is actively negotiating its curriculum with the community, are we working with the teaching and learning that is already happening in minority cultures? Churches, mosques, synagogues are all learning and teaching communities. On the obverse churches, mosques and synagogues are involved in more than confessional curriculum. Christian adult education, for example, has made a number of contributions to the adult educational tradition. It is not restricted to the academic study of theology any more than to promoting the confessional interests of a religious community. Many examples of education in political and social concern will be well known, for example in the development of Peace Studies. The relationship between different religious communities is well rehearsed, but is there a difference between Jewish economics and Muslim economics?

In both practice and theory, multicultural education is more developed in initial education than in adult education. Adult education has always claimed a "liberal tradition," and so the issue of variety and pluralism is not perceived as "our problem." The debate indicates otherwise, both for theology and for adult education it demands a more radical change of approach.

The Swann Report (1985) suggested six criteria for evaluating the curriculum.

— The variety of social, cultural and ethnic groups and a perspective of the world should be in evident in visuals, stories, conversation and information.

— People from social, cultural and ethnic groups should be presented as individuals with every human attribute.

— Cultures should be empathetically described in their own terms and not judged against some notion of "Ethnocentre" or "Eurocentre" culture.

— The curriculum should include accurate information on racial and cultural differences and similarities.

— All children should be encouraged to see the cultural diversity of our society in a positive light.

— The issue of racism at both institutional and individual level should be considered openly and efforts made to counter it.

In the United Kingdom the Race Relations Act, 1976, is purported to be one of the most comprehensive pieces of legislation in this area, although it is the "law of the land" it tends to be ignored in practice.

> This Act defines and distinguishes two types of discrimination direct and indirect. Direct discrimination occurs when a person is treated less favourably than another on racial grounds. For instance, to refuse a student entry to a school or college because he or she was black or to determine stream placement or exam entry on racial grounds would constitute direct discrimination. Indirect discrimination is more complicated and occurs when the application of a condition or requirement (e.g., job or entry to a school) applied to everybody regardless of race is such that a smaller proportion of a particular racial group than others can comply with it and it cannot be justified on non racial grounds. (Dorn, undated)

Only three out of twelve Anglican dioceses in England have equal opportunities policies. "Black people suffer discrimination in the Church of England because its institutions at every level—from parish to the General Synod—encourage it," (Guardian newspaper reporting, Seeds of Hope 1991).

We have now looked at the issue of diversity, and a diversity which is in practice "unfair." The issue may be illustrated from an after dinner speech: two Protestant Christians died, they arrived at the pearly gates of heaven to be greeted warmly by St. Peter, who gives them a conducted tour. It is everything they expected and more. Their only question is about a castle with a high wall, a moat and no drawbridge. Inside the castle they hear sounds of people enjoying themselves and so ask Peter, what is all this about. Just come away, was the reply, it's where the Roman Catholics are, and they don't think anyone else is here!

REALITIES IN DIVERSITY

In a plural situation, are we living and thinking in a ghetto? This accusation is often made—education is only concerned with teachers promoting and examining areas that they themselves already have been taught, and, therefore, simply prolonging an irrelevant tradition (Handy, 1985). Handy's arguments are made in the context of Higher Education and changing employment prospects. It is well recognized that much of Higher Education's curriculum was developed to meet the needs of effective administration of the British Empire. If we transfer Handy's observation to adult education, it prompts a reflection that much of the provision is restricted to what can be described as a cultural ghetto, "middle class, middle aged and middle brow," and predominantly White Protestant-Anglo-Saxon. Radical educators may well point to examples of practice at variance with this, but this ethos predominates. It has been argued that this phenomenon is the result of financial resource pressure and the demands of funding bodies to produce ever larger numbers of enrollments, but this is only partially true. For example, the University of the Third Age started with no financial resource dependency and yet has largely only reproduced a mainstream liberal curriculum. Signs of any curricular innovation are woefully missing. This begs a further question, within a· diverse social context who, does the choosing, and why?

The Church of England in practice is renowned for being elitist. Popularly dubbed as the Tory party at prayer, and for a short time in the mid 1980s the Social Democrats at prayer, there is much evidence that there is a clear distinction between the people of the parish congregation and the local community in which the parish institution exists. Church going is stubbornly static in terms of numbers and hidebound in terms of its cultural appeal and yet this is despite evidence of research that indicates a much higher figure of percentage population have theistic beliefs or claim to have what they describe as a religious experience (Hay, 1982). This is certainly confirmed by experience of such outreach initiatives as Industrial Mission and Further Education College Chaplaincies. Adult Education provision is likewise subject to the same situation. While a substantial percentage of the adult population perceive that it is undertaking educational activities, far fewer are attracted to formal teaching provision. "Formal adult education is the province of the better and longer educated" (McGiveny, 1990). Are we then confronted with a situation where both religion and adult education are claiming a universal significance and yet both are practicing in a cultural ghetto or even an ideological ghetto?

The Judeo-Christian tradition relies on divine initiative. Creation is understood as the response of a God whose nature cannot do other than offer a free creation the choice of a free response. In Christian theology the God of love creates free men, in order that his loving nature can be fulfilled. Choices within that creation are, therefore, by definition theocentric. This is reflected in the Hebrew traditions of the Old Testament expressed in terms of covenant. The history of Israel is one of berith, a covenant where Yahweh takes the initiative of choice and makes specific demands of the people he has chosen. (Wheeler Robinson, 1913) This concept of covenant was neither "fair," nor acceptable to an equal opportunities policy either ideologically or culturally. The history of Israel is set within a multicultural context which is difficult to understand from a dominant cultural position, let alone from an ethnic minority situation. Divine creation may be seen as a universal but divine election is a very different issue. Ewer's aphorism is pertinent, "How odd of God to choose the Jews." The notion of the true Israel perpetuates the election. For the Christian tradition the true Israel is personified in the person of Jesus. The Old Testament records a profound fear of syncretism, "and yet for the Christian tradition the person of Jesus Christ represents and individualises the divine election of a chosen people" (Black and Rowley, 1963). Christian theology tends not be helpful at this point. It focuses attention on Christological linguistics without grappling with what it means either to be human or divine. The same could be true of adult education when it professes to be human and interested in the promotion of self-development without ever describing what is meant by these ideas.

A multicultural perspective, however, demands that individualization is a real phenomenon and must be addressed. The attraction of individualism is that it is safe. An authoritative model can easily be created. Divinity is expressed in personal terms, this is loosely anthropomorphized. For example, Jesus becomes a friend and personal savior. We need to be aware of a range of issues at this point. Individualizing religious experience is open to the confusion between modeling and exemplification. A Jesus figure used as a model either as divine or human is a problematic concept. An individual in the context of time and place cannot be reproduced—a carpenter meeting the needs of an agrarian culture for an ethnic minority in the Roman Empire is not reproducible; the education and training for such a role is even more historically specific. We can, however, look at this process of individualization as example rather than model, to an instance that may be universalized rather than a system that must be reproduced, either by faith or learning. A second phenomenon is the reversal of starting points that the movement of individualization leads to, in that individual experience becomes the focus of attention rather than either theological, cultural or social tradition with their attendant ideologies. It is worth noting this in the following quotation from "Voice" a publication of "The Full Gospel Business Mens Fellowship," whose published purpose is

— to witness to God's presence and power in the world today through the message of the total gospel for the total man

— to provide a basis of Christian fellowship among men everywhere under the single banner of their experience in Jesus Christ and to strengthen them so they can go back to their respective churches refreshed and renewed. The FGBMFE is not a church nor a sect. It has no priests and does not start churches

— to bring about a greater measure of unity among Christians.

Here is a clear statement of this reversal. The individual takes priority. Indeed this is reinforced by what action this group suggests,

"You may have wondered if you too could know God personally and have peace in your heart. . . . . For this to occur you should. . . .

— acknowledge to God you have lived selfishly

— repent by turning to God and asking His forgiveness for your sins, and for Him to help to live as He desires

— believe that Jesus is the Son of God and that as He died on the cross, He took your sins upon Himself that you may obtain God's forgiveness

— confess to God that you can take Jesus to be your Saviour and Lord of your life"

For Christian theology, this is the traditional approach of fundamentalism, in this instance subtly marketed to appear as a serious attempt to address the issues of business ethics. Yet it is more than this in our context. It is a proposal to offer a full response to a total situation. That it clearly does not do this, in that it is highly seductive and elitist, matters less than its claims and its individual starting point. What kind of critique of the human experience does this approach have? What kind of curriculum of learning does it propagate?

— disillusion with and questioning of contemporary culture and its received values

— concentration on marital and sexual problems together with family relationships

— concerns about psychological stress and physical health

— success and enterprise and the lack of it

If we view this curriculum of concerns, then it takes us to a world that is far more familiar to the adult educator. There is little doubt we could offer the same analysis of concerns had we examined a published prospectus of an adult education program. It would have been couched in terms of self-development, human potential and awareness raising. Indeed, it would have been written in a different language, but in a language particular to a specific ideological critique of human experience. Here, in both theoretical and practical terms is a real issue. Are we actually to argue, come and learn our language and we will offer the key to human experience? From a more liberal position is it possible to tackle issues from the human experience without first learning the language of induction, to the ideology or the tribe? Sadly, there are many examples of this trap. It is perhaps best illustrated by negative examples in that if human beings cannot acceptably articulate ideological language then, they are not one of us. The constant reference to "non-Christians" by evangelical Christians is one example. A Council of Social Responsibility for an Anglican Diocese with episcopal support, consciously decided that the unemployed were not part of "their" interests, until real pressure was brought by unemployed church people and forced a U-turn in their policy. In the United Kingdom the Thatcher idea of people being "One of Us," and the perhaps newer notion of adults being "Politically Correct" is also central to this issue.

The 1990s, have seen an increase in theological fundamentalism, both from the Christian and Muslim traditions. Both Christian and Muslim liberal theologians have been eager to ascribe this to economic circumstances, and perhaps over eager in this regard. There is a desire to be assured of individual certainty and should this be accompanied by specific action plans and codes of ethics and this in turn produces a more attractive package to anyone reflecting on human experience.

ACCESS TO VARIETY

This brings us to a fundamental challenge, in that if we are in reality faced with a plural linguistic and cultural situation is the way forward couched in terms of becoming multilingual, not in a purely linguistic sense, but rather in becoming fluent in the linguistics of ideologies. This path, however, leads us to a gnostic problem, albeit one removed. It offers salvation by fluency and ignores the debate between commitment and understanding. This prompts us to ask a most important question, who has rights of access and how is that to be achieved? For the Christian tradition, the Areopagus Debate is vital. Christianity should have remained an insignificant Jewish sect. Notions of "gentiles" and "other" nations, in the face of the early Christian Church, should have placed Christianity alongside such other Jewish theological movements as the Zealots. The educational tradition of Christian "didache" should have remained firmly in its historical context and been of interest only to researchers into Romano-Hebrew traditions.

If what we have argued so far holds true, it should lead us to a "bowl of" ideology, in the sense that "life is a bowl of cherries," from which the individual can freely pick and choose, and no doubt spit out the stones. This is clearly not the reality, as access to belief and learning is profoundly restricted, individually, institutionally, culturally and ideologically. It is romantic to believe that the blocks in each instance are not there. Indeed, colleagues working in educational advice and guidance reflect on the folly of ignoring these in the interests of clients. They are only too aware of a tendency of colleagues talking of in terms of "our" courses, "our" clients and "their" students. The challenge is, however, still there. Within adult education the notion of access is high on the agenda. The plethora of access provision is now part of the adult education tradition. It, again is based on a philosophical or at least ethical right of adults, whoever they are, to progress in education. On sound analysis, the Accreditation of Prior Learning movement has cogently argued that progress in educational terms need not necessarily be along the lines of progression from formal initial education. This is more than a "Second Chance" philosophy of educational development, rather a recognition of varying developments within a lifelong learning spectrum. Access, and in particular access provision, is provided to meet this need. Elaborate structures are being devised to promote the concept so that provision can be offered. Cynically these are "crash courses for the failed," accountable to the system that is still providing the same courses for its successful learners, in order to increase levels of participation. In our argument, it could simply be seen as yet another way of increasing an elite that depends on its participation rate for credibility. Again, this is far from reality, but an argument that holds some truth.

For organized religion, whether informal or formal the same charge might be made against any initiative, that is, if you believe you are "right" you must limit your outreach, otherwise those who are "wrong" may well survive, either individually, culturally, socially or ideologically. The collapse of the Eastern bloc has shown that ideologically, there is no way forward either institutionally in the past, or organizationally in the present for belief in the ideology "wrong." Who do we baptise? Only those for our own congregation? Who do we interview? Only those with our kind of qualifications? Who do we enroll? Only those, who are our sort of people? Is it any longer possible to argue a right of access to any ideology whether theological or educational without prior linguistic qualifications? If the answer to this is problematic, it is questionable that the universality of such ideologies are at best problematic and at worst philosophically hypocritical. "Courses for All" and "All are Welcome" are advertisements that will not and cannot be maintained—rather "learning for people like us" and, "Everyone welcome who believes like us" are more honest mission statements.

RIGHTS OF ACCESS

We have to set this against the United Nations declaration (article 25) on Human Rights, (United Nations 1983) that a fundamental human right is the right to education. It is worth asking why this should be so. It is perhaps found in widely held popular beliefs in the intrinsic value of education to change the human condition for good. In the early 1960s this found popular expression in policies that greatly expanded both Higher, Further and Adult Education provision. The policy was based on a belief that this would enable a better society. The belief rested on a crude, but strongly held analysis that what was needed was "more education." Twenty years later confidence in this position had eroded. Education was judged not to have delivered, but interestingly the Reagan and Thatcher years have continued the belief but set it only in terms of the enterprise culture. The current expression is that while education may have failed, vocational training and economic awareness, driven by market forces, will lead to wealth generation and so societal well-being. The argument is narrower but it follows the same leaps of belief.

Both religious and educational institutions have their rites of initiation, entry qualifications, baptisms, interviews. Access courses, educational advice guidance and counseling services, the schemes to accredit prior experience all fall into this category of initiation. However, these are largely institutionally controlled in that there is self-interest in such provision in terms of institutional and organizational survival, or at least "grabbing more" of the market share. We need to address a more fundamental issue of access, expressed in the question asking whether there are basics, without which humans are denied the freedom to engage in a human right. There is a hidden, but ruthless logic that faces us. For example, "the Bible is the word of God" is a statement. "You believe you are a Christian," is a second statement. If therefore the first and second statements are true, the Bible cannot be questioned. If we put the argument the other way round you cannot be Christian unless you believe the Bible to be true. There are therefore, a series of assumed basics and if we put this in an educational context, unless you can read and write you are denied any access to education. If we are not computer literate are we denied access to the information society and if we are, are there core skills and competencies that need learning in the same way that a creed needs to be confessed? To push the point further, are these "basics" universal or particular to societal and cultural groups and can they be shared? The issue is highlighted by the concern about the proliferation of the English language as the international language of industry and commerce. International flights would not be possible without communication in English. The prognosis is that without English, business, commerce and industry would become impossible, and the world economy will depend on the economically active having English at least as a second language. One prognostication is that all paid work will depend on a knowledge of the English Language within the next twenty years. This is not a new phenomenon if we look at bilingual communities or Koine Greek in New Testament times. It does, however, raise the issue whether we are heading toward a single human culture, a kind of "brown world citizenship." There is a tradition of thought that can be traced to liberalism that promotes this concept. It is exemplified by a concentration on the brotherhood of man, and a desire to identify commonalities in culture and also importantly in theological ideologies.

ELITISM AND EXCLUSION

The Ecumenical movement has promoted common activities among Christian denominations, under a policy of "we have more in common than we have differences," and so it makes sense to do things together whenever possible. Church congregations have become "united" with common church buildings and joined congregations, but there is no Ecumenical Church. For example, there are currently Anglican-Lutheran, Anglican-Catholic, Anglican-Free Church and Anglican-Roman Catholic, dialogues taking place, alongside the work of the World Council of Churches. The interfaith dialogue is presented with the same issue, the 1991 Open Letter (Open Letter Group) is a fierce response to "brown world citizenship."

> Believing that Jesus Christ the incarnate Son of God, is both God and man, the unique revelation of God, the only Saviour and hope of mankind—we, the undersigned members of the Church of England, are concerned that his Gospel shall be clearly presented in this Decade of Evangelism.
> We desire to love and respect people of other faiths. We acknowledge and respect their rights and freedoms. We wholeheartedly support co-operation in appropriate community, social, moral and political issues between Christians and those of other faiths wherever this is possible. Nevertheless, we believe it to be our Lord's command that his Gospel be clearly proclaimed, openly and sensitively, to all people (including those of other faiths) with the intention that they should come to faith in him for salvation.

While this statement opposes the notion of shared Interfaith worship, 1993 has been designated "A Year of Interreligious Understanding and Cooperation" by the International Interfaith Organisations Coordinating Committee. COREC (International Consultancy on Religion, Education and Culture) is "an interfaith, intercultural consultancy" working for "greater understanding and appreciation of the variety of faiths and cultures of our world." Multifaith worship is an increasing phenomenon. The sharpness of the dilemma in practice is illustrated by the decision of the Red Cross to withdraw from Anglican worship.

> A strong national directive has forced the Surrey Red Cross to pull out of its annual service in Guildford Cathedral. The Equal Opportunities statement which led to the decision states—it is fundamental to the Red Cross that members of all faiths and none are welcome. It is important that no official single-faith Red Cross Service should be initiated and held which can give rise to any public perception. Where such celebrations currently exist, branches should seek alternative celebrations (Surrey Mail, 1991).

The name itself of this organization uses potent religious symbolism, so perhaps it should consider a change of title.

This takes us back to our original question, how plural can we be. We are witnessing the collapse of political ideologies that have significantly affected the opportunities for human development in both the East and West. Courses on "Christianity and Communism" which were flavor of the month in the 1960s are no longer relevant, but while the extremes of both right and left wing ideologies have disappeared, we are witnessing the growth of religious exclusiveness and fundamentalism alongside a growth in nationalism where the petty tyrant and despot assume ever greater importance.

There are those who wish to blur the difference between belief and learning. We may well profit by challenging this. It is the Christian preachers challenge that no one was ever argued into the "Kingdom of Heaven." Gnosticism does not lead to salvation, except for gnostics, but so too the universalist claims of the educator beg as many questions. The dilemma has no conclusion.

We can reflect on it as a puzzle rather than a problem. As a start we can be aware of the issues involved for, without awareness of this we are hopelessly subject to the marketing skills of those with vested interests.

It may have been very difficult and even revolutionary for Paul to claim he had to be all things to all men, but to practice the claim is more problematic still. Reflection leads to a complexity of issues and practice rather than clear answers. Illingworth's variety rather than a bland unity is the current order of the day, and it is the variety itself that presents both the theologian and the educator with vital questions of theory and of practice.

REFERENCES

Black, B. and Rowley, H. H. 1963, *Peake's Commentary on the Bible*. London, Nelson.

Dorn, A. undated, *The Race Relations Act and Education—a Code of Practice*. London, Commission for Racial Equality.

Guardian Newspaper reporting, *Seeds of Hope*. report by General Synod of the Church of England, Committee on Black African Concerns 23/10/91, London.

Handy, C. 1985, *The Future of Work*. Oxford, Blackwell.

Hay, D. 1982, *Exploring Inner Space*. London, Penguin.

Macquarrie, J. 1963, *Twentieth Century Religious Thought*. London, SCM.

McGiverny, V. 1990, *Education's for other people—Access to Education for Non Participant Adults*. Leicester, NIACE.

Open Letter to the Leadership of the Church of England. 1991, Open Letter Group.

Surrey Mail 1991, Vol. XI, No. 473. Godalming.

Swann Committee 1985, *Education for All*. Cmnd 9453. London, HMSO

Universal Declaration of Human Rights, Final Authorised Text. 1983, United Nations Office of Public Information.

Voice—Modern Journalism, undated, Full Gospel Mens Business Mens Fellowship International.

Wheeler, Robinson H. 1913, *Religious Ideas of the Old Testament*. London, Duckworth.

CHAPTER 15

Beyond God the Father and the Mother: Adult Education and Spirituality

MECHTHILD HART AND DEBORAH HOLTON

INTRODUCTION

In recent years, a handful of adult educators have developed critical theories of adult education. These attempts are influenced by the writings of Paolo Freire, by a number of primarily European critical theorists and New Left writers, and, to a limited extent, by feminist theory (see Collard and Law, 1991 for a summary). These writers share a concern for "critical," "emancipatory" or "transformative" educational paradigms and practices. Overall, these theories, and practical suggestions arising from them, dwell exclusively in the realm of cognition. Critical reflection, one of the key concepts in these writings, calls for a rigorous application of discursive reasoning, ultimately aimed at a critique and dissolution of false or "distorting" (Mezirow, 1990) beliefs and assumptions. While these attempts are extremely important and useful, their exclusive focus on cognitive processes is nevertheless unsatisfying. First of all, they have a tendency to neglect the fact that emancipatory or transformative processes involve more than critical insights (and the intellectual-conceptual processes that lead up to them), that is, more than the head or the mind, but heart and soul as well. While the involvement of heart and soul (and the rest of the body and person as well) are difficult to capture in critical-conceptual language, a truly comprehensive concept of emancipatory education needs to include an understanding of the noncognitive dimensions of trans-formative education as well.

Second, we believe that an exclusive focus on critique, on the power of reason in isolation from other human powers can lead to pessimism and a feeling of helplessness rather than lead people to social action as the implicit or explicit intent behind critical theorists (see, for instance, Collard and Law's critique of Mezirow, 1989). As Bahro (1989, p 96) pointed out: "Pure thought makes one melancholy, if only because it can store truth only in its dead form. It tends to darken and depress the entire psyche, and in its one-sidedness it is an inevitably melancholy fellow." Critical theory, with its emphasis on critique, and its lack of positive or utopian images, neglects the dimension of affirmation, which is particularly important for education. Every educational act has to start with an act of affirmation, at least in the form of a belief in the abilities of the learners and in the positive effects of education. Moreover, transformative education has to be affirmative in another sense as well: it has to allow for a creation of spaces where positive, future-oriented, utopian possibilities can take shape in people's imagi-nation. In Bahro's words (1989, p 97): "New cultures have always developed from those interior spaces where that which is to be saved assumes its subjective form." Bahro (1989) sees such an opening of interior spaces as essentially a spiritual process. While spirituality has cognitive dimensions, it "takes us beyond cognition" (Ochs, 1983, p 9); its primary medium is intuition, not (discursive) reason. Likewise, we believe that such a spiritual "opening up" takes place in a learning environment which encloses the critical task of transformative learning in the embrace of a fundamental affirmation of the learner by all participants of the learning process (teachers, learner, co-learners).

To some extent, the work on this chapter has simply made us aware of a spiritual dimension which is always present in educational situa-tions. In other words, we affirmed it rather than invented it or brought it into the educational situation from the outside. This is consistent with the introductory remarks (Preface) to this collection that "the experience of the human condition is a unity," and what divides edu-cators and theologians, for instance, are not the phenomena or experi-ences themselves, but their different interpretations. The themes that will be discussed below are therefore, not surprisingly, similar to the ones introduced at the beginning of this collection, in the preface, although they are formulated in a language of spirituality rather than theology: the birth of the self through social interaction, the seeking of meaning, the creation of order out of chaos, transformative learning, and transformation of reality (Preface). The points we are making in this chapter emerged from a close inspection of our actual practice as teachers and advisors of adult students.[1] This practice and experience served as the foundation, as the starting and end point of our deliberations. At the same time, aside from affirming existing spiritual dimensions retrospectively, as it were, a better understanding of these sharpened our awareness of possibilities for a more intentional, deliberate utilization of spirituality in the educational process.

WHAT IS SPIRITUALITY?

We, the authors of this chapter, bring a combination of cultural backgrounds (African American, European), religious upbringing (Catholic, Congregational Protestant), and disciplinary specialities (literature, adult education, women's studies, African American studies, theater and drama) to this project. In many ways our ideas have been shaped by these perspectives and traditions, resulting in cultural, intellectual, and personal differences between us. However, our experience as educators, our interest in spirituality, and our recognition of the connection between the two are shared, helping us to build bridges across, or to transcend these differences, which in turn become enriching rather than dividing.

Our own spiritual awareness developed through different experiences and processes, and the language we give it draws on different traditions. However, in both our cases an encounter with Eastern religious and spiritual traditions (mainly in the form of Zen Buddhism and Sidda Yoga) was one of the catalysts for our spiritual awakening. Moreover, we both encountered Eastern traditions through exceptional women who served as guides or mentors. In addition, for one of us the birth of her child become a transformative spiritual experience of pow-

---

1. We are both faculty members at a college offering a competence-based, individualized BA program to adult students. We teach courses on assessment of prior learning, research methods, and a variety of interdisciplinary courses organized around certain topics (e.g., Work and Leisure, Perspectives on Sexual Difference, African American Cultural History, and Theatre and Society).

er, creation, and the unification of body and soul; for the other, the loss of her child was similarly transformative, answering deep-rooted questions concerning nurturing and self-healing. Thus, our understanding of spirituality is inseparable from our experience as women.

Although images of nurturing, childbirth and motherhood are associated with female images of God, or of God the Mother (as suggested, for instance, in feminist theological writings on God the Mother, see Pagels, 1989, Daly, 1973, McFague, 1987), or of the Goddess (Christ and Plaskow, 1979, Kinsley, 1989), we do not propose a "women's" or a "feminist" spirituality. However, we believe that the experiences of women are particularly helpful for teaching us about a spirituality which resonates with the notions of life, creation, healing and nurturing, and which is gained through an immersion in daily experience rather than through a solitary journey to the desert (cf. Palmer, 1983; for a critique of this kind of ascetic spirituality see also Ochs, 1983).

However, as the title of our chapter indicates, we chose not to develop our ideas around the image of God the Mother. We believe that the concept of God the Mother is far from being an unequivocally positive counter-image to patriarchal notions of God the Father. In a society where motherhood or mothering are so intimately tied to female oppression, the figure of the mother is marked by this context of oppression, as is the experience of mothering itself. The cultural contradiction of idealizing Motherhood as a sacrosanct institution on the one hand, while treating the actual work of mothering with contempt on the other, and an exclusive social assignment of this work to women as a general low status group reverberates in probably every woman's experience. Feminist writings on mothering (e.g., Rich, 1976; Trebilcott, 1984), and on mother-daughter relationships (e.g., Joseph and Lewis, 1981) are replete with experiences of pain and disappointment, juxtaposed with experiences of unconditional love and maternal power. Within the context of this paper we cannot enter a discussion of the overwhelmingly complex and ambiguous meanings of mothering or motherhood. Suffice it to say that an acknowledgment of the complex and contradictory nature of the politics, economics, and psychology of motherhood is behind our decision to stay away from a language of God the Mother.

We will therefore not summarize our understanding of spirituality with the image of the mother, nor will we frame our discussions in theological language. Whether the image is God the Father or God the

Mother, both signify external, supreme authority or power, be it the power of ultimate judgment, or the power of unconditional love. In contrast, we see spirituality "as a practice, as a way of life" with "insights growing out of experience" (Ochs, 1983, p 3). As Ochs (1983, p 14) writes, spiritual life is "ordinary, readily available, and it surrounds us all." As such it is less clearly definable than an image of God (as mother or father) would suggest, and it also goes beyond the primarily conceptual constructions of a theological vocabulary which extrapolates important experiences and crystallizes or petrifies them into an external image. The spiritual, on the other hand, suffuses a person's entire existence within the world, integrating not only her entire organism as a unified system, but integrating her into the world as a whole (Bahro, 1989, pp 92–93). Thus, as an ongoing process, spirituality requires and simultaneously moves the individual toward self and community integration.

We recognize that the kind of spirituality we are discussing here has elements which can be found in a number of other religious and spiritual traditions, for instance Native American or African American (e.g., Brown, 1987, Levine, 1977, Long, 1981, Raboteau, 1978, Richardson, 1990).

Our goal here is not to give an account of the differences and similarities of these traditions, a task for which we would be ill-equipped. Rather, we consider our own spirituality in concert with spiritual approaches represented by these historically and culturally diverse belief systems as being alternatives to predominant Western, male-defined spiritual traditions. In a similar manner Harding (1986, p 165) notices "the curious coincidence of African and feminine 'world views.' " Unfortunately space will not permit our rendering of her intricate critique of the various attempts to explain this coincidence (which she chides as a-historical and as representing residues of patriarchal and colonial conceptual schemes), but merely refer to her conclusions. Her conclusions suggest (Harding, 1986, p 186) that "the feminine" or "African" should be considered "categories of challenge" where "the feminine and African world views name what is absent in the thinking and social activities of men and Europeans, what in relegated to 'others' to think, feel and do; what makes possible genderized and racial social orders." African and feminine world views therefore provide categories which are useful for a critique of masculinist Western world views which thrive on dualism, separation, and exclusion (Harding, 1986).

Our own "categories of challenge" are derived from a shared belief which ties together our varying interpretations and understandings of spirituality. It is the belief that, ultimately, diversity and interdependence, multiplicity and interconnectedness are inseparable, unifying all forms of life beyond the many artificial separations created by our culture among people of different races, sexes, ages, etc., and speaking to the existence of a profound spiritual connection among all living things.

This basic affirmation of life, of considering life itself sacred, is therefore at the center of our shared understanding of spirituality, although we may give it different names. At the same time, we also share an acute awareness of the many social and individual barriers that destroy or threaten life, and that disallow such an affirmation. Thus, affirmation is inseparable from critique.

Ultimately, then, it is *love* that supports and sustains our spirituality in teaching and learning. But it is the "tough love" Palmer (1983, p 9) describes:

> 'Love in action,' said Dostoevski, 'is a harsh and dreadful thing,' and so it can be. A knowledge that springs from love may require us to change, even sacrifice, for the sake of what we know. It is easy to be curious and controlling. It is difficult to love. But if we want a knowledge that will rebind our broken world, we must reach for that deeper passion.

The following discussions are developed out of a three-dimensional, holographic perception of love which is the core of our understanding of spirituality: self-love, or the valuing of the self; affirmation in community, and the love that is capable of acknowledging and moving beyond artificial barriers and divisions.

We believe that spirituality is essentially informed by such a multidimensional perception of love and that such love is bound to an attitude toward learning (and teaching) which is both compassionate and rigorous (Palmer, 1983). Elsewhere, one of us talked about the "rational love" of mothering which similarly combines the elements of critical judgment and empathetic intuition, reason and emotion, nearness and distance in a dialectical unity, and describes how the teaching-learning process can be conceived of in similar terms (Hart, 1992).

Thus, teaching becomes an act of faith, a distillation of love within given outward to learners. However, such an act of faith is difficult to achieve and to uphold as it requires a meeting between students and teacher from a perspective of belief and acceptance across the divisions that may exist based on differences of age, sex, race, creed, etc. It would also be naive to believe that the students perceive or unconditionally accept this act of faith. In fact, they may resist it as it places considerable demands on them, calls on them to be agents of their own learning, take risks, look inside themselves, and acknowledge connection with others. As we shall describe below, valuing one's contribution to the reciprocity of learning comes from mindful attention to learning, that is, a purposeful, almost meditative reflection on learning. But if the process of learning calls for reflection, it also asks students to trust—have faith—in the process and feel trusting enough in the environment to try something new, going beyond their own expectations. Once the learner begins to realize her potential she seeks affirmation in community, whether it be in the classroom with others like herself, or in more conventional locations. Community, however, puts one in touch with social barriers and attitudes that can hinder or destroy the spiritual connectedness each person (regardless of race, gender, class, or sexual orientation) has to the other. The ability to move beyond such powerful barriers is a challenge for learner and teacher alike. Yet, breaking through these limitations is at the heart of the spirituality of learning and teaching.

In the following we will illustrate these thoughts around three educational relationships we see as most affected by our interpretation of spirituality: the relationship of the learner to the act of learning, to her own experience, and to the community of learners. From a perspective of spirituality, the student has to come into a conscious relationship to these three dimensions of the learning process if learning is to become empowering and transformative. As we shall describe, the teacher's role is a special as well crucial one in making such learning possible.

Our discussions should be understood as suggestions, and as an attempt to formulate beliefs and practices some of which are still only tentative, are still in need of being comprehended and understood more fully. In addition, as mentioned above, the spiritual is not truly at home in the linear, cognitive medium of rational discourse we are using here. It tends to elude the confines of concepts, definitions, and unequivocal descriptions. Nevertheless, we hope to convey a sense of the power and meaningfulness the spiritual can have in the educational process.

VALUING LEARNING

For the teacher, self-love involves the act of looking within herself before imparting knowledge, or sharing experience. No easy task as it asks the teacher to *engage* in an affirmative inner awareness. Engagement may take the form of some type of meditation, reflective writing, personal transformation or spiritual devotional activity; all require a taming of external influences and a disciplined attention to self-valuing. Valuing one's self contributes to self-esteem and self-worth, which allows the teacher to mirror a loving attitude for students and incorporate it into her teaching style. Perceptive adult learners will recognize on some level of consciousness this attitude and will receive it as genuine, thus creating trust.

A similar conscious attitude of self-valuing is required from the students as well if true learning is to take place, allowing for an encounter with the self. In an explicitly educational situation, the act of self-valuing begins with a valuing of the activity of learning itself.

Initially, it is important to be conscious of the different experiences and meanings students associate with learning, or with taking a course. Most students are apprehensive, if not fearful or defensive. Institutionalized expectations about what constitutes education or learning are often at the bottom of these apprehensions, because conventional models of education, which most students have been exposed to, feed feelings of inadequacy and isolation, and draw students into a game of competition with winners and losers (Belenkey et al., 1983).

At the beginning of a class it is useful to spend some time talking about learning in a different way by suggesting that learning is a process of self-discovery and self-creation which deserves the utmost attention and care. Learning can be a vehicle for taking care of and paying attention to one's self. It can involve becoming aware of the way how each individual receives and creates knowledge about herself and about the world, how she perceives and relates to her own self. Similar to the process of focusing on one's body and becoming aware of aches and pains or centers of tension, such mindful attention to one's own learning may reveal areas of difficulty, blocks, and fears, or bring up painful memories associated with past learning experiences. However, such mindful attention may also reveal or release sources of creativity and competence not acknowledged or valued so far. Seen in this light, individual learning tasks can be reframed and cease to remain simply tasks or "chores" required to pass the course or get a grade. Instead, they become opportunities for self-discoveries and personal development.

We have found it useful to structure some time at the beginning, middle or end (whenever feasible) into class periods for self-reflection or "reflective withdrawal" (Lukinsky, 1990). For instance, at the beginning of a class period students (and teacher) can engage in a brief exercise of free-writing on the day they just spent and focus on the task at hand (other themes are possible as well). This ritual helps in the transition from the world "out there" to the classroom, and marks the classroom as a special place where the activity of learning and one's co- learners can be explicitly appreciated. One of us frequently uses music or sound as soft background during moments before class and lesson review, and as break interludes. Silence, structured at the beginning, middle, and end of class, sometimes coupled with journal exercises, also provides a needed transition from the day's activities and responsibilities which are particularly stressful in the case of adult students. In such a way, the energies students carry from their demanding worlds of work and family into the classroom can be refocused, and can enhance rather than hinder learning.

We have found that adult students are generally receptive towards these suggestions, although others find it difficult to break through habits of expectations towards teaching and learning which prevent such a positive, reflective attitude towards learning. It is particularly those students who learn for reasons that are disconnected to themselves, and that make learning fearful, oppressive, or an inevitable but ultimately futile effort. These are students who barricade themselves against letting any new idea or information enter their minds (not to speak of their hearts), and who present themselves as walled-off fortresses, occasionally letting down the draw bridge and delivering a product prepared to the teacher's or college's specifications. These are students who are dependent on authoritarian structures, and who are fearful or uncomfortable with introspective processes. They have great difficulty with assignments that are based on a trust in students' ability to reach the goals of the class or of an activity in their own unique way, and spend a great deal of time trying to figure out what the teacher "really" wants. Here the learning journal can be useful for guiding students to a more self-reflective mode.[2] For instance, the journal can provide a forum for engaging in a personal conversation with the students by responding to their entries with comments and questions that are not meant to judge but to draw out the implications of their recorded thoughts and feelings. In such a way it is possible for the attention and care given by the teacher to her students' comments eventually to be transformed into the students' own careful attention given to their own thoughts.

CLAIMING EXPERIENCE

To bring students into a conscious relationship to their learning requires a structuring of the learning tasks in ways which make this possible, and it therefore affects the way knowledge is conceived of and brought into the learning process. Clearly, knowledge cannot simply be transmitted, as in the "banking method of education" (Freire, 1970). Also, knowledge cannot simply come from one source alone, for instance, the teacher. If the student is to make this knowledge meaningful for herself it will ultimately have to be shaped in an encounter of external, "received" knowledge with the knowledge that is contained in the student's own experience.

Moreover, the student has to learn to relate to his own experience in ways that lead to self-knowledge, to a "finding of the self" (Bahro, 1989, p 97). To draw on the learner's experience is a familiar requirement in adult education. From a perspective of spirituality, however, this requirement needs to be carried further. Ochs (1983:10) writes that "an active, conscious, and deliberate process" of coming into a relationship with reality through one's own experience "is the beginning of spirituality." To establish such a close relationship with reality requires, therefore, "a conscious, deliberate transformation of the self" (ibid.). Meaning and value reside in this relationship with reality as "that which unites all our experiences (ibid., p 87).

One of the major obstacles that lie in the way of mindful attention

---

2. We need to thank our colleague Phyllis Walden for many of the suggestions for using learning journals. See also Lukinsky 1990 for a detailed description of the use of journal writing for "reflective withdrawal."

to one's experience comes from the tradition of education itself which places a premium on "mastering" a certain concrete body of knowledge, irrespective of the student's own experience, and the possible relationships the student can establish between personal experience and externally given knowledge. In our classes, such external knowledge and information is presented first of all as a general framework for examining one's own experience in light of the questions raises by this material. Thus, students have to be receptive to their own experience in order for them to become receptive to the material presented in class as well. In other words, they need to pay close attention to and "listen to" their experience, in relation to the knowledge received, and in order to listen to this knowledge equally attentively.

As a first requirement students need to do something they—most likely—have been told *not* to do in their learning: to *de-focus*, rather than to focus, to let the many different facets of their experience emerge and come into view *before* ordering their experience into objective, communicable interpretations. This means to be able to withstand periods of uncertainty or confusion, to accept—at least temporarily—"chaos" before creating order. If information or knowledge is to come in contact with one's experience, it must move through a period of symbiotic merging with the unfocused, boundaryless stuff of individual experience before it can be shaped once more into an "objective" form, allowing for critical distance and the possibility for scrutiny and critique not only by the individual learner but by the learning group as well. Wilshire (1989, p 98) describes this kind of knowledge creation in terms of finding a pattern:

> The minding, the consciousness is aimed beyond the facts into the murky darkness ·and uncertainty; concentration is on the misty, fuzzy, unfocused disorder of the collage, attending without prejudice to the chaos it temporarily presents, letting the assemblage form itself into its own PATTERN. When its own PATTERN emerges, the seeker-of-knowledge will know then and only then the proper questions to ask in order to produce an effective interpretation or answer.

We have found several techniques helpful that guide students towards a patient, "listening" or mindful attention to their own experience. One is the method of successive free-writes on a particular experience, gradually releasing more and more facets of this experience. Different kinds of narrative approaches such as story-telling or biographies can also be used to capture the "vividness of subjectivity" (Dominicé, 1990), laying out the "material" in a way that is relatively free of interpretational-conceptual constraints. Again, especially during free-writing periods, the use of music can assist in relieving tension (especially in the form of fear of writing), and in freeing up memory and imagination. Other methods which draw on visual capacities, such as mind-mapping, may be useful as well.

One of the obstacles teachers may face in their attempts to guide students slowly to an opening up of the meaning of their experience is the social habit of expecting "instant clarity" or "instant understanding." Very often, students (or teachers) do not accept a period of confusion or uncertainty as a necessary part of learning, but interpret it as a lack of clarity, a personal inability, or they simply attribute this lack of clarity to "bad teaching." Ultimately, the "allowing attitude" required for introspection and connection with one's experience speaks to the ability of letting go of the need to have everything under control, a need that is very often born from a sense of insecurity, and a lack of self-valuing or trust in one's ability. These are powerful obstacles, and the teacher's task is not only to mirror this self-valuing and trust to her students, but also to find practices which help create confidence where it is missing, and to support it where it already exists.

THE EXTENDED SELF

An inner calm and confidence which allows attentive listening to the self throughout periods of "chaos" and uncertainty simultaneously allows the person to "let go of the ego" (Wilshire, 1989, p 104), that is, of fears and apprehensions, but also of prejudices and misconceptions which keep the self closed and contained. Thus, mindful attention to the self leads to the fearlessness and ease necessary for the self to open up towards the world and be receptive for what the world has to offer, but also for what she has to offer to the world. In such a way, where students come to a true connection with themselves, they emerge with a new, enlarged sense of self which is capable of entering into community with others. Ochs (1983, p 18) describes this as a process of "de-centering the ego," where "the self no longer obstructs us," and where "we can enter into other people's concern with genuine interest." She calls this "shift from a concern from the self to what the self can contribute to the world" an act of creation (ibid., p 85). Although such a "de-centering" process may be preceded by feelings of fear or confusion, due to its creative nature, the moment of letting go of the ego is a joyous one as it relieves the pressure of self-protection and defensiveness and opens the view towards new possibilities.

Within a learning situation, as state of receptivity, ease, and fearlessness generally translates into an openness to new ideas coming from the teacher, outside sources, or one's co-learners and is therefore an important precondition for critical thinking. A student who has made progress in terms of a patient, allowing attitude towards himself naturally extends this ability to others. He develops acceptance and curiosity about others' ideas and experiences as well. In turn, his openness is dependent on his environment to be receptive and nurturing as well. This is where the building of a learning community is of crucial importance.

LEARNING AND COMMUNITY

In one sense, the building of a learning community in structured learning environments can be seen as mirroring the spiritual dimension of the teacher described earlier. Students are encouraged and empowered to seek diverse ideas to their learning and rely less on teacher as "authority." While the teacher develops guidelines and activities to help students support the communal learning setting, it is actually the students themselves who make it happen.

The difficulties that lie in the way of creating a trusting, communal learning environment cannot be overemphasized. First, we all have to struggle with engrained habits of self-protection and competition, behaviors that function very well outside of the classroom environment, and that may, most likely, have been functional in other educational contexts. In addition, attempts to create a learning community come face to face with individual as well as institutionalized differences of sex, race or ethnicity, age, etc., and therefore with a general social tendency to perceive difference as potentially threatening "otherness." Distrust towards one's own abilities, and the systematic "process of self-misunderstanding" (Myers, 1988, p 79) most of us fall victim to finds its counterpart in distrust towards and systematic misunderstanding of others. Active attention must therefore be given to the removal of barriers that may prevent the above from taking place. In this dimension, love becomes an instrument used to break down walls caused by societal ignorance that can hinder such connections and thus weaken the goals of the learning process. Failure to confront such barriers can lead to loss of community in the classroom which inhibits learning and devalues the individual—and collective—quest for knowledge (truth). Like "tough love," the teacher's consistent, respectful valuing of the differences existant in the classroom (be they cultural, social, racial, or developmental differences), cannot be emphasized enough. Such attention can neither be patronizing nor condescending, but must remain motivated by the spiritual dynamics of teaching and learning. Similarly, however, the same expectation is made of students with regard to the teacher, fostering a healthy respect among human equals. This third aspect of our "love hologram" mentioned at the beginning can be more demanding if one is a member of a "minority." Long held and deeply engrained ideas and stereotypes must be challenged and overcome in a manner both appropriate to the situation and in such a way as to positively reinforce the loving attitude without deprecation or denigration of anyone (see Thurman, 1981, pp 89–109).

Palmer (1983) discusses some ways of creating what he calls "a community of truth," and describes procedures which open "a hospitable learning space" (p 74). In similar ways, Belenky et al. (1983) describe processes of "connected teaching" that are oriented towards creating a community of learners. These suggestions are helpful, although they do not deal with the institutionalized barriers mentioned above. The philosopher Maria Lugones (1990) developed the concept of "playful 'world'-travelling" which provides a helpful description of the process of empathy, dialogue, and ultimately love which is required to establish such a community. She describes this concept in relation to her own mother whom she had for many years perceived "arrogantly," that is, whom she failed to love, and she uses this as an example for the failure of establishing a loving relationship between "women of color in the United States and White/Anglo women." She writes (1990, p 394):

> Loving my mother . . . required that I see with her eyes, that I go into my mother's world, that I see both of us as we are constructed in her world, that I witness her own sense of herself from within her world.

Only through this travelling to her "world" could I identify with her because only then could I cease to ignore her and to be excluded and separate from her.

As Lugones describes, the process of arriving at a loving perception of her mother is a hard and painful one. Likewise, the love Lugones sees as necessary to bridge the gulf between women of color and white women is difficult to achieve. It is the kind of love Palmer (1983, p 9) describes as "tough love":

> Love is not a soft and sentimental virtue, not a fuzzy feeling of romance. The love of which spiritual tradition speaks is 'tough love,' the connective tissue of reality—and we flee from it because we fear its claims on our lives. Curiosity and control create a knowledge that distances us from each other and the world, allowing us to use what we know as a plaything and to play the game by our own self-serving rules. But a knowledge that springs from love will implicate us in the web of life; it will wrap the knower and the known in compassion, in a bond of awesome responsibility as well as transforming joy; it will call us to involvement, mutuality, accountability.

The learning environment, then, must be a loving and trusting one. By confronting social barriers and controversial ideas within a "loving" context, the individual student is not alienated by the group if her views are divergent. Rather, the community seeks to understand differing points of view and reinforce the groups' commitment to learning. The teacher in this setting becomes facilitator but also learner, sometimes speaking in the voice of "the other" to support and move forward learning.[3] In these kinds of learning situations, unexpected learning opportunities are often revealed. Adults in the community of learning may develop new attitudes and behaviors that represent "stretches" or growth unrecognized as valuable by the individual before. While this may be true in more traditional settings as well, the

---

3. In a training workshop for cultural sensitivity (DePaul University, School for New Learning, November 1990), Dr. Samellah Abdullah, clinical psychologist, expressed an idea that is very similar to Lugones' concept of world-travelling. She said that compassion toward and experiencing of the "other" perspective is critical in managing diversity in a multicultural world; see also Myers, 1988, and Collins, 1990.

spirituality of community provides intrinsic motivations, reinforcing the students' connectedness to the world.[4]

We believe it is possible to develop approaches in an educational situation which are conducive to practicing "world-travelling," empathy and dialogue, and which seek connection among students and teachers as a community in search for knowledge. Some of the methods we try in our classrooms are having students write dialogues with fictitious people who are very different from themselves; asking them to assume the perspective of a certain character and write in her or his voice (a technique we learned from our colleague Phyllis Walden); another method is to ask students to repeat or paraphrase the opinions of a student or of students with whom they disagree until the latter are satisfied that they were truly understood. Often, sharing experiences on a similar issue by going around the circle contributes to a diminishing of defensiveness and to an appreciation of diversity. And, of course, role playing is an effective method in perspective-taking.

It is important to see these methods (and others we have mentioned or that are conceivable as valuable only within a holistic, comprehensive perspective of a spirituality of love as we outlined here. Regardless of the seemingly insignificant situational circumstances, careful thought and action involving all dimensions of our love hologram are always required (see Thurman 1981, pp 89–109) and need to be actively, consistently sustained. Without such a holistic approach, the transformative aspect of learning is compromised, false, and destructively dishonest, degenerating into a mere set of techniques with no spiritual purpose.

THE ROLE OF THE TEACHER

It remains a peculiar paradox, and one that is personally taxing, that the kind of classroom environment described above is not teacher-cen-

4. When difficult situations arise wherein a student may experience dissonance between more traditional ways of learning (teacher = authority) and less familiar communal learning, the group is also encouraged to help those students resolve their issues if and when appropriate. Finding the "if and when" is sometimes difficult, and can test the teacher's spiritual supports, if not drain them.

tered but highly teacher-dependent. By approaching students with an act of faith we already "model" the kind of learning we want to see happen in our students. By seeking connection we also want the students to become aware of the connection as well. In many ways, we, as the teachers, must be open and trusting at the beginning of the class, a difficult state to achieve, and one which requires spiritual preparation, a clarity of focus and purpose, and an ability to let go of the need to control and be ready for surprises, one of the "gifts of life" (Ochs, 1983, p 60). It requires acknowledgment and a truce, at best, with whatever personal demons plague the teacher. Furthermore, in the course of the teaching/learning transaction, faith, focus, purpose, and openness have to be sustained and constantly re-created as they are continually challenged by the many different responses and interactions that occur during a class period. In addition, teachers and students alike may be confronted with institutional limitations to their efforts and must find creative ways to deal with them.

We find that as women we draw from our own wellspring of love to achieve what we describe above. Belenky et al. (1986, p 217) appropriately speak of "the teacher as midwife," who "discerns truth inside the students" (ibid., p 223) and helps to bring their thoughts to maturity. However, our nurturing is also "tough," in the sense of Palmer's "tough love" described earlier, as it does not shun the claims of the truth that spring from love (Palmer, 1983, p 9).

Clearly, we described a process that is intrinsically satisfying and rewarding, but also highly demanding. It would be unrealistic to leave out the question of what the teacher needs to do to replenish and rejuvenate herself, thus assuring the constancy and quality of the learning process and its spiritual dimensions as outlined above. For without rejuvenation, one risks diminishing the very aspects of teaching that can spark student learning; without rejuvenation teaching becomes yet another "job" void of the spiritual "life" that makes it rewarding. While it is intrinsically rewarding to draw from one's pool of self-love and knowledge to support and sustain the various and challenging learning opportunities presented in the classroom and in advising situations, it must be acknowledged that there can be a physical, emotional, and psychic price for drawing so deeply from that well, unless rejuvenating outlets are developed and consistently utilized. The paradox lies in the fact that rejuvenation is assured if one mindfully attends to the activities associated with developing self-love, activities which require blocks of *quality* time often devoted to thinking about students and their learning. The attainment of enough time to balance oneself between the spiritual and mundane levels of "give and take" in the teacher/student relationship is nonetheless essential to maintaining the self and maintaining a healthy teacher/student relationship. Through rejuvenation energy is restored, faith renewed.

CONCLUSIONS

We hope that our descriptions contribute to some of the discussions on emancipatory or transformative learning, on different ways of knowing, on learning and social action, and on issues of multiculturalism which are currently taking place among adult educators (and elsewhere). We believe that a spiritual approach to these issues moves these discussions towards a broadly comprehensive, holistic concept of transformative education, bringing into focus dimensions that are left out in these discussions, or that cannot be addressed within the frameworks provided.

Above all, an emphasis on the spiritual dimension of education shows that the teacher is drawn into the same spiritual, ethical, and emotional requirements as the students, thus providing a model for a kind of interaction which is capable of opening up individual learning spaces within the context of a community of learners. Both, the specific tasks and demands placed on the teacher as well as the importance of community are generally neglected in discussions of emancipatory or transformative learning. In addition, the theme of social action, currently prominent among critical adult educators, here assumes a dimension which takes it beyond the dichotomy of education versus social action (Heany, 1990), which also sets up a false hierarchical opposition between individual and social change. A spiritual interpretation of transformative action, on the other hand, represents a more encompassing both/and approach (Collins, 1990) which acknowledges the vital importance of individual transformation without which all social movements are bound to eventually re-create oppressive relationships and structures regardless of their explicit intent. Furthermore, the motivation that lies behind social actions aimed at dismantling ideological as well as structural barriers created by violence or injustice can unfold its power—albeit in less spectacular or visible ways—in every social action or encounter, as it ultimately is, or should be, an act of love and an affirmation of life in all its diversity. This power unfolds wherever a diverse group of learners seriously addresses the issue of separation and connectedness, and engages in practices which strengthen the individual while simultaneously opening the view towards the world.

This dialectic of critique and affirmation has only been sketched by our discussion, and we see the need to explore further the idea of finding new ways of knowing and of knowledge creation within the field of adult education. In particular, the concept of "critical reflection," so important in writings on emancipatory or transformative education, needs to be released from its current confines of primarily cognitive processes. Ultimately, educational practices and approaches have to be developed which "are friendly towards the body, liberating for one's emotions, and training one's thinking" (Bahro, 1989, p 97). For education, which so centrally depends on knowledge and knowledge creation, this means to uncover traditions of knowing, employing "ways of thinking and seeing that for the most part have been excluded from western science and epistemology" (Wilshire, 1989, p 109). Palmer's suggestion (1983:9) that "we must recover from our spiritual tradition the models and methods of knowing as an act of love" is echoed by Wilshire's demand that "we learn to listen with empathy when we have been taught only to look with detachment" (1989, p 109), a familiar theme in many feminist critiques of Western masculinist epistemologies.[5] Some adult educators have begun systematically to explore nonverbal media such as music as contributing to emancipatory learning processes, both in terms of creating emotional openings for learning, in moving people to action, and in creating a sense of community or bondedness with others (Kaltoft, 1990). Wilshire (1989, p 109) further expands these suggestions by demanding that a "new learning" must include the "so-far bypassed knowledge in our bodies," not only the knowledge in our minds. The importance of the body, or of an embodied knowledge, cannot be addressed in this essay, but deserves the attention of adult educators. Many spiritual practices are oriented towards an integration of body and mind, and of a strengthening of the "biological core" (Bahro, 1989) of human existence. As far as we know, these experiences, and the literature that exists on the

5. One of us developed the concept of "subsistence knowing" as summarizing some of these alternative conceptions of knowing, see Hart 1992.

idea of knowing in the body has not been made available to adult education (see, for instance, Steinman, 1986, also Gardner, 1983), but can provide rich opportunities for arriving at liberatory, transformative educational theories and practices.

Finally, we want to reiterate that an awareness of the power of spirituality in the teaching-learning process has also made us acutely aware of limitations. In a paradoxical way, the more we expect from the teaching/learning transaction the more we have come to accept personal limits—those of the teacher as well as of the students. This is another aspect of "putting things in perspective," and it is one which keeps us in touch with our sense of humor, and a certain humility of what and how much we can achieve in light of the endless possibilities and variations of life, of encounters with life, but also in light of the many obstacles that lie in the path of this kind of learning. To be open for possibilities includes good as well as bad surprises, affirmation as well as disappointment. The ongoing process of personal and collective change or transformation we outlined above as being required by our spiritual beliefs can rarely be achieved by relatively short-lived educational encounters alone. However, an awareness of the magnitude of our spiritual task will inform or structure our interactions, methods, and practices, and thus contribute to the possibility of transformation.

REFERENCES

Bahro, R. 1989, *Logik der Rettung*. Stuttgart (Germany), Edition Weitbrecht.

Belenky, M. F., Clinchy, B. M., Goldberger, N. R., and Tarule, J. M. 1986, *Women's Ways of Knowing*. New York, Basic Books.

Brown, J. E. 1987, *The Spiritual Legacy of the American Indian*. New York, Crossroad Publishing.

Christ, C. P. and Plaskow, J., eds. 1979, *WomanSpirit Rising: A Feminist Reader on Religion*. San Francisco, Harper & Row.

Collard, S. and Law, M. 1989, The Limits of Perspective Transformation: A Critique of Mezirow's Theory. *Adult Education Quarterly, 39* (2), pp. 99–107.

Collard, S. and Law, M. 1991, The Impact of Critical Social Theory on Adult Education: A Preliminary Evaluation. *Proceedings of the 32nd Annual Adult Education Research Conference*. Norman, Oklahoma, The University of Oklahoma, pp. 56–63.

Collins, P. H. 1990, *Black Feminist Thought*. Boston, Unwin Hyman.

Daly, M. 1973, *Beyond God the Father: Toward a Philosophy of Women's Liberation.* Boston, Beacon Press.

Dominice, P. F. 1990, Composing Education Biographies: Group Reflection Through Life Histories. In: J. Mezirow, ed., *Fostering Critical Reflection in Adulthood.* San Francisco, Jossey-Bass, pp. 194–212.

Freire, P. 1970, *Peadogy of the Oppressed.* New York, Seabury Press.

Gardner, H. 1983, *Frames of Mind: The Theory of Multiple Intelligences.* New York, Basic Books.

Heany, T. 1991, Academics and Activism: Redefining the Link. *Proceedings of the 32nd Annual Adult Education Research Conference.* Norman, Oklahoma, The University of Oklahoma, pp. 319–320.

Harding, S. 1986, *The Science Question in Feminism.* Ithaca and London, Cornell University Press.

Hart, M. 1992, *Working and Educating for Life.* London, Routledge.

Joseph, G. I. and Lewis, J. 1981, *Common Differences.* Garden City, NY, Anchor Books.

Kaltoft, G. 1990, Music and Emancipatory Learning in Three Community Education Programs. Unpublished dissertation. New York, Teachers College, Columbia University.

Kinsley, D. 1989, *The Goddesses Mirror: Visions of the Divine from East and West.* Albany, NY, State University of New York Press.

Levine, L. 1977, *Black Culture and Black Consciousness: Afro-American Folk Thought From Slavery to Freedom.* New York, Oxford University Press.

Long, R. 1981, *African and American: Essays in Afro-American Culture.* Atlanta, GA, Center for African and African-American Studies, Atlanta University.

Lugones, M. 1990, Playfulness, "World"-Travelling, and Loving Perception. In: G. Anzaldua, ed., *Making Face, Making Soul.* San Francisco: Aunt Lute Foundation Books, pp. 390–402.

Lukinsky, J. 1990, Reflective Withdrawal Through Journal Writing. In: J. Mezirow, ed., *Fostering Critical Reflection in Adulthood,* San Francisco, Jossey-Bass.

McFague, S. 1987, *Models of God.* Philadelphia, Fortress Press.

Mezirow, J. 1990, How Critical Reflection Triggers Transformative Learning. In: J. Mezirow, ed., *Fostering Critical Reflection in Adulthood,* San Francisco, Jossey-Bass, pp. 1–20.

Myers, L. J. 1988. *Understanding an Afrocentric World View: Introduction to an Optimal Psychology.* Dubuque, IO, Kendall/Hunt Publishing.

Ochs, C. 1983, *Women and Spirituality.* Totowa, NJ, Allanheld.

Pagels, E. 1989, *The Gnostic Gospels.* New York, Vintage Books.

Palmer, J. 1983, *To Know as We Are Known.* San Francisco, Harper & Row.

Rich, A. 1979, *Of Woman Born.* New York, W. W. Norton.

Richardson, D. 1990, The Implications of African-American Spirituality. In: N. K. Asante and A. S. Vandi eds., *African Culture, the Rhythm of Unity.* Beverly Hills, CA, Sage Publications, pp. 59–79.

Raboteau, A. 1978, *Slave Religion: The "Invisible Institution" in the Antebellum South.* New York, Oxford University Press.

Steinman, L. 1986, *The Knowing Body.* Boston, Shambala.

Thurman, H. 1954, *The Creative Encounter: An Interpretation of Religion and the Social Witness.* Richmond, IN, Friends United Press.

Thurman, H. 1981, *Jesus and the Disinherited.* Richmond, IN, Friends United Press.

Trebilcot, J. ed. 1984, *Mothering.* Totowa, NJ, Rowman and Allanheld.

Wilshire, D. 1989, The Uses of Myth, Image, and the Female Body in Re-Visioning Knowledge. In A. M. Jaggar and S. R. Bordo, eds., *Gender/Body/Knowledge,* New Brunswick, Rutgers University Press, pp. 92–114.

CHAPTER 16

Moral Issues in Adult Education: From Life Problems to Educational Goals and Postmodern Uncertainty

WALTER LEIRMAN and LUC ANCKAERT

INTRODUCTION: IN SEARCH OF ISSUES AND PRINCIPLES

There was a time when adult educators seemed to know what the real issues of man and society were, and according to which principles the ensuing problems could be tackled via "critical and rational discussion, leading to conscientisation and from there to action." All citizens of a given society were called upon to enter into the "great discourse of personal and social emancipation." Thus, the European Council for Cultural Cooperation published a "final report" on continuing education in 1978, based on experiments in ten member countries. The report stated that continuing education was to be guided by a triad of principles: *égalisation* (equalization), *globalization* and *participation*. These three *"ation"*-terms were explained as follows:

- *equalization* points to unequal opportunities of large groups in society. Therefore, authorities and providers of adult education should

1. realize varied, sufficient and integrated offerings, and take measures of "positive discrimination" for those who never completed their basic education;

2. provide information, guidance and counseling to all possible clients;

3. enlarge accessibility to educational programs, for example, through forms of paid educational leave.

• *globalization* means the application of a holistic concept of man and society comprising both his lifeworld and societal systems and of a congruent learning model that takes its point of departure in human experience;

• *participation* points above all to the right of participants to define their own needs and to "take their education in their own hands."

In the terms of this report, "true" adult education had to correspond to these three principles.

Thirteen years later, we in adult education seem to be far less certain. Our uncertainty not only relates to the lack of firm principles, but also to our limited knowledge of the "real issues." Instead of taking a deductive stand, we now prefer to "listen" to the "potential clients or their representatives" or to "enter into a dialogue about their problems, needs and expectations."

The latter approach is being applied in a research project titled "Education '92: towards a needs-oriented and a better coordinated policy of continuing education" which two Flemish-Belgian universities undertook, upon the request of the Ministry of Education.

For that project, we opted for an inductive problem-oriented discussion approach, with a selected sample of about 300 "informed persons," most of whom are "actors" in the field of adult education in Flanders/Belgium. They exert one or more of the following roles: policy maker, educationist, educational researcher or critical commentator, and are involved in one of the following five sectors: basic adult education, professional adult education for 15–21-year-olds, professional adult education for persons over 21, social-cultural work, for example, general or liberal adult education and senior citizens' education.

In terms of contents, our approach was to move from the question "What are, according to you, the major *problems* and *challenges* confronting adult persons in the society of the 1990s?" to ensuing questions about *goals*, educational *offerings* and general and specific *policies* of the authorities, now and in the future. The method used was that of a "policy-developing Delphi," that is, three progressive rounds of written discussions based on questionnaires, whereby the data of

Round 1 are analyzed, reported to the Delphi-sample, and used as a basis for a second questionnaire in Round 2, which then is again analyzed and reported before starting Round 3.

The basic aim of such a tedious procedure is to come to precise proposals for a new policy based on solid information and cooperative discussion. Our research will end in a double set of hearings: four preparatory hearings with representatives from adjacent sectors, and a national colloquium about an adult education policy/policies for the 1990s.

PROBLEMS OF ADULTS AND POSSIBLE CONTRIBUTIONS THROUGH ADULT EDUCATION

After our first Delphi-round, a content analysis of the open questions about *problems* and *challenges* lead to the identification of 21 different problem areas, from "Demographic changes" and "mobility of persons" to "Environmental pollution," "Complexity of society" "Difficult access to information" and "uncertainty and lack of meaning to life."

In Round 2, we fed back this set of problems, and opened with two general questions: "To which degree do adults experience these problems?" and "To which degree can adult education help to solve these problems?" (on a 7-point scale). The overall results, which were similar for all our subcategories, are presented in the following figure. Our Delphi-panel sees three serious problems for adults in our society: the overload, for example, the inaccessibility of *information*, tensions in the field of *interpersonal relations* within the family and the work sphere, and the *complexity of society*. Fairly serious problems are those of *environmental pollution*, personal *uncertainty* and lack of *meaning to life*, the *continuous enlargement of national to international scale*, the *organization of work and labor*, the lack of *professional knowledge*, the difficult access to *technology*, the threats to *health*, the securing of a *personal identity* and continuing *specialization* and threats to *personal and family income*.

Presenting these data to an international forum, one may of course wonder whether this "problem scale" would look the same in other countries? In our view, two complementary answers are possible here:

1. we do not know, and should do comparative research in this area, and

2. although one can expect differences between different countries, and even more between specific target groups, we do expect that the overall picture will be fairly similar, at least in Western Europe and North America.

The next question was that of a possible contribution to solving these problems by means of (adult) education. Our figure reveals three trends:

1. our panel is fairly optimistic about three problem areas: *professional knowledge, information* and *technology* (in that order);

2. a moderate optimism reigns in areas like *complexity of society, personal relations, uncertainty, identity, environment, politics* and *health*;

3. our panel is moderately pessimistic in problem areas like *mobility, demography, income, housing.*

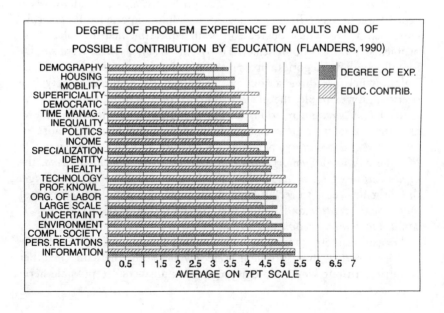

ADULT EDUCATION GOALS AND
THEIR IMPLEMENTATION

As we already indicated, in our research we moved from *problems* to *goals* and from there to their *implementation*. Since we did not yet know the real structure of the "problem set" of our sample, we used a specific framework of adult education goals (both general and specific), developed by Martin and Todd in the Alberta Adult Basic Education project (Todd, Martin, 1986). From the vantage point of our theme, this operation was very interesting. Our Canadian colleagues developed NINE major goal categories—from *"communicate"* and *"learn how to learn"* to *"earn a living"* and *"use mathematics."*

Looking at our first inventory of existential problems of adults, we were obliged to add *two* major categories which we felt were missing from a European point of view: *"give meaning to life"* and *"participate in culture."* In Round 2, we again asked our panel to tell us "How important are each of these goals in your eyes?" and "To what degree does the field of adult education effectively work on these goals?" We present the results in our next figure:

As one can see, all goals are found to be important to very impor-

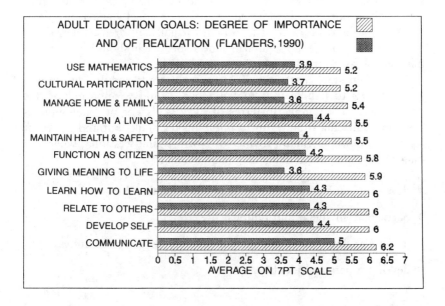

tant, with six top priorities: *communicate, learn how to learn, relate to others, develop self, give meaning to life* and *function as a citizen.*

Looking at the degree of "effectuation," one immediately notices that our panel thinks that the degree of attention in actual practice falls far below the degree of importance in most goal areas. Only one important goal appears to find a fair degree of attention: that of *communicating.* This is also the area where panel members signal most innovations in recent practice, especially in the sense of language learning and learning how to work in groups. However, the area revealing the smallest discrepancy in absolute terms is that of *earning a living*, especially in the sense of professional training. Here too, panel members signal a great amount of innovation in recent years.

The biggest discrepancy, on the other hand, is found in the area of *giving meaning to life*: this very important goal, described by our panel members in terms of reacting to uncertainty and the erosion of values and beliefs and the search for a profound life-orientation, receives rather poor attention, and panel members signal very few innovations in this area. Notice also that the same applies to *cultural participation* and to *manage home & family.*

When we added two "European" items to the original list of nine goal areas, we expected that these would be "strong points" of adult education in our country. Instead of that, our panel signals that there remains much to be done, and this in virtually all areas. One of the questions for our next round will indeed be: what should be done to narrow the greatest gaps which were signaled?

One might state that a set of 11 major goals for adult education is too complex to handle in actual practice. Could we not reduce this complexity, for example, in terms of "key skills" or of "major directions in adult education"? An example of key skills is found in recent legislation in the German province of North-Rhine Westfalia, where six major skills are enunciated:

- develop a profession and manage professional skills;

- participate in social and political life;

- living together in a family and in other types of communities;

- develop a personal identity;

- give shape to leisure time;

- acquire culture and scientifically based knowledge.

When we look at the above list, we notice indeed that most of the goals can be grouped into one or more of these six skill areas. On the other hand, aspects like "Communicate," "Learn how to learn" and "Give meaning to life" are not fully covered by this list where the focus is on cognitive and social "skills."

In view of a meaningful reduction, we also did a factor analysis on our "goal importance scale." This lead to the discovery of two basic clusters: one which encompasses our four most important goals plus "citizenship" and "cultural participation," and a second one which takes together "health and safety," "manage home & family" and "earn a living." We termed these two factors as follows:

F1: personal development towards communication, relational skills, and participation in culture and society;

F2: education in view of health, family life and professional work.

This two-factor structure transcends, to a certain degree, the traditional distinction between "general" or "liberal adult education" versus "technical and professional" or "vocational" adult education. On the one hand, it links personal development with culture and society, and on the other hand it combines professional life with family life. The first combination is not so new when one looks at the way general adult education has presented itself in Europe since World War II. However, in terms of importance, it is the personal side of development that is stressed by our panel, and this is in agreement with our so-called postmodern culture. The second link is more unusual, and we only can hypothesize here about its real meaning: in our Western societies the connection between family life and professional life is increasingly made by the "work" character of the first, especially for women in our society. And in this combination, physical and psychological health is a basic issue!

However, the basic conclusion from our research thus far seems to be that whereas policy makers and adult educators in our country are reasonably optimistic about the problem-solving potential of adult education, they are skeptical about the real contribution made by the different forms and sectors of adult education in terms of its different and important goals, and especially in the area of *giving meaning to life*.

ADULT EDUCATION AND ETHICAL UNCERTAINTY IN POSTMODERN TIMES

One of the "traditional" reactions to the conclusion that there is a wide gap between the importance attached to a certain educational goal and the attention paid to it in actual practice would be to address an urgent appeal to practioners: please, make up for the deficiency by offering new programs, using new methods and applying "modern" advertisement techniques. Another answer might be to interpret the gap as the expression of a serious hesitation and situate it within its cultural, anthropological and ethical context. This is exactly what we want to do (Anckaert, 1991).

We start our analysis with a specific example: the arguments pro and contra the Gulf War in the months preceding the event. On 15 January 1991, a Belgian retired admiral published an article on the legitimation of a war against Iraq in a newspaper. In this text, he argued that the Gulf War was a case of a *just war*. He made his evaluation by using the classical criteria of the just-war-tradition, for example, a just cause, the depletion of all other channels of conflict resolution, the protection of civilians, etc. His reasoning seemed very sound. On the same day, the Center for Theology of Peace of the Department of Moral Theology of our university, wrote an answer in which they argued that the Gulf War was *not a case of a just war at all*. They also used the classical criteria and their reasoning was also very sound. Who was right then: the admiral, the theologian, or both?

This example illustrates the interminable character of moral disagreements. In his famous book *After Virtue: A Study in Moral Theory*, MacIntyre (1981, 1984) describes and analyzes three characteristics of moral debates. Two of them are important to us. The first one is the conceptual incommensurability of the arguments. The conclusions drawn do follow premises which are of such a nature that we do not possess a *rational way* of deciding in favor of one or the other viewpoint. There is no objective norm (or common *mensura*) to prefer one of the types of reasoning, and the decision seems to be a matter of mere subjective choice. In other words: each party has its "good reasons" to stick to its position. The second feature of moral debates is that the rational arguments used in it seem to be impersonal and objective. They function as irrefutable truth statements. This second characteristic has a paradoxical relation to the first. The incommensurability suggests a subjective choice, whereas the rational character of the arguments suggests objectivity.

If people disagree in a moral debate, should they not (learn to) discuss rationally, and then decide in favor of the most "reasonable option"? In other words: should we not ascribe the fact of disagreement to a lack of knowledge and/or debating skills? We think that a better hypothesis for the explanation of disagreement may well be that moral disagreement is simply an expression of the disruption of modernity in what is commonly called "postmodern culture."

In our view, the decade of the 1980s has witnessed a transition from a perspective of *regularity/order* to a combined perspective of *creativity/innovation* and of *chaos/deregulation*. We explain this view by means of the following schema:

The first perspective, termed here *regularity/order*, represents the tradition of *Aufklärung*, and conceives of reality as Being-by-itself, whereby man acts as a constructive mason using the "available resources," takes order as his basic value, reveals an attitude of certainty and rest, and sees truth as fixed and unshakable. In the world of education, this perspective was maybe for the first time elaborated by Emmanuel Kant, who saw the act of educating as "leading ignorant people towards the use of their rationality under the guidance of wise masters."

In the second perspective, called here *creativity/innovation*, reality is seen differently, as "becoming-towards-new-being," whereby man acts as an innovator who replaces old and forworn ideas and systems by new and "better" ones, attaches the greatest value to creation and displays an attitude of playfulness, and does not believe in fixed truth, not only because different truths co-exist with one another, but also because new truth is "in the making." In the world of education, we have seen many examples of this perspective in the present century,

Perspective	Mode of being	Mode of action	Basic value	Basic attitude	Status of truth
Regularity/ Order	Being by itself	Construction	Order	Certainty	Fixed
Creativity/ Innovation	Becoming	Innovation/ Replacement	Creation	Playfulness	Paradox Unfixed
Chaos/ Deregulation	Nonbeing	Deconstruction	Power/ Violence	Fascination	Nonsense

from the "pedagogy starting from the child" (Pädagogik vom Kinde aus) and Freinetian or Summerhill schools to the pedagogy of Paulo Freire.

The third perspective is that of *chaos/deregulation*. Here, man finds himself in front of "le Néant" or "nonbeing," because there is no understandable essence. The central mode of action is deconstruction, that is, taking apart all ideas, systems and institutions, the basic attitude is one of endless fascination before a chaotic world, and the supreme value is power or violence, from where one can demonstrate the non-sensical dimensions of so-called reality. In education, it may seem difficult to find examples of this perspective, although some forms of "anti-authoritarian education" clearly stood in this perspective.

Looking at these three perspectives, we may ask ourselves now where we should place so-called postmodernity. This question can never be answered in full, for two reasons. First of all, postmodernity cannot be rationally defined, since it rejects fixed ideas, categories or schemes of thought. Second, postmodernism as a term, covers a whole range of tendencies, from "individualism" to "romantic traditionalism" (De Dijn, 1991). On the other hand, one cannot deny that there is a definite current of "anti-modernism," which reacts firmly against Cartesian rationality and fixed truths and moral principles. We can illustrate this with two examples: the new vision on subjectivity and on language.

In modern tradition, the independent human subject is the heart of the matter: man is the author of his own world, the creator of history, the maker of systems old and new. In postmodernism, the human subject is moved away from the center of reality. The absolute, almighty subject is de-centrated by asking the critical question of his origin: man is not his own origin, and his freedom is not any longer absolute, but situated and limited. This means that reason reaches its own limits in modern thought itself. Human finitude appears on the intellectual scene. This conclusion is apparent already in the philosophy of Schelling, and in the writings of Kierkegaard, the first existentialist thinker. But it has been formulated more penetratingly by such authors as Foucault, Derrida, Lacan and Girard.

Foucault speaks of the death of the modern subject and of the impact of institutions and epistemological schemes on the process of subjectivation (Foucault, 1975). Derrida stresses the problem of the origins of man and he deconstructs the tissue of existing texts and institutions: expressions are fluctuating rather than having a fixed meaning (Derrida, 1962). According to Lacan, subjectivity is not an original fact, but the result of the confrontation with the other, and therefore possibly a fiction (Lacan, 1966). Girard says that man is the result of *mimèsis* (imitation), which is the source of violence (Girard, 1978).

Postmodern thinkers stress the central role of interpersonal relations, rather than the idealistic relation between the original Ich and the Nicht-Ich (Fichte). The fluctuating reality of subjectivity undermines the concept of a fixed truth, grounded in modern subjectivity, and opens up a perspective of divergence and multiplicity.

Maybe the most important change is to be found on the level of language. In classical philosophy, language is seen as a function of interiority. Language is conceived of as internal Anschauung or as an instrument for communicating ready-made ideas. Classical philosophy attaches a central role to the direct and unequivocal relation between language and thought, or between word, meaning and reality. Nowadays, language is considered as an expression of and an instrument for multiple relations between men. Communication-theory investigates the different ways in which people exchange messages with each other. The literary critic considers a work of literature as a form of interaction between the author and the reader, and Umberto Eco even states that a reader *produces* a text by reading it (Eco, 1979). And in rhetorical analysis, one does not look for the meaning of the text, such as hermeneutics do, but for the ways in which meaning is produced.

There is also a revival of the importance of the story and of narration. Narrative can be seen as a way to explore and find meaning. But in Eco's brillant novel, *The Name of the Rose*, the book which contains the ultimate meaning, burns up in the flames of the library (Eco, 1983). Only disseminated fragments remain.

ADULT EDUCATION IN A NIHILISTIC PARADISE?

After this brief *de-scription* of our postmodern time, we are forced to ask how we can make moral decisions, which are more than a subjective utterance and which can have intersubjective and communicative validity. We thereby have to consider a context in which man, time and language have no longer a fixed meaning but are fluctuating on the waves of creativity and chaotic search. Can we escape from the paradox, indicated by MacIntyre, which consists of the incommensurability of arguments on the one hand and the objective claim of universally valid moral reasonings on the other hand?

We refuse to settle ourselves in the "nihilistic paradise of postmodern games of deconstruction." But we also refuse to write off postmodern thinking, because every refutation can be deconstructed. Postmodernity is irrefutable.

Postmodernity shows that humanism, progressive time and meaningful language are at least problematic. The end of modern man has become, to us, an inescapable reality. This may mean that the end of modern moral reasoning is a reality as well. In the following we will hold a plea for "a humanism of the other man" (Levinas, 1972), as a possible basis for current and future moral reasoning.

Jewish thinkers like Rosenzweig and Levinas propose a paradoxical view on man. On the one hand, man is a living protest against every possible totalization or fixed order, an irreducible entity. Rosenzweig describes man as meta-ethical or irreducible to any ethical system and to any unidimensional world-view (e.g., idealism); irreducible man lives "jenseits von Gut und Böse—beyond good or bad" (Nietzsche). Levinas sees man in his well-known analysis as "separation." On the other hand, human subjectivity is the result of an asymmetric relation. Rosenzweig describes man (Die Seele) as the result of the dialogue with transcendency or infinity.

Levinas says that human autonomy, the result of the existential protest against totalization, receives an ethical orientation through the confrontation with the Other. The Other is not the alter ego of pheno-menology, but the radically different Other who asks for the legitimacy of my own existence. "Est-ce que je ne tue pas par exister—do I not kill by just living?" The proper *conatus essendi*, which is originally oriented to the self-development of my existence, is questioned to its fundament and reoriented to the good of the Other. This is not a destruction of human autonomy, but a transformation of the humanism of the self into a humanism of the Other. The self receives a new kind of mission: it is fundamentally oriented to the well-being of the Other. The paradoxical relation between separation and transcendence makes this orientation possible. A radical new meaning is spoken to postmodern man. This meaning cannot be recuperated in a deconstruc-tive game because a certain deconstruction of man is necessary to detect this new meaning. The seeming paradox between subjectivity and objectivity is replaced by a fruitful paradox between the objective call for ethical engagement on the one hand and the autonomous an-swer of the subject to this call on the other. Solidarity with and re-sponsibility for the Other is the basis of every ethical reasoning. This responsibility opens up a new, diachronical time, in which every mean-ing is spoken to responsible man.

The search for meaning in life—a goal that many people seem to find important but for the realization of which people do not seem to receive much support or educational guidance—cannot be realized within the framework of global messages issued by great institutions, or by master's degree educational programs. In postmodern time, it can only be carried out in a narrative way at the grassroots level of local groups and communities, by individuals who use or create free spaces to express their experiences, feelings, and thoughts, and to share them with others.

However, such a "project" contains its risks as well. The main risk, as one moral philosopher recently stated, is that one would rely too exclusively on feelings, on local communities and on wild metaphors. Feelings—as we witness in the rise of nationalism in Eastern Europe can become exclusive and aggressive. Communities, as we witness in certain sects or closed groups, can become very oppressive to their members, and the endless use of metaphors and symbols can alienate us from reality—as certain forms of modern theatre prove (Dewachter, 1991). We should not wonder, therefore, that one of the traditional methods of adult education—the "reading circle" or *Studienkreis* or "révision de vie"—is receiving new attention nowadays. As long as it is not used in an instrumental way (a "good recipe"), it can help to create the "open space" that postmodern man needs to find both independence and inclusion.

REFERENCES

Anckaert, L. 1991, *Moral reasoning in postmodern times*. Achen, unpubl. article
Conseil de l'Europe. 1978, *Education permanente. Repport final*. Strasbourg, CCC, 79 p.
De Dijn, H. 1991, 'Post-modernismen: de vlag en de lading' (Post-modernisms: the flag and what it covers), *Kultuurleven*, 58, nr 6, p. 19 f.
Derrida, J. 1962, *Traduction et introduction à E. Husserl, L'origine de la géometrie*, Paris, Presses Universitaires de France. ID. 1972, *Marges de la philosophie*, Paris, Minuit, 1972.
Dewachter, F. 1991, 'Een ethiek zonder principes?' (Ethics without principles?), *Kultuurleven*, o.c., p. 34–41.
Eco, U. 1979, '*How to Produce Texts by Reading Them?*', in: *The Role of the Reader. Explorations in the Semiotics of Texts*, London, Hutchinson.
Eco, U. 1983, *The Name of the Rose*, London, Secker & Warburg.
M. Foucault, *Les mots et les choses. Une archéologie des sciences humaines*, Paris, Gallimard, 1966; M. Foucault, *Surveiller et punir. Naissance de la prison*, Paris, Gallimard, 1975.
Girard, R. 1978, *Des choses cachées depuis la fondation du monde*, Paris, Grasset.
Lacan, J. 1966, *Le stade du miroir comme formateur de la fonction du Je*, in: *Ecrits I*, Seuil, Paris.
Levinas, E. 1972, *Humanisme de l'autre homme*, Montpellier, Fata Morgana.
MacIntyre, A. 1981; 2nd ed., 1984, *After Virtue. A Study in Moral Theory*, Notre Dame, University of Notre Dame Press.
Todd, Anna Kae and Martin, Patricia, 1986, *The Alberta adult basic education Project*. in W. Leirman ed., *Adult education and the challenges of the 1990s. Project presentations*. Leuven, Social Pedagogy.

CHAPTER 17

Prophecy: Radical Adult Education and the Politics of Power

DAVID DESHLER

INTRODUCTION

Throughout Judeo-Christian history, the prophets have been those who have stood for justice and proclaimed it, at whatever the personal cost. This proclamation has usually not been welcomed within the ranks of either politics or religion, let alone the educational establishment. While prophets have drawn their critical perspectives from religious traditions, they have been persecuted by their own religious establishments as well as by their contemporary political, economic, and often educational power structures. Religious prophetic voices are often in leadership positions within social movements, bringing theological and ideological dimensions to social action. This chapter will provide a brief review of some of the theological roots of prophetic religion from biblical sources and church history and from several expressions of contemporary theology. This will be followed by a brief description of prophetic expressions of adult education in relationship to labor movements, liberation movements, peace movements, and the environmental movement. The chapter will conclude with a discussion of several parallel paradoxes found in both prophetic religion and radical adult education.

THEOLOGICAL ROOTS OF PROPHETIC RELIGION

Prophetic Theology in Judaism

The prophetic themes from Judaism are primarily in the Torah, Amos, Hosea, Jeremiah, Isaiah, Jonah, and the Psalms. The message is a proclamation of liberation from bondage and slavery, castigation of the establishment for oppressing the poor, and warnings about genocide and nationalism.

The story of the liberation of the Jews from the oppression of the Egyptians under the leadership of Moses is probably the best known liberation epic for Judaism, Christianity, and Islam. Exodus (3:7–9) states:

> Then the Lord said, "I have seen the affliction of my people who are in Egypt, and have heard their cry because of their taskmasters; I know their sufferings, and I have come down to deliver them out of the hand of the Egyptians, and to bring them up out of that land to a good and broad land, a land flowing with milk and honey, to the place of the Canaanites, the Hittites, the Amorites, the Perizzites, the Hivites and the Jebusites. And now, behold, the cry of the people if Israel has come to me, and I have seen the oppression with which the Egyptians oppress them.

Probably the oldest prophetic literature of the Bible is the book of Amos. Amos, a sheep herder of Tekoa during the days of Uzziah, King of Judah, stood on the steps of the temple (a nonformal educational setting) in the midst of a holiday crowd and shouted against Damascus because they "threshed Gilead with threshing sledges of iron." The people cheered because they hated the government of Damascus. Then he turned on the transgressions of Gaza for they "carried into exile a whole people." He accused Tyre for "not remembering the covenants of brotherhood when it delivered a whole people to Edom;" and accused Edom for "pursuing his brother with the sword and casting off all pity." He accused the Ammonites for "ripping open women with children in Gilead that they might enlarge their border;" Moab had "desecrated the bones of the king of Edom." The people undoubtedly cheered his pronouncements on their enemies. Then Amos proclaimed against his own government; "Judah had rejected the law of the Lord, they had lied. Israel had sold the righteous for silver and the needy for a pair of shoes, they had trampled the head of the poor into the dust of the earth and turned aside the way of the afflicted." He said, "hear this word, you cows of Bashan (wives of the wealthy), who are in the mountain of Samaria, who oppress the poor, who crush the needy, who say to their husbands, 'Bring, that we may drink!' Take away from me the noise of your songs; to the melody of your harps I will not listen. But let justice roll down as waters, and righteousness like an everflowing stream" (Amos 5:23–24). Note that in Amos's message that ethical responsibility lies not only with individuals (wives of the wealthy, and soldiers) but with collective decisions of governments.

With the eighth-century B.C. prophets Amos, Isaiah, and Jeremiah came an application of monotheistic universal ethical standards. The consequences of evil and the obligation of righteousness apply equally to Israel as well as to all other people. Isaiah (6:1–13) assumes that the meaning of the concept, "Holy," as an attribute of the "Lord of Hosts," is not only mystery, awe, and wonder, but the sense of reverence that comes with the awareness of ultimate universal righteousness, the obligation to do justice. These prophets proclaimed that social, economic, military, and political catastrophe and destruction were the consequences of ignoring the righteousness of God. Kingdoms rise and fall, based on their just treatment of other nations and their respect for the rights of the poor. Clearly God, who is just, is on the side of the victims, the poor and the oppressed.

The nations have sunk in the pit which they made; their own foot has been caught in the net which they hid. The Lord is made known! The Lord has executed judgment! The wicked are snared in the work of their own hands. The wicked shall depart to Sheol, all the nations that forget God. For the needy shall not always be forgotten, and the hope of the poor shall not perish for ever. Arise, O Lord! Let not mortals prevail; let the nations be judged before you! Put them in fear, O Lord; let the nations know that they are mortal! (Psalm 9:15–20)

. . . those who decree iniquitous decrees and write oppression, who turn aside from the needy from justice and rob the poor of my people of their right, that widows may be their spoil and that they may make the fatherless their prey. What will you do on the day of punishment in the storm which will come from afar. To whom will you flee for help, and where will you leave your wealth? (Isa. 10:1–3)

God is seated in the divine council; and in the midst of the gods holds judgment: "How long will you judge unjustly and show partiality to the wicked? Give justice to the weak and the orphan; maintain the right of the afflicted and the destitute. Rescue the weak and the needy; deliver them from the hand of the wicked. (Ps. 82:1–4)

Happy are those whose help is in the God of Jacob, whose hope is in the Lord, their God, who made heaven and earth, the sea, and all that is in them, who keeps faith for ever, who executes justice for the oppressed; who gives food to the hungry. The Lord sets the prisoners free; the Lord opens the eyes of the blind. The Lord lifts up those who are bowed down; the Lord loves the righteous. The Lord watches over the sojourners, and upholds the widow and the orphan, but the Lord brings the way of the wicked to ruin. (Psalm 146:5–9)

The prophets complained about how oppression is practiced by the establishment:

Everyone is greedy for unjust gain; and from prophet to priest, every one deals falsely. They have healed the wound of my people lightly, saying "Peace, peace," when there is no peace. Were they ashamed when they committed abominations? No, they were not at all ashamed; they did not know how to blush. Therefore, they shall fall among those who fall; at the time that I punish them, they shall be overthrown. (Jer. 6:13–15)

But you have eyes and heart only for your dishonest gain, for shedding innocent blood, and for practicing oppression and violence. (Jer. 22:17)

Justice is turned back, and righteousness stands afar off; for truth has fallen in the public squares, and uprightness cannot enter. Truth is lacking, and he who departs from evil makes himself a prey. The Lord saw it, and it displeased the Lord that there was no justice. (Isaiah 59:14–15)

Every one deceives his neighbor, and no one speaks the truth; they have taught their tongue to speak lies; they commit iniquity and are too weary to repent. Heaping oppression upon oppression, and deceit upon deceit, they refuse to know me says the Lord. (Jer. 9:5–6)

One practice against oppression and for liberation, especially from poverty, was the Torah's tradition of the year of the Jubilee. This tradition was designed to provide liberation from economic oppression and perpetual indebtedness (Lev. 25:1–55).

Then you shall send abroad the loud trumpet on the tenth day of the seventh month; on the day of atonement you shall sound abroad the trumpet throughout all your land. And you shall hallow the fiftieth year, and proclaim liberty throughout the land to all its inhabitants, it shall be a jubilee for you, when each of you shall return to his property and each of you shall return to his family. (Lev. 25:8–10)

The underlying concept of Jubilee is the assumption that "the land should not be sold in perpetuity, for the land is God's, for you are strangers and sojourners with God" (Lev. 25:23–24). Under these rules those who had lost their land could return to their property to redeem it. If brothers became poor, the community had the obligation to maintain them until the year of the Jubilee. All people who were bound through indebtedness were to be released. It is clear that justice applies to the economic system and to the treatment of the poor. Another dimension of the year of the Jubilee is compassion for the poor:

If there is among you a poor man, one of your brethren, in any of your towns with your land which the Lord your God gives you, you shall not harden your heart or shut your hand against your poor brother, but you shall open your hand to him, and lend him sufficient for his need, whatever it may be. Take head lest there be a base thought in your heart, and you say, "The seventh year, the year of the release is near, and your eye be hostile to your poor brother, and you give him nothing, and he cry to the Lord against you, and it be sin in you. You shall give to him freely, and your heart shall not be grudging when you give to him; because for this the Lord your God will bless you in all your work and in all that you undertake. (Deut. 15:7–10)

Another dimension of the Judiaism's monotheistic prophetic message was its attack on what we would call today "racism," or bias against non-Jews. In the story of Jonah, a stubborn, self-righteous and bigoted figure, we have a message that challenges religious and racial prejudice. In the story, God asks Jonah to preach repentance to Nineveh, a foreign city. He is incensed because of his bigotry. He runs away by boarding a ship bound for Tarshish (most distant seaport in the Mediterranean) and cannot escape the universal imperative and concern that God has for non-Jews. He is thrown overboard during a storm, swallowed by a large fish, is cast out on the land, and finally does what the Lord has asked him to do: preaches grudgingly to the Ninevites. The citizens of Nineveh, much to Jonah's dismay, repent and find favor with God. Jonah returns home and sulks under a booth where a shade plant grows and then the plant mysteriously dies. He is furious over the hot sun and his fate. He is told by God that he cares more for the death of a shade plant than he does for the foreigners in the city of Nineveh. There are also stories from the period of captivity when plots of genocide toward Jews were averted through courageous acts (Esther; Daniel).

Prayers on behalf of the oppressed and declarations of ethical responsibility of individuals and nations to deliver justice and mercy to the poor and oppressed are found throughout the book of Psalms:

> Give the kind your justice, O God, and your righteousness to the royal son! May he judge your people with righteousness, and your poor with justice! Let the mountains bear prosperity for the people and the hills, in righteousness! May he defend the cause of the poor of the people, give deliverance to the needy, and crush the oppressor! . . . For he delivers the needy when they call, the poor and those who have no helper. He has pity on the weak and the needy, and saves the lives of the needy. From oppression and violence he redeems their life; and precious is their blood in his sight. (Ps. 72:1–4; 12–14)

> O Lord, you will hear the desire of the meek, you will strengthen their hearts; you will incline your ear to do justice to the orphan and the oppressed, so that people on earth may strike terror no more. (Ps. 10:17–18)

> In the holy habitation, God is father of orphans and protector of widows. God gives the desolate a home to dwell in, and leads out the prisoners to prosperity; but the rebellious dwell in a parched land. (Ps. 68:5–6)

With these challenges to the establishment, it is little wonder that any of these prophets survived for long. Indeed Jeremiah protests the silencing of the prophets and social critics. "Your own sword devoured your prophets like a ravening lion" (Jer. 2:30).

Prophetic Theology in the New Testament

The birth stories of Jesus include several liberation themes. First of all, when Mary, the expectant mother of the baby Jesus, is given a blessing by her cousin Elizabeth, she, in turn, exclaims:

My soul magnifies the Lord, and my spirit rejoices in God my Savior, for he has regarded the low estate of his handmaiden, for he who is mighty has done great things for me and holy is his name. And his mercy is on those who fear him from generation to generation. He has shown strength with his arm, he has *scattered the proud in the imagination of their hearts, he has put down the mighty from their thrones, he has exalted those of low degree; he has filled the hungry with good things, and the rich he has sent empty away* (emphasis added).

This clearly is not a mandate to preserve the status quo. It is a warning to the proud, the mighty, and the rich. It is a proclamation on behalf of the oppressed, the hungry, and the poor. The context of the birth of Jesus is described as oppressive. A Roman governor, Herod, upon hearing of the birth of a potential prophet, ordered the death of all male children in Bethlehem and in all that region who were two years old or under (Matt. 2:16–18). This provides a foreshadowing of the persecution and death of Jesus later by the Roman government, which would view Jesus as politically dangerous.

Another major liberation passage is depicted at the beginning of Jesus's teaching career at Nazareth:

And he came to Nazareth, where he had been brought up; and he went to the synagogue, as he custom was, on the sabbath day. And he stood up to read; and there was given to him the book of the prophet Isaiah (61:1–4). He opened the book and found the place where it is written, "The Spirit of the Lord is upon me, because he has anointed me to preach *good news to the poor*. He has sent me to proclaim *release to the captives and recovering of sight to the blind, to set at liberty those who are oppressed*, to proclaim the acceptable year of the Lord (Luke 4:16–30).

This narration builds on the prophetic tradition of Amos, Hosea, Isaiah, and Jeremiah who insisted that the powerful exercise righteousness and that God has compassion for the oppressed. This option for the poor is present in the teachings of Jesus. He calls the rich, who pursue riches and build many barns, "fools" who have not become rich toward God (Luke 12:13–21). He describes a rich man who for many years ignored a homeless beggar named Lazarus who sat at the rich man's gate. When the rich man died and was buried, and in hell being in torment, he sees Lazarus, the homeless beggar held in esteem by Father Abraham, and calls to him to have mercy. But Abraham responds:

Son, remember that you in your lifetime received your good things, and Lazarus in like manner evil things; now he is comforted here, and you are in anguish. And besides all this, between us and you a great chasm has been fixed, in order that those who would pass from here to you may not be able, and none may cross from there to us. And he said, "Then I beg you father, to send him to my father's house, for I have five brothers, so that he may warn them, lest they also come into this place of torment." But Abraham said, "They have Moses and the prophets; let them hear them." And he said, "No, father Abraham; but if someone goes to them from the dead, they will repent." He said to him, "If they do not hear Moses and the prophets, neither will they be convinced if some one should rise from the dead.

Again, a preference for the non-elite, the poor, and the homeless is shown in Jesus's parable of the man who prepared a great banquet and invited important guests who made excuses for not coming. He then asked his servant to "go quickly to the streets and lanes of the city, and bring in the poor and maimed and blind and lame." Those who were invited, and did not come are warned that they will not taste the banquet of the kingdom of heaven (Luke 14:15–24).

In the Gospels, Jesus is depicted as a person who seeks out those whom society's elites have rejected. He talks to tax collectors, to harlots, and to the sick, the poor, and those who experience racial and religious discrimination. In Jesus's parable of the Good Samaritan, it is not only the ethic of compassion that is advocated, but a challenge to religious and racial bigotry that is boldly proclaimed by selecting a non-Jew as the exemplar of mercy (Luke 10:29–37). This same challenge to racial and gender bigotry is shown in Jesus's willingness to give attention to a maritally unfaithful Samaritan woman at the well (John 4:5–15).

Jesus confronted the patriarchal attitudes of his time toward women by confronting the self-righteousness of those who were stoning an alleged adulteress (John 8:3–11). He advocated the equality of the marriage partnership by challenging the legal rights of men to write a certificate of divorce as hardness of heart permitted by Moses (Matt. 19:1–12).

However, it is in the means for bringing about this overturning of the powerful, rich oppressors that Jesus is most prophetic and radical. Jesus insists that righteousness is more than keeping the law, it is overcoming evil with good by even loving one's enemies:

If someone does evil to you, do not pay him back with evil. Try to do what all men consider to be good. Do everything possible, on your part, to live at peace with all men. Never take revenge, my friends, but instead let God's wrath do it, for the scripture says, "I will revenge, I will pay back, says the Lord." Instead, as the scripture says: "If your enemy is hungry, feed him; if he is thirsty, give him to drink; for by doing this you will heap burning coals on his head." Do not let evil defeat you; instead, conquer evil with good (Rom. 12: 17–21).

Radical Christian Pacifism

The early Christians were pacifists who tried to practice the admonition to love their enemies, to return good for evil, and to do good to those who hated and reviled them. They refused military service until Constantine declared Christianity to be the state religion. Tradition holds that when Constantine ordered his army to be baptized into the Christian faith, he also commanded them to withhold their sword arms so that they could continue to serve the state. This contradiction between the pacifism of the early church and the demands of the state led Augustine (*City of God: Book 19:7*) to make the distinction between a *just* and an *unjust war*. Aquinas (*Summa Theologica II: Rep 2–3*) later proscribed the conditions, which are theoretically difficult to satisfy, for justifying a *just war* on the part of the state. Although the Vatican until the modern era has used this concept along with many governments to justify war, the prophetic pacifist tradition in the church has never embraced this concept as consistent with the teachings of Jesus. The Jewish prophetic tradition on the other hand has embraced the concept of *just war*.

Prophetic Reformation Theology

Among the many prophetic voices during the Renaissance, there were two reformers who stand out; Erasmus the humanist and Luther the ecclesiastical reformer and declarer of the freedom of the Christian. The two opposed each other vehemently toward the end of their careers. Luther, a religious reformer with courageous zeal, attacked the corruption of the church, and called for popular public secular education for all (McGiffert, 1917). However, when the peasants revolted due to economic oppression, he tragically failed to see the economic and political aspects of the Reformation and thus did not support the peasants' rebellion. His major prophetic contribution was his stand on human freedom. Erasmus's prophetic voice was directed toward scholasticism. He was dedicated to stripping off unessential accessories of ritual and dogma. He promoted the imitation of Jesus in unselfish labor for one's fellows. He was not a political warrior; however, he sounded a prophetic note regarding ethical reform of schools and universities. He remained within the fold of the Roman Church and thus evoked the wrath of Luther. Against the background of feudal and ecclesiastical oppression, these and other prophetic voices were truly courageous.

Prophetic Theology of Vatican II

Religious prophetic voices were encouraged by Pope John (Abbott, 1966), who in 1961 called an Ecumenical Council that met between 1963–1965. The Council, known as Vatican II, produced sixteen major documents that were addressed to the church as well as modern society, some of which contain strong prophetic elements. In the document on the church today, peace is equated with justice and not simply the absence of war, the arms race is condemned, and war is banned, not only because it is an utterly treacherous trap for humanity, but also because it injures the poor to an intolerable degree (p 295). The declaration on religious freedom also sounded a universal voice that has contributed to human rights. Pope John's "Pacem in Terris" pastoral letter has been quite influential; however, the stand of the American Catholic bishops against the production of nuclear weapons is a much stronger document.

The Prophetic Theology of the World Council of Churches

Following World War II, the World Council of Churches played a significant role worldwide in the resettlement of refugees. Its most consistent prophetic voice, however, has been raised in regard to war, the arms race, and the plight of the poor. Its prophetic declarations on economic justice also have been favorite targets for political conservatives (Duchrow, 1987). The fact that the World Council of Churches includes the Eastern Orthodox traditions, including the Russian Orthodox Church, has made it a scapegoat for anti-communist claims that it has been the tool of the international communist conspiracy. When Freire fled from Chile following a U.S.-led, right-wing military coup, he joined the Geneva staff of the World Council of Churches to continue his popular education work among non government organizations including church international development efforts.

Modern Jewish Prophetic Voices

Remarkable portraits of Jewish prophetic voices of the last century have been provided in a work by Vorspan (1960). They include Simon Wolf, Louis Brandeis, Louis Marshall, Lillian Wold, Albert Einstein, Stephen Wise, Henry Morisky, Henry Cohen, Henrietta Szold, Edward Isreal, David Dubinsky, Samuel Mayerberg, Abraham Cronback, and Herbert Lehman. What these leaders had in common, he asserts, is that they were critics of society. Aware of their own immigrant backgrounds, they pointed the spotlight on any evil, injustice, cruelty, or inhumanity and in the name of decency they demanded change. They did more than talk; they fought for improvement. Additional portraits of Jewish women who were activist promoters of equity in agriculture and protesters of the holocaust are provided by Bryer (1986). The prophetic tradition within reformed Judaism in the United States has been especially vocal on human rights issues.

Contemporary Prophetic Theology

Contemporary theology and philosophy for some time has been addressing what has been called the "crisis of modernity." Griffin, Beardslee, and Holland (1989) suggest that the modern world as a coherent period of social history began seminally with the sixteenth century, matured after the eighteenth century, and now in the late twentieth century is coming to an end. Some who call themselves "postmodern" are engaged in "deconstructive or eliminative" analysis. Others are engaged in "constructive or revisionary" work. The conservatives are attempting a "restoration," while the radicals are attempting to be "liberationists." It is the liberationist prophetic stream that we are concerned with in this chapter. There are at least four liberationist streams that have carried on the prophetic theological tradition during this century. They are the protestant social gospel that fed Christian liberalism, Neo-orthodoxy, Roman Catholic liberation theology, and process and creationist theology.

The first liberationist stream can be described at the Protestant social gospel. In Europe, it was the great German theologian Ritschl who proclaimed a social gospel that focused on the Kingdom of God as the ideal society on earth. He believed that to know God was to work with God in building the Kingdom of God on earth. In the United States it was Walter Rauschenbusch, a strong prophetic voice at the turn of the century who is known as the father of the social gospel in America. Rauschenbusch was a product of German piety until he came to the conclusion that the "Hell's Kitchen" neighborhood of New York City, where he was pastor of Second German Baptist Church between 1886 and 1897, was "not a safe place for saved souls." He came to believe that the task for the twentieth century was to focus on social salvation even as the latter part of the eighteenth century had focused on individual salvation. He saw the religion of Jesus as a force for realizing a society built upon individual worth, human solidarity, service, and love of humankind. He complained about the privitization of contemporary religion in his books on *Christianity and the Social Crisis* in 1907, and *A Theology for the Social Gospel* in 1917. From 1918 to the end of his life, he taught social ethics at the Colgate Rochester Divinity School in New York State. His interpretation of Jesus within a social political context was a lonely voice during a period of privatization of religion in America. The social gospel encouraged Christian activism in the cooperative movement, the labor movement, the settlement house movement, and prison reforms. There were many who followed, including Sherwood Eddy, Kirby Page, Harry F. Ward, and Jerome Davis who saw the Kingdom of God as Christian socialism.

The second liberationist prophetic stream can be referred to loosely as neo-orthodoxy. During and following World War II, several notable theologians struggled with the meaning of human nature and the social responsibility of the church for the demonic rise of Nazism including the holocaust and the militarization of Japan. The prophetic voice of Dietrich Bonhoeffer (1954a, 1954b, 1963), who was imprisoned and executed by the Nazis for an assassination attempt on Hitler, became a symbol of a Christianity that was worldly, politically responsible, and the servant of society. Karl Barth (1957) in the prophetic tradition of the Bible, called for conviction of the social sins of modern life and civilization, condemned human self-sufficiency and complacency, and criticized the optimism of earlier liberals. Reinhold Niebuhr (1932, 1937), a Baptist minister in Detroit, came to a conclusion, similar to that of Rauschenbusch, in his classic work titled *Moral Man in Immoral Society*, pointing out that individual morality and religious privatism was insufficient while social structures destroy human life and dignity. He brought together the concepts of love and justice along with emphasizing the role of the prophetic church in confronting the centers of oppressive power. His brother, H. Richard Niebuhr (1937, 1951), who taught at Yale Divinity School, also explicated the relationship of religion to social structures and American culture in his work on the *Kingdom of God in America* and *Christ and Culture*. They both attacked privativistic Christianity, as did Rauschenbusch. Reinhold Niebuhr taught for many years at Union Theological Seminary including the years that Myles Horton of Highlander Center was a seminarian. Paul Tillich (1951, 1957, 1963), was another prophetic voice. He was a German who fled the Nazis and taught at Harvard for many years. He saw his task as describing the boundaries, similarities and differences between the meaning of prophetic Christian theology and philosophy, Christianity and other religions, Christianity and culture, Protestantism and Catholicism, and between liberalism and neo-orthodoxy. Through his three volume *Systematic Theology*, he built bridges of meaning between Christian language and the language of sociology, psychology, and political science as well as divergent movements both past and present. Tillich proclaimed prophetic judgment against religious pride, ecclesiastical arrogance, and secular self-sufficiency and their destructive consequences.

The third liberationist stream came out of a radical segment of the Catholic Church in Latin America. Liberation theology was in response to the economic, political, and cultural oppression of the poor. It was also in response to a church that for centuries had gained power and privilege through collusion with the wealthy establishment. Under repressive governments, the church was the only vehicle of expression to look for the disappeared. One of the first outspoken expressions of liberation theology came from Peruvian theologian Gustavo Gutierrez

(1986?) who defined liberation at two levels: (1) the economic and political; and (2) the theological, an effort to root out social injustices as salvation in present historical conditions as a free gift of the Lord who becomes flesh in the life of a people fighting for its human dignity and its status as offspring of God. Another prophetic voice was that of Brazilian Dom Paulo Evaristo Arns, who was the protector of the Commission for Justice and Peace (assistance in locating the disappeared). He was the most outspoken critic of the Brazilian military regime and a supporter of the Christian Basic Communities (CEB's). Between 1968–1978 two church conferences, the Medellin Conference and Puebla Conference, gave space to the defenders of the "new" prophetic church. This theology has been an expression of utopian prophetic hope. It has been a movement that rejected do-goodism and palliative reforms in order to commit itself to the dominated social classes and to radical social change. It declared liberation not only for exploited individuals, but for exploited countries as well. It was at these conferences that the preferential option for the poor, the fight to lessen the social inequities, the support for the creation of grassroots communities, the fight against imperialism (internal and external), and the personal choice for a political theology was taken. The Pueblo Conference particularly acted to certify this prophetic, revolutionary church. It denounced regimes of force, and the national security doctrine. It announced liberation including women's liberation, option for the poor, and Christian Basic Communities. Conservatives considered it as a strategy of the communists to destroy family, faith, and democracy (Boff, Leonardo and Clodovis, 1986, p 6).

The theology of liberation is more than just a theology, according to Boff, Leonardo and Clodovis:

> It represents the church of a whole continent—a church caught-up in the historical process of a people on the move. There are people behind liberation theology, there is struggle, there is a process at once ecclesial and social. Behind liberation theology there are no books, but people. What is at stake is that "telltale difference" between theory and practice. (Boff, Leonardo and Clodovis, 1986, p 6)

The practice of liberation theology begins with the gathering of the poor into Christian Basic Communities (groups of 10 to 40 persons) to read the liberation scriptures described in the first section of this paper. The people are encouraged to identify themselves with this message, to interpret the meanings in terms of the social political contexts in which they live their lives, and to discuss actions to be taken by the communities.

Another theological expression that shares the perspective of liberation theology is the work of Harvey Cox (1984) who has consistently challenged privatistic religion particularly in his classic work, *Religion in the Secular City: Towards a Postmodern Theology.*

Although unacknowledged and under political pressure by the Roman Catholic hierarchy, Mathew Fox (1983), a Dominican, has provided an alternative prophetic voice that presents the central message of the Christian faith as proclamation of what he calls "creation spirituality," a theological response to ecological crisis and a call to befriend the creation. He rejoices in global ecumenism, justice and liberation movements, and the feminist movement. He rejects the "fall/redemption" theology that concentrates on sin as a "rather substantial lacuna, ironically, the very trivializing of sin, the inability to grasp sins like genocide and ecocide and biocide of which the human race is fully capable" (Fox, 1983, p 19). He claims that creationist theology predates redemption theology and is rooted in the eight-century prophets. His work is unsystematic and sporadic, and eclectic; however, it is a sourcebook for many Christians involved with the environmental movement.

SOCIAL MOVEMENTS, ADULT EDUCATION, AND PROPHETIC THEOLOGY

Social movements may or may not be religious in their origin but they often use prophetic religious ideology and attract prophetic religious leadership to their causes and ranks. Adult education that incorporates social justice dimensions is most often an expression of a social movement. Examples include: the worker's education movement in England and the United States; liberationist movements including the abolitionist, civil rights, popular education, and feminist movements; the antiwar and peace movements, and the environmental movement. The intention here in discussing each of these social movements is to briefly describe the linkages among social movements, adult education efforts of a few movement leaders, and their use of prophetic theology.

Worker's Education in England and North America

The roots of many adult education programs lay initially in a concern for social justice and radical change both reformist and radical in conjunction with workers' education. Although the main stream of adult education has concentrated on fulfilling individual needs, preparing workers for the existing labor market, and responding to increased leisure hours of the middle class, there are many historical examples of adult education that have raised prophetic voices regarding unjust structures of society and have emphasized collective political and economic achievement of equality and social justice. Examples include the Folk High School Movement in Scandinavia, Societa Umanitaria de Milan in Italy, the WEA and NCLA in England, Frontier College and the Antigonish Movement in Canada, the Highlander Center in the United States, the American Labor College, community development, and settlement houses (Lovett, 1988). Often the leadership of these expressions of prophetic adult education has come from the clergy.

The Folk High School Movement in Scandinavia has been an important influence in numerous education programs on behalf of workers. Danish Folk Schools, started by Bishop Gruntvig, were populist and intended to redress cultural, social and political inequalities. Theology and social ethics permeated the curricula of Folk Schools. They figured heavily in the transformation from Scandinavian monarchy to the Scandinavian socialism we know today. The Folk School Movement along with other Scandinavian approaches, including study circles, have had close links with both the labor movement and the cooperative movement.

Highlander Folk School in Tennessee, now called the Highlander Research and Education Center, has played a central role in the history of popular education in the United States. Its founder Myles Horton, a graduate of Union Theological Seminary at Columbia University in New York, became a radical adult educator who played a critical role in the growth and development of the trade union movement in Tennessee while suffering attacks by the Ku Klux Klan and other reactionary elements in the South. The Center played an even more crucial role during the civil rights movement through intensive, short-term residential workshops, providing a place for strategic planning, training in nonviolent methods, and in forging movement solidarity. "It has sought to educate people away from the dead end of individualism into the freedom that grows from cooperation and collective solutions to problems. It placed great stress on culture and art, particularly local working-class culture" (Lovett, 1988, p xviii). It is now engaged in economic development and environmental conservation efforts.

Another radical adult education expression occurred through the Societa Umanitaria de Milan in Italy, which "convened the first European conference on unemployment; the first on adult education; set up the first labour exchanges in Italy; the first cooperative housing scheme, the first institution of the unemployed; trained cooperators; had a large People's Theatre; started the Italian People's Universities, the first adult education unions; and promoted People's Libraries, all before 1910" (Lovett, 1988, p xvi). These efforts can be linked to Christian socialist ideology.

In North America a concern for women workers led Hilda Worthington Smith, Dean of Bryn Mawr College, to organize a Summer School for Women Workers from 1922–1928 (Saul and Bernhardt, 1991). Schied (1991) has traced the origins and roots of socialism in the United States to the secret French workers clubs (League of the Just) that the German artisans, journeymen, and skilled workers organized. By the 1840s workers' clubs had spread throughout German speaking lands including the United States. The center of activity was in Switzerland. Large-scale German settlement in the United States in the late 1840s and 1850s was due to the bad economic conditions and the failure of the 1848 revolution. Between 1850–1900 Germans were 25% of the U.S. population. Wilhelm Weitling the best known of the utopian artisan communists. He broke with Marx and immigrated to the U.S. in 1847 and organized workers' clubs (Arbeiterbund).

The Antigonish movement of Nova Scotia in Canada became world famous during the 1930s. The leading figures of this movement as well as the Danish Folk Schools were clergymen, Father Moses Coady and Father Jimmy Tompkins. Coady was the intellectual figurehead of the movement, operating from the Extension Department of St. Francis Xavier University. Tompkins was the fieldworker building the foundations of the movement amongst the poor people of the region in the 1920s. According to Lovett (1988, p xiv), Antigonish believed:

> . . . . that reform would come about through education, public participation and the establishment of alternative institutions, i.e., cooperatives and credit unions. For Coady adult education was an aggressive agent of

change, a mass movement of reform, the peaceful way to social change. It was a populist movement, strongly anti-communist but with a vision of a new society . . . The Antigonish movement did succeed in engaging large numbers of workers in a extensive educational programme linked to social action. (Lovett, 1988, p xiv).

The industrial revolution filled the cities with immigrants and often masses of unemployed. Another response to the industrial revolution's impact on immigrants and working class people was the settlement house movement started by Jane Addams. Both Jews, particularly the Reformed, and Christians expressed their prophetic tradition through settlement houses which gave birth to the social work profession. That movement was a response of Protestant social gospel adherents to the oppressive conditions of both urban and rural areas. According to Stackhouse (1985) the Christian sociologists responded to the industrial revolution in conversation with the best social theories available to them. They were fully committed to the biblical witness as the source and norm for their efforts, a witness that articulated a doctrine of "person in community." The community development movement in the United States was built on religious commitment to a just community that respected persons as subjects. It also emphasized local democratic control within a doctrine of "person in community" (Biddle and Biddle, 1965).

Liberation Movement

Although slavery has existed since recorded history, the efforts to abolish it legally in the United States began during the nineteenth century in the abolitionist movement. This movement had its roots in the work of Quakers, and other radical Protestants who organized underground railway operations for freed slaves making their way to abolitionist states and to Canada. Following the Civil War, an alternative system grew up along side the dominant system including black churches, Freedman's Bureaus, black colleges, vocational schools, fraternities, and the largest black educational movement in America, Marcus Garvey's Universal Negro Improvement Association. The birth of the National Association for the Advancement of Colored People in 1909 brought into the open the conflict between the more radical W.

E. B. Du Bois and the more conservative Booker T. Washington. The civil rights movement in the United States, especially during the late 1950s and 1960s, has been recognized as one of the most successful reform movements in U.S. history. Adult education and the black church were at the heart of the movement through mass meetings, songs and group discussions, citizenship and freedom schools, and strategic training in conjunction with nonviolent action (Gyant, 1991). In the 1960s, Martin Luther King, Jr., a Baptist minister, educated at Boston University School of Theology, was the prophetic voice of the civil rights movement. King's nonviolent approach was made explicit in his book *Strength to Love* (1964). Drawing from both liberation themes from the Exodus, the eighth-century prophets, and the teachings of Jesus, he made specific applications to oppression in America. Just prior to his assassination he publicly opposed the war in Vietnam from a Christian pacifist perspective long before mass antiwar protests. The Southern Christian Leadership Conference was the central organizing force of black church leadership behind the protests. Other leaders of the civil rights movement included Whitney Young (Urban League), Andrew Young (SCLC), James Farmer (CORE), H. Rap Brown (SNCC), and the militants Floyd McKissick, Stockley Carmichael, Malcomb X (Black Muslims), and Ron Karenga (Hough, 1968), Fannie Lou Hamer, Rosa Parks, Dorothy Cotton, Annie Devine, Victoria Gray, Martha Mae Carter, Septima Clark, and Bernice Robinson (Gyant, 1991). The educational activities of these leaders for civil rights and the black church for the most part were one and the same. Spirituality and belief in liberation themes of Christianity provided the underlying motivation for the public accommodations' sit-in's, Citizenship Schools, Freedom Schools, voter registration drives, activities of the NAACP, and the National Council of Negro Women. As mentioned, the role of Myles Horton and Highlander Center (Adams, 1975) was central in the coordination, planning, and leadership development of the civil rights movement in the United States.

Simultaneous with the civil rights struggle in the United States, another extensive liberationist movement known as popular education emerged in Latin America in conjunction with liberation theology. Popular education intends to increase the ability of people to: (1) consciously appropriate their own reality; (2) influence and control the processes in their daily lives, including equal distribution of goods and services; (3) defend their own interests and to define the type of society that would serve them best; and (4) to make the society less hegemonic and more responsive to them (Cardena, 1984). Popular education in North America has been adopted by many community-based adult education programs.

Although there are many persons who have articulated the themes of popular education, none is better known internationally than Paulo Freire. An analysis of the theological foundations of Freire, from the sources he cites, suggests that he has drawn from (1) personalism, especially as evidenced in the writings of Emmanuel Mounier, (2) existentialism, (3) phenomenology, (4) Marxism, and (5) Christianity (Blackwood, 1987). Blackwood contends that prophetic Christianity is in the first position of priority, but that it does not function independently as a controlling variable. From Mounier's Christian personalism, Freire emphasizes a critical optimism and hope that leads to engagement for transformation of society instead of apathetic fatalism that lets things simply run on. His goal is to inject a faith, a vision, a positive concept of the person and society as created in the image of God. Freire draws from the existentialism of Buber, Marcel, Jasper, Sartre, and Camus, an emphasis on transcending massification, manipulation, and alienation through authentic reflection and action upon concrete existential situations so that persons become subjects instead of domesticated objects (Blackwood, 1987, p 210). Freire's emphasis on conscientization is closely linked to phenomenology which concentrates on how a human interprets and perceives his or her world. Drawing from Marx does not mean that Freire is a communist or a supporter of any specific political regime. Rather he has found the idea of class struggle as a rubric for interpreting social structures especially in a Latin American context. Freire rejects Marxist atheism while admitting that "God" and religion are often used by the powerful to control the poor, as an opium of the people. Freire's universe is unmistakably theocentric. A concept of God comprises the integrating point from which the other truth sources radiate. Steeped in Catholicism from his childhood, Freire espoused the theology of more progressive Catholics such as Teilhard de Chardin, Maritan, Lonergan, and the Christian existentialists and personalists. The relationship with God can never be a relationship of domination or domestication, but it is always a relationship of liberation. God is the God of the Exodus, the Jubilee, the prophets, Jesus and the book of James. The biblical witness is an often overlooked influence upon Freire. Although he rarely quotes Scripture directly, his language only thinly masks its biblical origin.

"Such terms as incarnation, logos, conversion, born again, salvation, faith, hope, trust, love, justice, the Kingdom of God, God, Jesus Christ, freedom, transformation, commitment, creation, humility, sin and reconciliation all reflect the foundation of biblical theology" (Blackwood, 1987, p 213). Christ, according to Freire, is a prophetic leader of holistic revolution by praxis dialogue with people at the point of their struggle with evil. Jesus did not conform to the status quo of the social order, even and especially the religious social order, but opposed it through praxis dialogue, even to the point of being put to death by it (Schipani, 1984, p 68). Freire's revolutionary education is prophetically religious, an intentional critical intervention into the unjust state of power differentiation in order to transform it from within. Nothing short of an all-pervasive revolutionary pedagogy will accomplish the dissolution of class interest and forge a new social order. Both oppressors and oppressed will be liberated in this process, and a new social synthesis will be produced (Freire, 1972, p 180). While Liberation theologians in the Catholic Church of Brazil were organizing Christian Basic Communities, Freire was organizing culture circles with the poor. The two phenomena are intertwined ideologically within the Latin American context.

The feminist liberation movement has been challenging the patriarchal tendency of both Christianity and Judaism. Religious feminists within the religious establishment have been questioning ordination restriction and practices against female religious leadership, representation on regional and national ecclesiastical structures, and the examination of gender offensive language in the Bible as well as in worship liturgy and hymnody. Coffman (1991) has reported the stress in McCormich Theological Seminary in Chicago when inclusive language was introduced throughout the curriculum and worshiping community. The feminist movement is challenging the patriarchy of the prophets themselves. Adult education in the churches has been disturbed by the radical feminists who have raised issues of homophobia, as well as issues of sexism within the ranks of the church.

Peace and World Order Movement

One of the major outcomes of the Reformation was the rereading of the New Testament uninterpreted through the eyes of the ecclesiastical hierarchy. The Quakers (Yarrow, 1978), Mennonites, and Brethren particularly focused on the words of Jesus regarding overcoming evil with good, and refraining from violence. They saw themselves as the revival of first-century Christianity with their inspiration coming from the words of Jesus. George Fox, the founder of the Quakers, refused to join the army. These pacifist Protestants have provided the major leadership for peace work in Europe and North America since the 1700s (Bainton, 1960). The Quakers have sponsored peace conferences and seminars, conflict resolution sessions for diplomats during the cold war, India/Pakistan war, Nigerian civil war, North Vietnam/United States, and have provided leadership for the Canadian Peace Research Association; British Conflict Research Society; The Peace Science Society (international); the Conference for Peace Research in History; and the Consortium for Peace Research, Education and Development (Yarrow, 1978, p 280).

Pacifism came with immigrants to America (Brock, 1968a; Brock, 1968b). Although there are many who are lesser known, the name A. J. Muste has come to symbolize peace activism in North America. Many call him the American Gandhi. Muste was born in the Netherlands in 1885 and came to the United States in 1891. He is best known for his work as the executive secretary of the Fellowship of Reconciliation, an organization that united the peace activists of the Quakers, Brethren, Mennonites, and many others. He advocated direct nonviolent action and was instrumental in starting the Congress of Racial Equality. Civil rights leader, Martin Luther King, Jr., said that he was profoundly influenced by Muste. Although Muste was sympathetic to the aspirations of socialist and labor parties, he criticized them for their lack of opposition to military establishments the world over. At the age of 75 he engaged in civil disobedience against civil defense drills during the cold war hysteria of 1960 (Hentoff, 1963). Another pacifist who had extensive influence was Kirby Page; he published over 48 books and organized numerous peace study tours including one to the Soviet Union in 1928. He brought world leaders together with peace activists. He was one of the first to protest the rise of Hitler and to interpret Gandhi to North Americans. He advocated informal conversation in the midst of violence and anger, unhurried prayer, clarification of the mind, strengthening of commitment to peace, and the engendering of courage in direct action.

The American Catholic peace movement has spoken out against the uncritical acceptance of the just war tradition within the Catholic

Church (McNeal, 1974). Dorothy Day, the founder of the *Catholic Worker* expressed pacifism through that newspaper throughout World War II. Thomas Merton has taken a strong position of nuclear pacifism. Two American priests, Daniel and Philip Berrigan, were prominent in their antiwar action against the U.S. involvement in the war in Vietnam.

In spite of the cold war following World War II, peace activists organized conferences to share resources and prepare strategy. The first Christian peace conference for socialist countries was held in 1958 in Czechoslovakia under the sponsorship of the Department of the Christian Peace Conference at Prague (Roer, 1974). The next major conference in 1966 included Roman Catholics, representatives of the World Council of Churches, and the socialist peace activists. These Church and Society Conferences overcame difficulties in spite of the anti-communist stance of Pope Pius XII (Roer, 1974). In North America, a response to World War II, peace activists held regular American church study conferences for well over twenty years (Lunger, 1988).

More recently many universities have provided peace studies courses (Reardon, 1982). The World Policy Institute has published several editions of curriculum guides and syllabi for universities and community colleges on peace and world order studies (Wien, 1984). The voices of feminists on peace and peace education have provided a new prophetic dimension (Brock-Utne, 1989).

Perhaps the strongest antiwar document by a major religious group in recent years has come from the United Methodist Council of Bishops (1986) in their pastoral letter titled, "In Defense of Creation." They built on the American Catholic Bishops' antinuclear pastoral letter and the World Council of Churches Sixth Assembly in Vancouver in 1983 (Gill, 1983), which said:

> We believe that the time has come when the churches must unequivocally declare that the production and deployment as well as the use of nuclear weapons are a crime against humanity and that such activities must be condemned on ethical and theological grounds. (Gill, p 137)

The United Methodist position on nuclear war is framed within the larger issue of life sustainability on the planet and commitment to the doctrine of creation.

In Europe and North America the peace movement has been active in protests against the Vietnam War, the invasion of the Falklands, Grenada, and Panama, and against the 1991 Middle East war.

Environmental Theology

The roots of contemporary environmental theology are found in the monistic doctrine of F. D. E. Schleirmacher, Alfred North Whitehead, and Henry Bergson, who emphasized divine immanence and the rejection of the natural/supernatural dichotomy. Contemporary American theologians John Cobb, Jr. (1983) and David Ray Griffin (1989) are probably the best known process theologians taking seriously the religious stance toward issues of the creation and planetary sustainability and survival as well as issues of justice and equality. Some environmental leaders have been extremely critical of Christian theism regarding the environment. Naes and Sessions (1989) state that:

> Christian theism has done much to bring about the dangerous situation to which the world has come. In various forms it has supported anthropocentrism, ignored or belittled the natural world, opposed efforts to stop population growth, directed attention away from the urgent needs of this life, treated as of absolute authority for today teachings that were meant to influence a very different world, aroused false hopes, given false assurances, and claimed God's authority for all these sins. (p 399)

A response to this charge comes from theologian John Cobb and economist Daly who have advocated an ethical criteria for evaluating the behavior of nations in regard to global sustainability (Daly and Cobb, 1989). They have proposed an index of sustainable economic welfare that factors in the costs of environmental degradation, and sustainability as well as income distribution as an alternative to GNP. It is a prophetic challenge to conventional capitalism, militarism, and materialistic life styles. The categories include natural resource depletion, foreign versus domestic capital-net capital growth, environmental damage, value of unpaid household labor, and value of leisure. Their biospheric vision and thinking is based on "deep ecology" community with other living things. They declare that the rise of this vision, especially influenced by ecological and feminist sensitivities has been one of the great advances of this generation.

Giving voice in the tradition of the eighth-century prophets, Daly and Cobb state:

> Yet there is hope. On a hotter planet, with lost deltas and shrunken coastlines, under a more dangerous sun, with less arable land, more people, fewer species of living things, a legacy of poisonous wastes, and much beauty irrevocably lost, there will still be the possibility that our childrens' children will learn at least to live as a community among communities. Perhaps they will learn also to forgive this generation its blind commitment to ever greater consumption. Perhaps they will even appreciate its belated efforts to leave them a planet still capable of supporting life in community (Daly and Cobb, 1989, p 400).

Prophetic Oriented Adult Education Organizations

Illich (1977) is known for his prophetic voice against the professionalization and comercialization of education worldwide. He points out that when education becomes the servant of the establishment, it erects a barrier between itself and the poor:

> Imperceptibly all countries, East and West, have adopted a system of knowledge capitalism. Wealth is redefined in terms of hours of instruction purchased with public funds and poverty is explained and measured by the individual's failure to consume. In such a society, the poor are those who lag behind others in education. The rich man [sic], the knowledge capitalist, cannot bridge the gap which separates him from Lazarus.

This tension between establishment adult education organizations and those represented by "Lazarus" has been part of the history of contemporary adult education organizations. For instance, the International Council of Adult Education was created as an addition to the UNESCO government-oriented perspective on adult education. The International Council, although less conservative than the UNESCO sponsored organization, does officially represent the various national and regional professional adult education associations. Remarkably, however, this establishment professional organization, through the leadership of its past executive director Budd Hall, has made possible the participation of many prophetic voices through the creation of networks, which are now called working groups. These working groups have voiced the concerns of the illiterate, women, indigenous naive people, the incarcerated, the impaired, refugees, subsistence farmers, slum dwellers, and others who experience oppression. These working groups have supported peace efforts, transformative training, and popular education. Its Participatory Research Working Group and the Transformative Research Working Group have focused attention on the relationship between power and knowledge creation and have advocated research that benefits the less powerful and contributes directly to social justice. Many of the working groups publish newsletters and sponsor events that focus attention on social justice issues and popular education advocacy. Their publications have provided an international prophetic voice among adult educators. As a result of representation from the Council's working groups, the tension between establishment and prophetic perspectives was quite evident at the 5th World Assembly of the International Council of Adult Education held in Bangkok, Thailand, in January, 1990.

Another international organization, The International League for Social Commitment in Adult Education (ILSCAE), came into being in 1984, in response to a sense of the erosion of commitment to social justice on the part of professional adult education national organizations in North America. ILSCAE became an affiliate organization of the International Council of Adult Education. It has held international conferences in Sweden, England, Netherlands, Canada, and Nicaragua. The conferences have introduced participants to forms of popular adult education in host countries and have facilitated international contacts among adult educators committed to social transformation.

Again, in 1990 a group of social activist leaders of adult education met at Highlander Center and formed a new organization called North Americans for Popular Adult Education, to promote democratic social change through education as an alternative organization to the Canadian Association for Adult Education and the American Association for Adult and Continuing Education. Their first organizing conference was held in Toronto in 1991. Their existence is a prophetic challenge to establishment adult education in North America.

RADICAL ADULT EDUCATION AND PROPHETIC RELIGION: DYNAMIC SIMILARITIES

There are at least the following similarities between the experiences of radical adult educators and those who have served the prophetic functions in religion: persecution, co-optation, privatism, contextuality, reflectivity, and vision. Brief comments on each follow:

Persecution

Prophets are never honored in their home country. The same traditions that give rise to prophetic voices also persecute or ignore their prophets. The dynamics of power and privilege are always at work to silence the prophetic tradition. It is the religious establishment itself that kills the prophets, along with the political and economic establishments. The prophets for social justice in both religion and adult education have always been present within their respective traditions as minority voices, often "crying in the wilderness." The prophets are silenced and killed by religion as well as by the secular order for their critical messages. There is irony and historical reality in the observation and warning of Jesus (Luke 11:47–49) that God sends prophets, who are persecuted and killed by the religious establishment itself. After the killing, the establishment then builds tombs and monuments to them while at the same time it prepares to kill new ones. It is similar in radical education. The Highlander Center in Tennessee was burned down. Freire and others had some success among the poor with a popular education literacy movement in Brazil, then he was imprisoned and exiled. Similar persecution occurred to popular educators in Chile under Penochet. Popular educators are accused and persecuted as communists in the Philippines along with Christian Basic Communities.

Resistance to Co-optation

The dominant forces and voices in religion and the educational establishment have usually accommodated themselves to, been co-opted by, or have sometimes enthusiastically participated in, the perpetuation of political, economic, and social oppression of the poor; nationalistic military fervor for holy wars; intolerance, racism, bigotry, discrimination, colonialism and imperialism. All of these accommodations have usually been justified on the basis of ecclesiastical or organizational self-preservation. Most of the declarations of the biblical prophets are outcries against corrupted religion and government that have betrayed the vision of justice and righteousness. Although there are prophetic exceptions, the dominant voice of Christianity tolerated and sometimes actively promoted a variety of social wrongs and injustices. For example, anti-Semitism, for which there are scriptural justifications in the Fourth Gospel, itself has had frequent expressions in mainstream Christianity. Although the early church held a pacifist stance toward violence and war, with the adoption of Christianity as a state religion under Constantine, the church has provided religious legitimacy for many so-called "just" and "holy" wars during which unspeakable atrocities and brutalities have been committed. The crusades of the Middle Ages can be compared to present-day examples of "holy" wars. An incestuous relationship between organized religion and the state has often resulted in a religious hegemony to justify the status quo of oppressive governments. The co-optation of Russian Orthodoxy by the Czars of Russia is an example. The relationship between missionaries and the colonizing invaders of Asia, Africa, and Latin America is another example of both prophetic protest and political accommodation on the part of Christianity to the brutality of European imperialism, including cultural as well as physical genocide. Genocide against native peoples and efforts to erase their culture through assimilation has been actively promoted by many Christian groups or passively accepted as inevitable by others. The Christian establishment, from its early beginnings during the time of the Roman Empire to modern times, failed to vigorously oppose slavery, contrary to universal imperatives in the teaching of Jesus or in the letters of Paul. The dominant white Protestant churches in the United States, for many years, turned a blind eye toward slavery. While some white Protestants, after the Emancipation Proclamation during the Civil War, were engaged in massive adult literacy efforts among blacks, the vast majority actively participated in creating a segregated society, and were not the major players during the civil rights movement of the 1960s. The South African government has been successful in co-opting some forms of Christian religion to justify apartheid even though the South African Council of Churches has called apartheid a heresy. The dominant forms of organized religion have not been prophetic, yet these same traditions continually give rise to prophetic voices who challenge both religious and secular justifications for the practice of oppression, injustice, brutality, war, and inhumanity. Much adult education in Europe and North America serves the reproduction of existing social inequities, the industrial military complex, and the materialism that threatens the survival of our planet. It is preoccupied with means and methods, oblivious to the ends or ultimate purposes which are being served by the commercial, or governmental enterprises. The prophets who criticize the system are treated like unwanted "whistle blowers."

Privativistic Individualism

During the last 200 years, the dominant influence of privativistic individualism has pervaded both religious and educational perspectives particularly in North America. This emphasis on privativistic individualism obscured the need to focus on or to criticize the structural weaknesses and injustices of society. For religion, personal or individual salvation was emphasized in the Sunday Schools. Religious instruction included interpretation of the Christian tradition and personal spiritual development. Liberation emphases, which included articulating a vision of the Kingdom of God, recognizing forms of oppression, and criticizing privativistic individualism was, for the most part, ignored or down played. The emphasis was on personal morality, not social ethics. It was assumed that if individuals became moral, then society would become just. The advocates of the social gospel and the neo-orthodox theologians challenged this notion. However, the conflict between the personal/individualistic and the social/collective was further complicated in North America by the doctrine of the separation of church and state as an aspect of pluralistic public education. American public education emphasis on individual achievement implied that a just social and political order would emerge if education produced individually enlightened, competent, and skilled citizens and workers. The reconstructivists and reconceptionists in education challenged this. However, they were minority voices. In North American adult education there has been a historical movement away from a social commitment on the part of the Adult Education Association and its successor the American Association of Adult and Continuing Education with the popularity of Malcolm Knowles's individual self-directed learning, and the domination of human resource development. In both adult education and in the establishment religion there is a tension between the emphasis on personal fulfillment and personal salvation on the one hand and collective ethical decisions and social justice or the Kingdom of God on the other hand. This division in religion can be seen in relationship to

302   ADULT EDUCATION AND THEOLOGICAL INTERPRETATIONS

the separation between establishment theology and the field of social ethics. Griffin (1989, p 81) states that "one pervasive feature of modern theology has been a separation of systematic theology from theological ethics, especially social ethics." Most individualistic theology, he contends, appears to be irrelevant to racism, sexism, social and economic justice, imperialism, war, nuclearism, and ecological destruction. The discussion of these has been left to the ethicists, due to intellectual fragmentation of modernity. The modern university with its many specializations and the neglect of ethics is an example of the same individualistic dynamic. More recently, however, parts of the environmental movement have placed an emphasis on bridging the gap between the personal and the social; concrete individual beliefs/behavior and global social policy/demands for collective action.

Contextuality and Ideology

Theology is the religious ideology of a specific community, born out of specific experience. When theology has been codified for all time and generalized, it has often been ignored as irrelevant, or worse become authoritatively oppressive. Most theologians have long noted that their task has been to interpret the faith for specific communities at specific historical times if the faith is to be relevant and vital. The same can be said regarding ideologies and social movements and radical adult education. One of the things that the Highlander center staff learned was that "ideology, no matter how firmly rooted in objective reality, was of no value if it was separated from a social movement of struggling people" (Lovett, 1988, p xviii). Popular education has taught adult educators that it is not very helpful to take principles and apply them to situations, but rather to examine situations to discern the imperative for action. Both prophetic religion and popular education within social movement contexts attempt to make ideology contextually specific. This is the practice to theory bridge.

Disjuncture and Reflectivity

The starting point for learning according to both the prophetic voices in religion and adult education is some kind of disjuncture, gap, or dissonance. For the prophet it is the observation of societal behavior that does not fit the religious imperative of righteousness in the Kingdom of God. The disjuncture or dissonance must be encountered by society in order to achieve a new heaven and a new earth. The religious prophet may start with the biblical narrative, contrasting it with contemporary observations and critical reflections. The proclamation that follows is the outcome of the demands of God for radical social change. For the radical adult educator and learner, the disjuncture or dissonance may occur in the social contradictions of one's concrete existence. It may be an awareness of injustice or inconsistency between belief and behavior, or the experience of resistance that emerges within individuals and groups as they sense that they are being manipulated, that can become the occasion for critical reflection resulting in praxis or an imperative for action. Whether we consider the Christian Basic Communities, or Freire's Culture Circles, the prophetic imperative comes from a disjuncture that is the occasion for critical reflection.

Vision of the Future

Images of the future reflect our values. If you are materialistic, your image of the future likely will focus on high technology, rapid rocket transportation, electronic controlled housing, robotic slaves, and star wars military hardware. However, if you are a prophet, within the Hebrew tradition like Amos of the eighth century B.C., your image of the future will likely focus on a world where the poor catch up to the rich, where all have enough to eat, where cities destroyed by war are rebuilt, and where there are no more refugees:

> "Behold the days are coming," says the Lord, "when the plowman shall overtake the reaper and the treader of grapes him who sows the seed; mountains shall drip sweet wine, and all the hills shall flow with it. I will restore the fortunes of my people Israel, and they shall rebuild the ruined cites and inhabit them; they shall plant vineyards and drink their wine, and they shall make gardens and eat their fruit. I will plant them upon their land, and they shall never again be plucked up out of the land which I have given them," says the Lord your God. (Amos 9:13–15)

Today's prophets have images of the world that includes a focus on adequate food, clothing and shelter and health care for all humans, with health care provided as a right to all, without war and the fear of war; without refugees, without the abridgment or denial of human rights, with dialogue among those from different religious traditions, a conservationist and sustainable future, a compassionate community, a multicultural leaning society.

Prophets for social justice in both religion and adult education have always been present within their respective traditions as minority voices, often "crying in the wilderness." The dominant forces and voices in religion and education have usually been co-opted by and have served the interests of an unjust and wasteful establishment, yet the voices of the prophets have never been silenced for long. Their visions of the future awaken us from our hegemonic sleep.

REFERENCES

Abbott, W. M., ed. 1966, *The Documents of Vatican II*. New York, Association Press.

Adams, F. 1975, *Unearthing Seeds of Fire*. Winston-Salem, NC, J. F. Blair.

Aquinas, T. *Summa Theologica II: Rep 2–3*. London, Enclopaedia Britannica, Inc. Great Books of the Western World, Vol. 20.

Augustine. 1952 (Marcus Dods, trans.), *City of God: Book 19:7*. London, Enclopaedia Britannica, Inc. Great Books of the Western World, Vol. 18.

Bahro, R. 1986, *Building the Green Movement*. (Translation by M. Tyler). Philadelphia, PA, New Society Publishers.

Bainton, R. 1960, *Christian Attitudes Toward War and Peace: A Historical Survey and Critical Evaluation*. Nashville, TN, Abingdon Press.

Barth, K. 1957, *The Word of God and the Word of Man*. New York, Torchbooks.

Benauer, J. 1990, Nazi Ethics. *Continuum*, Vol. 1, No. 1, pp. 15–29.

Bennett, J. C., and Seifert, H. 1977, *U.S. Foreign Policy and Christian Ethics*. Philadelphia, PA, Westminster Press.

Biddle, W. W. and Biddle, L. J. 1965, *The Community Development Process: The Rediscovery of Local Initiative*. New York, Holt, Rinehart and Winston.

Blackwood, V. 1987, "Historical & Theological Foundations of Paulo Freire's Educational Praxis." *Trinity Journal*, 8 New Series, 201–232.

Boff, Leonardo, and Boff, Clodovis. 1986, *Liberation Theology: From Confrontation to Dialogue*. San Francisco, Harper and Row.

Bonhoeffer, D. 1954a, *Prisoner for God*. New York, Macmillan Paperbacks.

Bonhoeffer, D. 1954b, *Life Together*. New York, Harper.

Bonhoeffer, D. 1963, *The Cost of Discipleship*. New York, Macmillan Paperbacks.

Brayer, M. M. 1986, *The Jewish Women in Rabbinic Literature: A Psychostructural Perspective*, Vol. 2. Hoboken, NJ, KTAV Publishing House.

Brock, P. 1968a, *Pacifism in the United States: From the Colonial Era to the First World War*. Princeton, NJ, Princeton University Press.

Brock, P. 1968b, *Radical Pacifists in Antebellum America*. Princeton, NJ, Princeton University Press.

Brock-Utne, B. 1989, *Feminist Perspectives on Peace and Peace Education*. New York, Pergamon Press.

Brown, R. M. 1952, *Making Peace in the Global Village*. Philadelphia, PA, Westminster Press.

Brown, M. 1988. *Spirituality and Liberation: Overcoming the Great Fallacy*. Philadelphia, PA, Westminster Press.

Bruggerman, W. 1980, *The Prophetic Imagination*. Fortress Press.

Cardena, F. 1984. "Popular Education and Peasant Movements for Change." *Convergence*, 27 (3), 31–36.

Childress, J. F., and MacQuarrie, J. eds. 1986, *The Westminster Dictionary of Christian Ethics*. Philadelphia, PA, Westminster Press; SCM Press.

Cobb, J. B. Jr. and Griffin, D. R. 1983, *Process Theology: An introductory Exposition*. Philadelphia, PA, Westminster Press.

Cobb, J. B. Jr. 1983, *A Christian Natural Theology: Based on the Thought of Alfred North Whitehead*. Philadelphia, PA, Westminster Press.

Coe, G. A. 1919, *A Social Theory of Religious Education*. New York: Charles Scribner's Sons.

Coffman, P. M. 1991. "Inclusive Language and Perspective Transformation," in M. Langenbach (ed.); *Proceedings: 32nd Annual Adult Education Research Conference*. Norman, University of Oklahoma.

Cort, J. C. 1988, *Christian Socialism: An informal History*. Maryknoll, NY, Orbis Books.

Cox, H. 1984, *Religion in the Secular City: Towards a Postmodern Theology*. New York, Simon & Schuster.

Daly, H. E., and Cobb, J. B. Jr. 1989, *For the Common Good: Redirecting the Economy Toward Community, The Environment, and a Sustainable Future*. Boston, MA, Beacon Press.

Duchrow, U. 1987, *Global Economy: A Confessional Issue for the Churches?*. Geneva, World Council of Churches Publication.

Elliot, H. 1953, *Can Religious Education Be Christian?* New York, Macmillan.

Evans, A. F., Evans, R. A., and Kennedy, W. B. 1987, *Pedagogies for the Non-Poor*. Maryknoll, N.Y., Orbis Books.

Foucault, M. 1983, On the Geneology of Ethics: An Overview of Work in Progress. In H. Drefus and P. Babinow, eds. *Michael Foucault: Beyond Structuralism and Hermeneutics*, 2nd ed. Chicago, IL, Chicago University Press, pp. 229–252.

Fox, M. 1983, *Original Blessing: A Primer in Creation Spirituality*. Santa Fe, New Mexico, Bear and Company.

306 ADULT EDUCATION AND THEOLOGICAL INTERPRETATIONS

Freire, P. 1978, *Pedagogy of the Oppressed*. New York, Seabury Press.

Galilea, S. 1988, *The Way of Living Faith: A Spirituality of Liberation*. San Francisco, CA, Harper & Row.

Gill, D., ed. 1983, *Gathered for Life: Official Report, VI Assembly World Council of Churches*. Geneva: World Council of Churches.

Giroux, H. 1983, *Theory and Resistance in Education: A Pedagogy for the Opposition*. South Hadley, MA, Bergin and Garvey.

Gorai, D. C. 1984, The Experience of the Churches in Development. *Religion and Society*, Vol. 31, No. 4, pp. 23–32.

Griffin, D. R., 1989, *A Process Christology*. Philadelphia, PA, Westminster Press.

Griffin, D. R., Beardslee, W. A., and Holland, J. 1989, *Varieties of Postmodern Theology*. Albany, State University of New York Press.

Gutierrez, G. 1986, Liberation and the Poor: The Puebla Perspective. In Deane William Ferm (ed.), *Third World Liberation Theologies: A Reader*. New York, Maryknoll Press, Orbis Books, pp. 22–73.

Gyant, L. 1991, "Contributions of African American Women to Nonformal Education During the Civil Rights Movement, 1955–1965." in Langenbach (compiler) *Proceedings: 32nd Annual Adult Education Research Conference*. Norman, University of Oklahoma.

Hentoff, N. 1963, *Peace Agitator: The Story of A. J. Muste*. New York, Macmillan.

Hough, J. C. Jr. 1968, *Black Power and White Protestants*. New York, Oxford University Press.

Illich, I. 1977. Education: A Consumer Commodity and a Pseudo-Religion. *The Christian Century*, Vol. 88, December 15, pp. 1464–1466.

Joy, D. M., ed. 1983, *Moral Development Foundations: Judeo-Christian Alternatives to Piaget/Kohlberg*. Nashville, TN, Abingdon Press.

King, M. L. 1964, *Strength to Love*. New York: Harper & Row.

King, P. G., Kent, M., and Woodyard, D. O. 1988, *Risking Liberation: Middle Class Powerlessness and Social Heroism*. Atlanta, GA, John Knox.

Lovett, T. 1988, *Radical Adult Education: A Reader*. London, Routledge.

Lunger, H. L. ed. 1988, *Facing War/Waging Peace: Findings of the American Church Study Conferences, 1940–1960*. New York, Friendship Press.

Lyotard, J. 1984, *The Post-Modern Condition: A Report on Knowledge*. (Translated by Geoff Bennington and Brian Msssumi). Minneapolis, University of Minnesota Press.

McGiffert, A. C. 1917, *Martin Luther, The Man and His Work*. New York, the Century Co.

McNeal, P. F. 1974, *The American Catholic Peace Movement 1928–1972*. New York, Arno Press (Doctoral Thesis, Temple University).

Minus, P. M. 1988, *Walter Rauschenbusch: American Reformer*. New York, Macmillan.

Moore, A. J. 1982, Liberation and the Future of Christian Education. In J. L. Seymour and D. E. Miller, *Contemporary Approaches to Christian Education*. Nashville, TN, Abingdon, pp. 103–122.

Moore, A. J., ed. 1989. *Religious Education as Social Transformation*. Birmingham, AL, Religious Education Press.

Nairm, T. A. 1988, Hartshorne and Utilitarianism: A Response to Moskop. *Process Studies*, Vol. 17, No. 3, p. 170.

Naes, A. and Sessions, G. 1989, "Principles for the Movement" in H. E. Daly, and J. B. Cobb, Jr. 1989, *For the Common Good: Redirecting the Economy Toward Community, The Environment, and a Sustainable Future*. Boston, MA: Beacon Press.

Niebuhr, R. 1932, *Moral Man in Immoral Society*. New York: Charles Scribner's Sons.

Niebuhr, H. R. 1937, *The Kingdom of God in America*. New York: Harper and Brothers.

Niebuhr, H. R. 1951, *Christ and Culture*. New York: Harper & Row.

Noll, M. A. 1988, *One Nation Under God? Christian Faith and Political Action in America*. San Francisco, CA, Harper & Row.

Rauschenbusch, W. 1917, *A Theology for the Social Gospel*. New York, Abingdon Press.

Rauschenbusch, W. 1907, *Christianity and the Social Crisis*. New York, Abingdon Press.

Reardon, B. 1982, *Militarization, Security, and Peace Education: A Guide for Concerned Citizens*. Valley Forge, PA, United Ministries in Education, Publisher.

Roer, I. 1974, *Christian Peace Conferences: A Plan of Ecumenical Peace Work*. Prague, Czechoslovakia, Information Department of the Christian Peace Conference.

Saul, J. and Bernhardt, J. 1991, "Hilda Worthington Smith: Pioneer Educator for Women Workers." In M. Langenbach (ed.); *Proceedings: 32nd Annual Adult Education Research Conference*. Norman, The University of Oklahoma.

Schied, F. M. 1991. "Education and Working Class Radicalism: the Immigrant Origins of American Socialism," in M. Langenbach (ed.); *Proceedings: 32nd Annual Adult Education Research Conference*. Norman: The University of Oklahoma.

Schipani, D. S. 1984, *Conscientization and Creativity*. Lanham, MD, University Press of America.

Seymour, J. L., and Miller, D. E. 1982, *Contemporary Approaches to Christian Education*. Nashville, TN, Abingdon.

Spretnak, C., ed. 1982, *The Problems of Women's Spirituality: Essays on the Rise of Spiritual Power Within the Feminist Movement*. Garden City, NY, Anchor Books.

Stackhouse, M. L. 1985, "Jesus and Economics." In J. T. Johner, ed. *The Bible in American Law, Politics, and Political Rhetoric*. Philadelphia, PA, Fortress.

Stout, J. 1981, *The Flight From Authority*. Notre Dame, IN, University of Notre Dame Press.

Sullivan, R. R. 1989, *Political Hermeneutics: The Early Thinking of Hans-Georg Gadamer*. University Park, Pennsylvania State University Press.

Surin, K. 1990, A Certain "Politics of Speech": "Religious Pluralism" in the Age of the McDonald's Hamburger. *Modern Theology*, Vol. 7, No. 1, pp. 67–100.

Thomas, M. M. 1984, Theological Aspects of the Relationships Between Social Action Groups and Churches. *Religion and Society*, Vol. 31, No. 4, pp. 17–22.

United Methodist Council of Bishops, The. 1986, *In Defense of Creation: The Nuclear Crisis and a Just Peace*. Nashville, TN, Graded Press.

Vorspan, A. 1960, *Giants of Justice*. New York, Union of American Hebrew Congregations.

Whitehead, A. N. 1929, *The Aims of Education*. New York, Macmillan.

Whitehead, A. N. 1933, *Adventures of Ideas*. New York, Free Press.

Wien, B. J., ed., 1984, *Peace and World Order Studies: A Curriculum Guide*, 4th ed. New York, World Policy Institute.

Wogaman, J. P. 1989, *Christian Moral Judgment*. Louisville, KY, Westminster/John Knox Press.

Xavier, A. 1984, Social Action Groups and the Churches in India. *Religion and Society*, Vol. 31, No. 4, pp. 33–41.

Yarrow, C. H. M. 1978, *Quaker Experience in International Conciliation*. New York, Arno Press. (Temple University Doctoral Thesis, 1974).

Joy (1983) provides an alternative to the moral development approaches of Piaget and Kohlberg who focus on personal moral development. Raises questions about education that encourages a prophetic criticism of existing culture and social structures, and a transcendent vision of the future.

Perhaps the next challenge for radical prophetic social transformative adult education will be to fashion new pedagogies for the non-poor (Evans, Evens and Kennedy, 1987).

CHAPTER 18

And I Saw A New Heaven and A New Earth

PETER JARVIS

In the previous chapter, the role of prophecy and its relationship to radical adult education were explored. The prophet tended both to denounce and then to announce the coming of a new age, of a new Kingdom—the Kingdom of God. Christianity, certainly, (and Judaism before it), has always been a very realistic faith—it has looked at the present world and seen its imperfections; it has then proclaimed the Kingdom of God rather than the kingdoms of humankind. Throughout the Old Testament, God was king in the heavens and his kingship would only be finally manifest when the "Day of the Lord" came. This, however, gave rise to eschatological expectations and to the idea of the coming of a Messiah.

Christianity inherited many of these ideas—indeed the passage from the Revelation of St. John the Divine, from which the title of this chapter is taken, appeared in the writings of the trito-Isaiah: "For behold, I create new heavens and new earth" (Isa. 65:17). In the New Testament, the theme of the Kingdom of God is quite central. In Christ's teaching, the Kingdom demands high ethical standards of living and a total religious commitment. In a sense, the Kingdom is about a way of life foreign to that discovered in ordinary daily living, allegiance to a way which is different from that of the normal everyday standards but it appears to be both logical and realistic, so that it remains as both a promise and a possibility: it is both present and future.

It is, therefore, hardly surprising at a time when the early Christians were persecuted for their beliefs, and they were being persecuted during the time when the Revelation of St. John the Divine appeared, that the eschatological hope for the future played a significant part. From the beginnings of Christian scholarship, this theme has been discussed, such as Augustine's *City of God*, the hope for the future has continued to the present day. Whenever people are persecuted and deprived of their rights as human beings these hopes reemerge and take hold of some of the adherents in a very significant manner. 'And I saw a new heaven and a new earth' was re-echoed in that famous speech of Martin Luther King: "I have a dream. . . . " To the depressed and underprivileged of the world, the vision of a better world is something of a dream, a hope, hardly to be anticipated but most certainly to be prayed for!

Throughout the history of the Christian Church this hope has always been present in some way: it has proclaimed the Kingdom; it has anticipated this eschatological future; it has proclaimed a new heaven and new earth on earth. The mainstream church has always sought to work within the established social systems to make the Kingdom manifest, although there have been times in its history when this has not always been possible. It has been persecuted and ostracized and sidelined from the seats of power, but even then its hopes for a better world have not been destroyed. Those who have been relatively successful in the world have not always been willing to stand outside it, and so mainstream Christianity has frequently proclaimed its message of a new Kingdom from within the systems of the world. It has had a prophetic role, which it has not always fulfilled with distinction—it has both denounced and announced—and it has not always been popular for its proclamations. The Christian Church has not only attracted those people who have been successful or happy in the social systems of the world, it has attracted those who have been less successful, the lower classes and the colonized, and who, for whatever reason, have wanted to change those social systems that have labeled them unsuccessful. Indeed, it is perhaps easier to embrace such a prophetic religious position if social success has not been achieved. Many of these have had little to lose and have found it easier to renounce and denounce the world. These are among the many who have looked for a new heaven and a new earth. For some it has been a matter of trying to create a more perfect community on earth, while for others it has meant that their religion has been millenarian in nature since, apart from divine intervention, they could see no other way for the world to be changed and purified.

Among the former, there have been communities that have separated from the world, have treated it as evil, and have tried to establish their own perfect society on earth. Many examples of this phenomenon may be found throughout the history of the Church, such as the Shakers, the Oneida Community, and the Bruderhof (Whitworth, 1975). Others, such as the Church of the Latter Day Saints, have grown and become large, significant institutions, but many have been no more than small communities that existed for a generation or longer, seeking a better way of life on earth. In the same way, other sects have emerged that have looked at the world, considered it to have an evil system of government and a sinful life-style, but thought that they could not change it apart from praying for divine intervention. Their members, therefore, have embraced their own forms of perfection, have announced that the end was nigh and that the Lord would return to earth to administer judgment and justice and then to establish a new heaven and a new earth, of which they would be a part. This is the message of the Pentecostal movement, the Jehovah's Witnesses and a variety of other sects that have proclaimed this same idea throughout the history of Christianity. Sociologists of religion have studied these sects, both historical and contemporary in advanced countries and among primitive peoples, but this is not the place to explore them further (See, however, Wilson, 1967; Burridge, 1969; Needleman, 1970; Evans, 1973; *inter alia*).

A clear division exists within sociological studies of religious organizations between those which have embraced and worked in the world—defined as churches; and those which have rejected the ways of the world as evil and which have, consequently, looked for a better world, either today or tomorrow—defined as sects. Sociologists of religion studied these groups quite extensively especially in the 1960s and 1970s, as the books cited above illustrate, although this interest has broadened more recently. At the same time, however, the study of utopianism has grown and developed, perhaps reflecting something of the significance of these early sociological studies of religion. It also illustrates how society has changed and how people are now beginning to question the direction in which it appears to be developing.

Utopian studies have highlighted the fact that these early concerns of the Hebrews and the Christians were not a cultural phenomenon exclusive to the Judeo-Christian heritage. Indeed, Kumar notes that while Plato's *Republic* is a utopian study, it actually comes quite late in the development of Greek utopian thought. He notes (1987, p 3) that:

> Utopian themes reach back to the earliest Greek writings. From Hesiod's *Works and Days*, of the early seventh century BC, came the canonical depiction of the Golden Age, the bitterly lamented age of Kronos' reign: when men "lived as if they were gods, their hearts free from sorrow, and without hard work or pain"; when "the fruitful earth yielded its abundant harvest to them of its own accord, and they lived in ease and peace upon their lands with many good things."

Shades of the Garden of Eden! (See Chapter 9). From the earliest recorded literature, the people looked back to a golden age but also looked forward to another. Before and after time, there is a utopian vision! In the *Republic* there is an ideal city-state, according to Plato, with its carefully thought out system of governance, and in Revelation there is also an ideal city. Kumar points out that the city was a significant concept in the development of utopian thought, since it was an escape from the natural world. He (1987, p 5) cites Lewis Mumford who regarded the city as the first utopia because it expressed both humankind's escape from nature and the opportunity it presented to design its own perfection. Consequently, architecture has always played a major role in utopian thought. In the Middle Ages, with the beginnings of secularization, even more utopian writings began to appear, including the fourteenth-century English poem "The Land of Cokaygne" where

> There are rivers broad and fine
> Of oil, milk, honey and of wine . . .

This then is the paradise of the glutton that mocks the life-style of the monastery. Of course, the most influential piece of the Middle Ages about utopia is probably More's *Utopia*, which he actually viewed as an extension of the *Republic*. Here More expounds a form of social communism where all people are equal, where there is no money and where everyone's education is the same. In "The Land of Cokaygne" and Utopia the visions are different reflecting their different origins, but in both instances the vision lies beyond the reality of everyday life and this points to one of the problems of the idea—it is not an easy concept to define (Levitas, 1990) nor is its function in society easy to determine.

Levitas concludes that the idea of utopia embodies form, function and content and that any understanding of the term must embrace all three. In order to understand it, she (1990, p 183) suggests that utopianism "has as a precondition a disparity between socially constructed need and socially prescribed and actually available means of satisfaction," and she goes on (1990, p 191) to write:

> Utopia expresses and explores what is desired; under certain conditions it also contains the hope that these desires may be met in reality, rather than merely in fantasy. The essential element in utopia is not hope, but desire—the desire for a better way of being. It involves imaging a state of being in which the problems which actually confront us are removed or resolved, often, but not necessarily, through imaging a state of the world in which the scarcity gap is closed or the "collective problem" solved.

She points out that this definition is analytic rather than descriptive, although it is hardly a conceptual definition. At the same time there have been many expressions of desire about creating at least a new earth throughout the history of utopian thought and while not all that writing will be examined here, a few of the significant writings will be mentioned. It is interesting to note, however, that one study was written especially for adult education classes, and that was Ross's *Utopias Old and New* (1938)—according to Levitas (1990, pp 20–21).

Levitas regards utopianism as desire and this relates quite closely to the idea of wish fulfillment (Mannhein, 1936, pp 184–190). Mannheim treats the utopian element as the nature of the dominant wish and it is this which organizes the way that people think: he thinks that utopian ideas differ from ideological ones because they break the bonds of the existing order whereas ideologies do not. The history of utopian writing finds a variety of different desires being fulfilled: from the Land of Cokaygne and *Big Rock Candy Mountain* where food is in abundance, to the sexual freedom, to the abolition of property in Morris's *News from Nowhere* and Marx's classless society. In all of these the bonds with the existing social order are to be broken, either through revolution or merely through imagination. Mannheim's discussion on ideology is perhaps suspect in some ways (see Geuss, 1981 for a full discussion on ideology) since many of the writers who construct their own utopias are actually seeking to embody their own ideology in their utopian writing. Nevertheless, the distinction he draws in relation to the continuity with the social order is a significant one, differing just slightly in emphasis from that of Levitas. She seems to suggest that there is some possibility of social continuity in the fulfillment of the desire. Perhaps these two positions are not that far apart in as much as it might be theoretically possible for there to be social continuity but, in practice, it is most unlikely indeed. Mannheim goes on to distinguish four possible different types of utopian mentality: the orgiastic chiliasm of the Anabaptists; the liberal humanist ideal; the conservative idea; the socialist-communistic utopia. Mannheim (1936, p 198) suggests that:

> For Chiliasm the spirit is a force which suffuses and expresses itself through us. For humanitarian liberalism it is that 'other realm' which, when absorbed in our moral conscience, inspires us. Ideas, not bare ecstacy, guided by the activity of the epoch. . . . (give) itself over to the reconstruction of the world. This modern humanitarian idea radiated from the political realm into all spheres of cultural life culminating finally in the "idealistic" philosophy is an attempt to achieve the highest attainable stage of self-consciousness.

The first of Mannheim's types has been discussed above within the framework of millenarianism. Mannheim locates the philosophy underlying the French Revolution in the humanitarian liberal tradition and this is certainly correct. The revolutionary violence, however, and the failure to achieve a utopian society in France indicate some of the problems of utopianism within such a liberal and rational tradition. Many who would espouse the humanitarian liberalism of the French Revolution would also regard the revolutionary actions and violence as unacceptable, preferring to see a peaceful transition to a better world. It seems to them perfectly rational that people should live together in peace and harmony and that even those who exercise power should regard this as a logical end, especially since the holders of power often clothe their rhetoric in the language of service and equality. But with the revolutionary outcome of what may appear to be logical and fair propositions, the rhetoric may have become exposed. The violent nature of change, even the discontinuity of the social system, also becomes more apparent and certainly seems to be closer to Mannheim's definition of ideology and highlight some of the problems of his distinction. Indeed, it does point out that it is a utopian vision and that it might not logically be expected to happen in the real world!

Mannheim (1936, p 206) goes on to suggest that conservative mentality has no utopian vision although it gives rise to counter-utopias. He does appear to be a little inconsistent here in as much as it would be possible for those who hold conservative positions, for example, Hayek (1944), to have their own utopian conceptions. Hayek (1988), for instance, argues that there could be no freedom without several (private) property which is at the heart of the morality of civilization. Indeed, Hayek actually wants to see the state rolled back so that individuals can be free, and this is significant. Freedom is, of course, one of the themes of the socialistic-communist utopia and significantly in some aspects of utopian thought extreme right and the extreme left appear to converge. They both seek freedom for individuals, opportunity for self-fulfillment, and so on—but one believes it can only be achieved through private property while the other claims that private property is at the heart of the problem and should be abolished. Kumar (1987), by contrast, suggests that anti-utopias are the distorted image of utopia and can only arise after utopian thought has appeared. In a real sense, the writings of Hayek and others are an attempt to demonstrate weaknesses in the socialist-communist position by exposing something of their own ideals, and so must be part of any debate on utopianism and anti-utopianism.

Mannheim's final form of utopian thought, and one upon which this chapter will focus a little longer, is the socialist-communistic one found in the writings of Morris and Marx, amongst others. From the previous discussion, it may be seen clearly that Marx was not unique in postulating a classless society, and he was by no means the first to write about a better world, but because he was such a fine scholar and because his writings were taken seriously he gained a large following. Many who have called their ideologies Marxist have only expressed their own interpretations of his writings. Because he himself also changed his perspectives during his scholarly life, something that any scholar engaging in real debate must do, it is difficult, if not impossible, to determine an orthodox Marxism. (See, for instance, Tucker (1972) for a discussion about whether there are two Marxisms, or one.) Indeed, after Marx's death there have also been many revisions of his thinking. But this is no different to what occurred after the death of Christ!

For the sake of clarity, brief summaries of both *The Communist Manifesto* and *News from Nowhere* follow in order to demonstrate the two positions. McLellan (1979 pp 44–50) summarizes the former thus:

The Communist Manifesto of Marx and Engels (1969) falls into four parts: the first provides a history of society since the Middle Ages as a class society and they describe the revolutionary nature of the proletariat which itself changed during this period; the second and third provide an overview of bourgeois literature devoted to socialism, including utopianism which indicate the yearnings of the people for a better society; the fourth indicates the attitudes of communists to various opposition parties. However, the point is that the workers of the world need to unite to overthrow the bourgeoisie because the classless society will not just appear. Indeed, even after the revolution there must first be a dictatorship of the proletariat to rule during the time of social adjustment; then the need for a state would disappear. The state itself would wither away so the dictatorship of the proletariat could be abdicated and the people could live in a classless society.

William Morris, a radical from the Romantic tradition, also produced a communist-type study, in this case a novel, which embodied the socialist-communist ideal and Slapper (Coleman and O'Sullivan 1990, pp 35–42) likewise summarizes *News from Nowhere*. This is a novel depicting a utopian society in twenty-second century England; it is in the form of a dream in which William Morris finds himself in a utopian society. On seeking to cross the Thames by boat, the participant discovers that there is no need for money, that the waterman is helpful and acts as his guide, introducing him to this strange world. Morris discovers everybody is helpful, that education is lifelong but exists without schooling, that the Houses of Parliament serve as a vegetable market and a "storage place for manure" since there is now no state, that people only seek what they need and that there is no acquisition of wealth, no private property and no marriage as such although there are loving relationships. Finally, the vision dims and dies. However, before the Equality of Life period had commenced there had been a revolution and it was the workers who had organized themselves to strike and to fight against the rulers for what they regarded as right.

In both the novel and the political manifesto, there are similar pro-cesses; the utopian position cannot be reached without some form of social discontinuity. The revolution will come, the state will wither away, the rational and basically good working people will assume con-trol, and, finally create a situation where pure anarchy can reign—not chaos but total equality. Perhaps the vision of humankind, perfect and selfless in contra-distinction to the idea of sin and evil is one of the most significant parts of the dream. Clearly, however, there is the feeling that power corrupts and few people who have power wish to lay it down voluntarily for the sake of the others whom they often profess to serve, and so they have to have it removed from them.

Few appear to consider that utopia can actually be achieved through rational and logical progress—there must be some form of social dis-continuity; either humankind can achieve the utopia through a revolu-tion or else it will appear as a result of divine intervention. When there has been a revolution, however, utopia has not resulted; still the vision presents itself as something that might be achieved but has not yet happened. What then are the functions of utopian thought? Utopian writing serves at least three functions: it acts as a critique of contem-porary society indicating that however high the standards, the present has not yet achieved perfection and that there are other sets of values than those embodied in capitalism. Second, it points to something more that lies beyond the present which is not really economic in nature, something which appears achievable and quite rational, although it has not yet appeared. Third, however, for those who feel that it can only come with divine intervention or in the after-life, it does serve as a sedative offering the people hope in their despair and a sense that ultimate reality is fair and loving even if those who rule the present world are greedy and self-seeking, even though they would claim oth-erwise. However, the significance of these types of religious hope has declined as contemporary society has secularized. Indeed, the millenar-ian sects appear to be more illogical than ever in a world of rational values. Perhaps, the socialist-communist-utopian perspective approaches the religious one in many ways, without being classified as quite so irrational. At the same time utopian thinking has certainly been an aspect in the motivation of radical adult educators, like Myles Horton and Paulo Freire.

In the dialogue between them (Bell, Gaventa, and Peters, 1990) the following points are made:

I thought maybe that's the answer, these utopian colonies, these communes, getting away from life, and kind of separating yourself and living your own life. I was attracted to it but I was very sceptical from the very beginning. It seemed to be too precious, too "getting away" from things. I ended up visiting all the remains of communes in the United States—Oneida, Amana, New Harmony in Ohio. . . . I ended up concluding that they were just like I had already concluded—that a person shouldn't live within himself. . . . And I discarded utopian communities . . . .

. . . .

. . . . Finally, it just became very clear that I would never find what I was looking for. I was trying the wrong approach. The thing to do was just find a place, move in and start, and let it grow. (Horton, Bell et al. 1990, pp 52–3)

Highlander started when Horton recognized that the religious commune would not produce the new earth and that he had to work for change and just let the situation develop: citizenship schools, human rights, the rights of black people, the rights of the workers, and so on all happened. In many ways Highlander has helped to change the face of America. The vision remained, but the revolution was transformed into a lifetime's struggle to create a better world.

I asked myself why, why is it possible that some children should eat and some others don't.

It was too much for me to understand that, but when I think of that, I once again see how much I liked to know, to think, to ask questions, to imagine, to realize, and how much I see I've begun to build the dream I still have. That is, I've begun to dream with a different society. . . . . .

. . . .

I was, in fact, beginning to have a vision of a different kind of life, of a different kind of society—a society less unjust, more humanized. . . . (Freire, Bell et al. 1990, p 58)

Like Horton, Freire has spent his lifetime trying to achieve that vision through radical adult education. Freire (1972) has clearly outlined the revolutionary potential of what he was seeking to do but at the same time there has been throughout his writing a radical Christian vision of a human world made by people. His being imprisoned and exiled by those who had power in Brazil demonstrates that they recognized what he was doing too. For both Horton and Freire, some form of utopian vision has been a motivating factor in their adult education work—an ideology that drove them on—but is motivation the only place for utopianism in adult education?

Utopianism is more than just a motivating factor, however significant that has been in the lives of people such as Horton and Freire. E. P. Thompson writes:

> And in such an adventure two things happen: our habitual values (the 'commonsense' of bourgeois society) are thrown into disarray. And we enter Utopia's proper and new-found space: *the education of desire*. This is not the same as 'a moral education' towards a given end: it is rather, to open a way of aspiration, to 'teach desire to desire, to desire better, to desire more, and above all to desire in a different way.' (Thompson, 1977, pp 790–91, cited in Levitas 1990, p 122)

Utopian thought has been both a sedative and an inspiration—this is something of its paradoxical nature, so that the education of desire is not its only function, although it is one which adult educators must examine. Levitas (1990, p 124) has nicely summed up this position:

> . . . . . the function of utopia, which is not just the expression, but the education of desire. Utopia entails not just the fictional depiction of a better society, but the assertion of a radically different set of values; these values are communicated indirectly through their implications for a whole way of life in order for utopia to operate at the level of experience, not merely cognition, encouraging the sense that it does not have to be like this, it could be otherwise. Utopia contradicts bourgeois common sense and facilitates a "leap out of the kingdom of necessity into an imagined kingdom of freedom in which the desire may actually indicate choices or impose itself as need." (quotation cited from Thompson, 1977, pp 798–99)

However, as Levitas (1990, p 124) points out, there is no purpose in educating desire for its own sake; its outcome must be the realization of utopia. But herein lies the problem, perhaps by its very nature it is unrealizable, so that while it might have a transformative and emancipatory function for some people, such as Horton and Freire, Horton's realization was that it will not happen, but he had to start where he was to make the world a better place.

No adult education course should have the education of a specific desire as its aim—that would be indoctrination—but courses can be organized about utopian thought and writing which are educational.

Utopian thought, however, serves another function for education—there are other ways of communicating and enriching experience than just the rational, cognitive domain; its presence acts as a type of informal teacher from whom its message is occasionally caught. Indeed, human experience is more rich than just rational cognition, and utopian thought points education, especially with its recent emphases upon experiential learning and education for work and wealth production, to a much wider domain of learning from experience which may indeed emancipate and transform. It suggests also that future experience is to be made and discovered in the present, and that it is important not to take the values of the present for granted but to treat the taken-for-grantedness not just critically but problematically. Citicism is not sufficient; it is not sufficient merely to be a critical thinker, for there is a whole new world to be built and that demands creative and constructive thought—there are other values and other ways of life.

> Then I saw a new heaven and a new earth: for the first heaven and the first earth had passed away, and the sea was no more. And I saw the holy city, the new Jerusalem, coming down from heaven, from God, prepared as a bride adorned for her husband; and I heard a great voice from the throne saying, "Behold the dwelling of God is with men. He will dwell with them, and they shall be his people, and God himself will be with them; he will wipe away every tear from their eyes, and death shall be no more, neither shall there be mourning not crying nor pain anymore, for the former things have passed away." And he who sat upon the throne said, "Behold, I make all things new." (Revelation of St. John the Divine, 21:1–5a)

REFERENCES

Bell, B., Gaventa, J., and Peters, J., eds. 1990, *We Make the Road by Walking*. Philadelphia, Temple University Press.
Burridge, M. 1969, *New Heaven, New Earth*. Oxford, Basil Blackwell.
Coleman, S., and O'Sullivan, P. 1990, *William Morris and News from Nowhere*. Bideford, Green Books.
Evans, C. 1973, *Cults of Unreason*. London, Harrap.
Freire, P. 1972, *Cultural Action for Freedom*. Harmondsworth, Penguin.
Guess, R. 1981, *The Idea of Critical Theory*. Cambridge, Cambridge University Press.
Hayek, F. A. 1944, *The Road to Serfdom*. London, ARK Paperbacks (1986 edition)

Hayek, F. A. 1988, *The Fatal Conceit*. W. W. Bartley III ed. London, Routledge

Kumar, K. 1987, *Utopia and Anti-Utopia in Modern Times*. Oxford, Basil Blackwell.

Levitas, R. 1990, *The Concept of Utopia*. New York, Philip Allan.

Mannheim, K. 1936, *Ideology and Utopia*. London, Routledge and Kegan Paul.

Marx, K., and Engels, F. 1969, *The Communist Manifesto*. A. J. P. Taylor ed. Harmondsworth, Penguin.

McClellan, D. 1979, *The Thought of Karl Marx*. (2nd edition). London, Macmillan.

Morris, W. 1973, *News from Nowhere*. London, Lawrence and Wishart.

Needleman, J. 1970, *The New Religions*. London, Allen Lane, The Penguin Press.

Ross, H. 1938, *Utopias Old and New*. London, Nicholas and Watson.

Thompson, E. P. 1977, *William Morris: Romantic to Revolutionary*. London, Merlin Press.

Tucker, R. 1972, *Philosophy and Myth in Karl Marx*. (2nd edition). Cambridge, Cambridge University Press.

Whitworth, J. M. 1975, *God's Blueprints*. London, Routledge and Kegan Paul.

Wilson, B. R. ed. 1967, *Patterns of Sectarianism*. London, Heinemann.

PART VII
REFLECTIONS

CHAPTER 19

Endeavors in a Theology of Adult Education: A Theologian Reflects

NICOLA SLEE

INTRODUCTION

One of the most striking features of the foregoing essays to me is the rich range of human experience and traditions of reflection which they represent, and the open and self-consciously autobiographical context of much of the writing. The writers do not observe coolly from a distance something to which they have no commitment; rather, they write with passion and conviction, fueled by their own experience as adult educators and their various religious and philosophical commitments. Thus the volume as a whole acknowledges very explicitly what for me is a truism; namely, that all academic endeavor is hermeneutically committed, and that such hermeneutical bias is shaped inescapably by the personal life-experience of the individual, which is itself, of course, profoundly shaped by the wider cultural, social and political context within which the individual is situated. This is no less true of me, whose reflections upon the essays in this volume are born out of my own particular and limited theological and educational commitments. So it seems important to begin these reflections with a declaration of my own ideological biases as they emerge out of my own experience.

I write as a Christian and a theologian, as a teacher and adult educator, as a woman and a feminist, and all these commitments are crucial to the way in which I look at the world. As an Anglican teaching in an Anglican college and preparing Anglicans (as well as some Methodists and United Reformed Church members) for ordination, I write with a mixture of loyalty to, and frustration with, the tradition within which I have been nurtured. As an adult educator, I write with an understanding of, and convictions about, education which have been shaped by nearly ten years of teaching adults in the various contexts of higher education, parish life and theological training. As a woman and as a feminist, I write from the distinctive perspective of one-half of the human race which is still largely marginalized in theological and educational discourse but which is slowly finding its voice and claiming its power.

Having acknowledged my own theological and educational commitments, it will be helpful now to outline the methodology I intend to adopt in the remainder of this chapter. Rather than comment on the essays individually, which would, in all likelihood, result in a somewhat superficial and fragmentary overview, I have chosen to reflect more broadly on the enterprise represented by the volume as a whole. Thus, I begin with some general comments on the nature of the enterprise undertaken in this volume, understood in terms of the development of a "theology of adult education." This will lead on to the identification of a number of tensions or polar opposites which are perceived within the collection as a whole, and which represent important subjects on the agenda of the theology of education requiring some further clarification and analysis. Finally, I shall attempt to map out a range of biblical and theological resources—some of them identified by the authors of previous chapters, but others neglected—which might helpfully be called upon in the enterprise of the theology of education in order to address and resolve these, and other, fundamental issues. By adopting this rather broad-edged response to the essays, I hope to offer some fruitful suggestions for carrying forward the significant but as yet unsystematic work begun in this volume. I am only too aware that these reflections are wholly impressionistic, and do no more than sketch in general terms some possible themes and resources which others must develop more fully.

A THEOLOGY OF ADULT EDUCATION: REFLECTIONS ON THE ENTERPRISE

The attempt by the authors of this volume to engage in a serious and critical dialogue between the literature and experience of adult education and Christian theological traditions respectively is to be both welcomed and praised. The enterprise marks a significant landmark in the development of a theology of adult education in the English-speaking world.

As Leslie Francis and Adrian Thatcher (1990) comment in their recent reader in the area, "the concept of 'theology of education' sounds comparitively strange both to educationalists, who are familiar with such areas of discourse as 'psychology of education,' 'philosophy of education' and 'sociology of education,' and to theologians, who are familiar with the application of their discipline to many other applied areas of social and personal life" (p 1). As a theologian, I have always been surprised and disappointed that theologians in the English-speaking world have demonstrated a peculiar disinterest in the nature of education as a subject of central theological concern. This is not to say that theologians do not interest themselves in the *practice* of education. Many of them do, as is evident from the continuing involvement of the churches in the provision of education in school, parish and home setting. Yet what is lacking, apart from one or two notable exceptions,[1] is any sustained and serious *theological* consideration of education per se. This dearth of theological reflection upon the nature and processes of education is as lamentable as it is puzzling. For Christian faith has at its center a deep concern with matters educational. The Hebrew scriptures which Christians share with fellow Jews are testimony to a profound religious concern with the nature and acquisition of true wisdom and knowledge of God, which runs throughout the rich diversity of biblical traditions. Whatever else they are, Christians are disciples, that is, learners, who walk in the steps of a Master teacher, whose own educational praxis as narrated in the gospels is an extraordinarily rich, and largely untapped, resource for understanding the nature of teaching and learning. "Rabbi" may not have become one of the chief Christological titles, presumably because it could not indicate the theological distinctiveness of Christian confession about Jesus, but notions of teaching, learning and wisdom certainly lie close to the heart of New Testament understandings of what it means to walk in the way of Jesus.

---

1. One thinks of the work of Gabriel Moran, Thomas Groome, Maria Harris, and other Christian educationists in the United States. If there is an established tradition of a Christian theology of education in general, and adult education in particular, it is represented by such work.

The reasons for this lacuna within the theological establishment are difficult to identify with any precision, though they can be speculated upon. A number of possibilities suggest themselves for consideration. First, there is no obvious institutional context within British universities and theological circles, at least, where a theology of education could naturally take root and flourish. With the exception of some Scottish universities and in contrast to their Continental counterparts, British faculties of theology do not generally include departments of *practical theology*, where educational issues would arise in the analysis of the praxis of faith within church and society. Lacking such an institutional setting, it is hardly surprising that the theology of education has not flourished.

A second reason for theological disinterest in matters educational is probably to be attributed to the secularization of education in our own day. Whereas educational provision in most nations in the west was initiated and developed by the churches, it has become in this century very largely the responsibility and the concern of the state. Despite their continuing involvement in the provision of state education in the United Kingdom, the churches appear to have lost the vision for education which fueled the pioneering efforts of the great educationists of the nineteenth century. This is reflected in theological circles as much as political, in the lack of intellectual inquisitiveness about education demonstrated by academic theologians. At the same time, educational discourse has been established on its own, independent intellectual foundations, and no longer sees the need to draw on religious resources for its reflection and analysis. What all this means is that, outside the walls of the religious communities, education in our schools and colleges has largely lost touch with its religious roots, and the spheres of theology and education have become largely segragated.

My third hypothesis is rather more speculative and certainly more contentious than the previous two. It attributes the underdevelopment of the theology of education, at least in part, to the impact of patriarchy on church and society. Education, and particularly the work of teaching, has been conducted in Western societies and certainly within the churches, very largely, if not exclusively, by women. As such, it has been undervalued and its significance, both at the level of theory and practice, severely underplayed. Along with other areas of "women's work," education has been badly paid, insufficiently resourced, and inadequately recognized. Perceived as a low-status activity within church and wider community, it has not attracted the interest of academic theologians.

Perhaps a final reason for the late emergence of a recognizable area of discourse which we might term "theology of education" lies in the complexity of the enterprise which demands a thorough grounding and competenence in two specialized and, themselves, complex and wide-ranging disciplines, and the ability to interrelate concerns and methods in both fields in fruitful ways. Few would claim to have mastered the range of knowledge and skills required to engage in a sophisticated dialogue between the two disciplines. Still, the complexity and demand of interdisciplinary dialogue have not prevented the development of those other "-ologies" of education—philosophy, sociology, psychology and so on—so there is something more than the sheer difficulty of the enterprise at work here.

Whatever the reasons for the neglect, it is encouraging to detect signs of change. Francis and Thatcher identify a growing movement of interest in the interrelationship of the two disciplines:

> Throughout the English-speaking world educationalists and theologians have begun to demonstrate how their two very different disciplines can fruitfully interact. Educationalists are recognizing how theology can make a valuable contribution to the development and critique of educational theory, while theologians are recognizing the need to take educational discourse seriously (p ix).

The essays in the present collection, exploratory and piecemeal as they are, represent another hopeful sign of this movement.

A THEOLOGY OF EDUCATION: TENSIONS AND CONFLICTS

Writing as they do, and necessarily must, from the specific contexts of educational and theological discourse to which their own autobiographies have exposed them, the writers in this collection draw on a rich but inevitably selective range of theological and educational resources. One of the tasks of reflecting on the collection as a whole is to examine the ways in which the various perspectives represented by the different writers and chapters interact and suggest further questions and issues for debate. I should like to do this by commenting on what I perceive as a number of tensions within the collection as whole, tensions which, in some cases run within, as well as across chapters, tensions which arise partly out of the different philosophical traditions to which the writers are committed, but which also might be seen as representing polar opposites within which the enterprise of education is always conducted, and with which any theology of education must deal.

Individual versus Communal Perspectives

A first tension I note is that between learning perceived as essentially an individual quest and learning as communal activity. There is, clearly, a movement within the collection as a whole from the personal perspective in the earlier chapters to broader social and political considerations at the end; but throughout the collection runs an uneasy alliance of two rather different models of education. The first (which appears to underlie the analysis offered by Jarvis in Chapters 1, 6 and 9, is a predominant perspective in Stubblefield's chapter, despite his emphasis on dialogue, and is clearly expressed by Walker in Chapter 11) speaks of education in terms of the individual's quest for meaning in an existentially ambivalent world-order and the creation of the autonomous and self-reflective person in this process through the exercise of freedom and self-determination in acts of responsible choice. The primary unit of education is the independent human subject, variously defined as "the self-transcending" or "self-actualizing" subject whose task is to "achieve moral self-transcendence, authentic existence and real self-value" (Walker, quoting Lonergan). Human beings are understood as "meaning-seeking animals" whose primary educational vocation is the formation of the self and the forging of meaning for their lives (Jarvis).

In this perspective, although the individual may be *located* within a broader social setting, the metaphors and images chosen to describe the educational process tend to emphasize the separation of the individual from the community. Thus, Jarvis speaks of humankind as "a restless wanderer always seeking meaning for existence" and again, in his analysis of the fall narrative, suggests that "learning leads to individuation and part of the process of becoming an individual involves breaking the ties that bind people together". Because the basic unit of learning is perceived as the independent human subject whose quest is the creation of his own selfhood, the individual is primary and the community is secondary, both in a philosophical and a pragmatic sense. Philosophically, the individual takes pride of place at the heart of the model of education in operation, but pragmatically, the process of education is understood to work outwards, starting from the illumination or actualization of the individual and from there to a wider transformation of society. Thus, according to Stubblefield, "the purpose of adult education is to enhance the ability of persons to act as agents", and thus, presumably to act *upon* the world in some sense, yet the process starts with the subjectivity of the individual.

In contrast to this model, the second (which may be detected in the analyses offered by Clark, Welton, Leirman and Anckaert, Walters and Deshler, as well as in parts of Stubblefield) thinks of education more as an activity of the whole community, constituted by a network of persons-in-relation, where the process of education is seen in terms of the creation and transformation of society through protest, prophecy, vision and action, within which individual growth has meaning, but only insofar as it contributes to wider structural change. Thus, both Walters and Deshler stress the wider social and political commitments of education to equality, justice and transformation of society. Stubblefield and Hart and Wood Holton lay emphasis on the dialogical methods of adult education which take place within a mutually supportive learning community. In his account of adult education understood through the metaphor of conversion, Welton brings both dimensions together when he asserts that the heart of conversion, and implicitly, of adult education, is the "entry into a transformative learning community sharing a common life and attuned to the least of God's creatures". Conversion is "being opened up to the world and to God in a new way, a being-in-relation-to-God-and-the-world that is played out in one's fundamental option and action".

Cognitive versus Affective Perspectives

Closely allied to the first tension between individual and communal emphasis is a tension between learning perceived as an essentially cognitive process and learning understood more broadly as the development and integration of the whole person. On the one hand, a number of essayists set high store by the development of cognitive skills, and emphasise in particular the crucial importance of critical thinking in the development of adult autonomy (e.g., Jarvis in Chapter 6, Stubblefield, Walker, van der Veen). Thus, both Jarvis and Walker characterize the process of adult education largely in terms of "search for meaning" and "critical reflection," and it is these two elements, according to Walker, "that transform the use of self-directed processes into true self-directed learning" and lead to "the most basic autonomy, the most fundamental freedom and responsibility". Where Freire's understanding of education as conscientization is dominant, as it is in several of the discussions, there remains a fundamental emphasis on coming to "right consciousness" as an essentially cognitive insight and experience, even though this has radical political overtones and arises out of an analysis of experience.

On the other hand, other writers in the collection wish to speak of the task of adult education much more in terms of the development of the whole person, in which the education of the body and the emotions and the acquisition of a reflective spirituality is every bit as vital as logical thinking and where the capacity for critical *affirmation* is considered of equal value to the exercise of critique as it is more commonly understood (Hart and Wood Holton, Leirman and Anckaert). Thus Hart and Wood Holton propose an alternative to Jarvis's root metaphor of education as the "search for meaning" by speaking of "the human experience of wonder which leads us beyond our immediate knowing". Arguing that "a truly comprehensive concept of emancipatory education needs to include an understanding of the non-cognitive dimensions of transformative education", they suggest that "educational practices and approaches have to be developed which 'are friendly towards the body, liberating for one's emotions, and training one's thinking' ". Leirman and Anckaert likewise emphasize the notions of education through emotion, narrative, community and metaphor in a postmodern perspective, though they see some potential dangers in these emphases.

Developmental versus Conversion Perspectives

A third tension is evident more in the *language and terminology* employed than it is one fully worked out in analysis or discussion. This is a tension between a language of development and growth, on the one hand, and a language of conversion and transformation on the other. To a certain extent, this tension is symptomatic of the tension between the two realms of discourse, educational and theological, which the authors are attempting to bring into fruitful interchange, but it does also represent a tension *within* the two disciplines themselves. In the first case, the predominance of growth and developmental images and metaphors (as we find in Jarvis in Chapter 1, Ferro, Stubblefield, Courtenay and Walker) emphasizes movement, dynamism and change in the educational process, implies a goal or end to which education aspires, and is inherently optimistic about the capacity of the human being for perpetual, even endless, self-transformation. In contemporary psychological and educational discourse, this root metaphor is so pervasive that we frequently fail to recognize it *as* metaphor. Gabriel Moran (1990) has recently suggested that the notion of "development" is a central metaphor in modernity, "the modern world's alternative to providence, predestination, and heaven," and that "theories of development are a fervent belief, backed by scientific data, that human life will get better if we do our part by clearing away the obstacles to continued growth" (p 150). Where the growth metaphor is not checked by other, complementary or even conflicting imagery, it tends to promote an aggressively competetive and achievement-oriented mentality, and to ignore the need for stability, stillness and contemplation in the educational process.

Alternatively, to speak of education more in terms of metaphors of conversion and transformation (as is suggested by Clark, McCaffry, Welton, Hart and Wood Holton, Deshler, and Jarvis in Chapter 18) invites us into a very different kind of discourse, where mystery, contemplation, imagination, gift and grace become keys to the educational process, and where a rather different model of the human being is suggested, emphasizing the possibilities of creative imagination as the door to vision and the renewal of society, rather than developmental stage or cognitive ability as determinative of the capacity for insight and transformation.

To speak of education in terms of "conversion," "prophecy" and "utopia," as Welton, Deshler and Jarvis do, is to enlarge the vision of both the human person and the purpose of education within society as a whole. Tony McCaffry has suggested that "not all metaphors are worthwhile, metaphors can die while others can be dynamically prophetic; some can be partial others extended; some indicate a single aspect of significance, others go to the root of the matter and offer a paradigm within which the totality can be experienced". To speak in terms of this alternative metaphoric language of conversion and transformation does not so much deny the notion of development or growth or decry cognitive ability per se but rather provides a wider context within which to set these concerns. Thus, McCaffrey speaks of the truth of the gospel which underpins a Christian understanding of adult education as "the mystery overarching and underpinning all that is, that has been and that will be", a mystery which "does not insult the human intelligence so much as challenge it". And Hart and Wood Holton insist that "transformative education has to . . . allow for a creation of spaces where positive, future-oriented, utopian possibilities can take shape in people's imagination".

The three tensions which I have noted—and space forbids me from developing others—are themselves symptomatic of a more basic tension between various competing philosophical and theological traditions upon which different authors draw for their reflections. On the one hand, the emphasis on education as an essentially cognitive and developmental process of individual meaning-making has its roots in the traditions of Enlightenment rationality, Existentialist philosophy, and Protestant liberalism, among others. Whilst these traditions are by no means uniform, they share an axiomatic faith in, and common vision of, the independent human subject, characterized by freedom, rationality and moral responsibility, acting upon the world to shape and define it and to "make" meaning. In somewhat different ways, these traditions express an implicit optimism about human progress through the exercise of rationality and freedom.

At back of these traditions is the image of the lonely, male subject, the "tragic agent" (Stubblefield), set in the midst of an alien universe whose task is to achieve his own autonomous personhood through the excercise of freedom, conflict, choice and commitment, and to forge meaning and better human community in the world through the exercise of rational thought and the exploitation of all its fruits, especially those of science and technology. "He" is perfectly described by Leirman and Anckaert as "the author of his own world, the creator of history, the maker of systems old and new". His freedom is both created and guaranteed by "a thrust of the person to act in a way that achieves moral self-transcendence, authentic existence, and real self-value" (Lonergan, in Walker). Such a vision of the human being is enshrined within a larger view of reality but is very much at its center: the world is the stage for human history, and "man" is "master," not only of his own destiny, but also that of the world as a whole. His relationship to the wider cosmos is described in largely hierarchical and dualistic terms of distance, separation and otherness, issuing in a benign responsibility (at best) or manipulation and control (at worst).

On the other hand, the emphasis on education as an activity of the whole person in community through the activities of creative imagination, vision and contemplation leading to political action, arises out of very different philosophical traditions, namely those of Marxist socialism, postmodernism and feminism, and related forms of liberation and feminist theologies. Again, these traditions, disparate as they are, share a common view of the human person-in-community, constituted by relationship to other persons, to social structures and to the earth itself, and by their action in the world. At back of these traditions is a very different image of *persons* (in contrast to the individual male self) located in community and in relationship, set within social structures which frequently militate against personhood, but with the capacity for joint vision, imagination and action to change and overturn unjust structures. Put at its simplest, this view of humanity is based on the conviction that "we cannot exist without one another" (Clark), so that "[a person] is a being that can only 'be' by virtue of others" (Ratzinger, in Clark).

This vision of the human being is, in its own way, every bit as optimistic as that arising from Enlightenment rationality, but the seeds of its optimism lie elsewhere, in communal bonding rather than in lonely individual quest, in story and ritual rather than in abstract concept and rational thought, in visionary utopianism rather than scientific achievement, in committed action rather than "objective" analysis. This vision of the human community is also part of a wider vision of reality, which, attempting to overcome the limitations of Cartesian dualism, emphasizes the interconnectedness and interdependence of all things in a single, complex and fragile cosmos, envisaged more as a living organism than an inert, though cleverly constructed, machine. Hart and Wood Holton express this beautifully when they say, "ultimately, diversity and interdependence, multiplicity and interconnectedness are inseparable, unifying all forms of life beyond the many artificial separations created by our culture". In such a world-view, human relationship to the cosmos as a whole is spoken of in terms of mutuality, shared inheritance and vulnerability, leading to an ethic of responsibility and celebration.

Perhaps it is misleading to polarize the tensions quite so baldly as I have done here. To separate and analyze is inevitably to simplify. The theology of education must speak about the individual quest for meaning as well as the creation of human community, the exercise of rationality as well as the use of the senses, the development of the human person and society as well as the gift of personhood and community, and, to that extent, may legitimately draw widely on a range of philosophical and theological traditions in order to do so. Yet the basic philosophical framework chosen will determine the vision of the human person espoused and will set the agenda of issues with which theology of education must deal. No conceptual framework is neutral, as this collection repeatedly acknowledges, and some provide a richer, fuller and ultimately more authentic language for expressing and reflecting on the gospel than others. In our own time, the languages of Enlightenment rationality, Existentialist philosophy and liberal Protestantism have been shown to be fatally flawed insofar as they represent the illusory autonomy of a minority of privileged, white, middleclass and male elites, and fail to address the needs and insights of large groups of people, and even of the earth itself. The independent human subject crowned by the glories of rationality and standing in splendid isolation from the rest of creation has been deconstructed decisively by postmodernist thought, though he does not seem to want to lie down! As Leirman and Anckaert say:

In postmodernism, the human subject is moved away from the centre of reality. The absolute, almighty subject is de-centrated by asking the critical question of his origin: man is not his own origin, and his freedom is not any longer absolute, but situated and limited. This means that reason reaches its own limits in modern thought itself. Human finitude appears on the intellectual scene.

Neither post-Enlightenment scientific rationality nor Existentialist subjectivity will serve any longer for the creation of a vision of education which is authentically and fully Christian. For this, we need philosophical traditions which take seriously the material and bodily nature of human existence, our rootedness in relationship and community, and our capacity for vision and action as well as critical reflection.

Such traditions are gaining new recognition in our time, and there are encouraging signs of their presence in this volume, but, new as they are, they have deep roots in ancient wisdoms, including many neglected biblical and theological traditions. It is to these which I now turn in the final part of this paper.

A THEOLOGY OF EDUCATION: RESOURCES FOR THE ENTERPRISE

The particularity of paradigms represented by the writers in this collection reflects not only their own autobiographically-shaped hermeneutical commitments, but also the fragmentary and underdeveloped state of the theology of education itself. There is, as yet, no consensus regarding the agenda, the methodology and the resources which might circumscribe such a theology, and few have even attempted to sketch out what such parameters might be (but cf. Hull, 1977). It would be foolish to attempt such a task in the short space of this essay, but it might be worthwhile to identify something of the range of theological resources available in Christian traditions which a systematic theology of education would need to utilize. This might provide some clues towards analyzing and resolving the tensions and conflicts noted above and seeing where the major themes in a theology of education might lie, at least as these are suggested from *theology's* side. (I recognize that the subdisciplines of education also need to be considered in the working out of a theology of education, but that is not my brief here.) I would like to attempt such a sketch, first, by outlining a few major resources available within the Bible, and then pointing out some post-biblical theological themes which could provide some starting points for reflecting on the nature and activity of education. It will be evident that some of these resources have already been called upon in this collection, yet I am struck by the wider possibilities offered by Christian traditions which have *not* been utilized by the writers.

Biblical Traditions

A major result of modern critical study of the Bible is the insight that the Bible does not speak with one voice but many. It contains traditions representing well over a thousand years of a people's history and is characterized more by diversity than uniformity, both in terms of literary qualities *and* theology. This makes the use of the Bible as a theological source problematic in many ways. This fundamental hermeneutical issue cannot be discussed here, though a theology of education would have to address it. All that is attempted here is to call attention to three central biblical traditions which offer a primary theological resource for theological education.

Wisdom Traditions

The Bible is centrally concerned with what it means to "know God," to have understanding and wisdom, and this must provide a primary resource for a theology of education which wishes to be informed by biblical insights. This concern with the "knowledge of God" is reflected, not only in the designated "Wisdom writings" themselves, but throughout the biblical corpus. Many of the stories in the so-called historical books can be read as the tale of Israel's struggle to learn "knowledge of God," and the legal and cultic codes as the attempt to prescribe the parameters within which the way of the Lord may be learnt and practiced.

Wisdom within the Judeo-Christian biblical traditions is not thought of primarily as abstract knowledge or speculative thought, but as personal, moral, experiential and pragmatic knowledge. It is intrinsically relational (cf. Clark's and Stubblefield's analysis). To "know God" is to recognize his authority and live according to his laws, that is, to be in right relationship to and with God. Wisdom is personified in the later Wisdom writings as a female principle who actively seeks out those who will listen to her, who, like the Logos in the Johannine prologue, "pitches her tent" amongst Israel and reveals the secrets of God to those who will accept her. Closely associated with the work of God in creation, Dame Wisdom is the fulfilment rather than the contradiction of "natural" or "sensual" knowledge. She exemplifies the biblical understanding of relational and experiential wisdom at its best.

From a New Testament perspective, Mark and Paul are particularly concerned with wisdom. For Mark, the "secret of the kingdom" is consistently misunderstood by the disciples, those "on the inside," but is grasped by those on the edges—the Gentiles, the women, the socially or religiously marginalized, and this is a theme with obvious political as well as pedagogical overtones. For Paul, the "wisdom of God" is in direct conflict with the "wisdom of the world" and is manifested above all in Christ crucified and the folly of the cross. What might a theology of education look like which took these Markan and Pauline themes seriously?

Prophetic Traditions

David Deshler has already surveyed fully the roots of the prophetic impulse in Christianity in the biblical traditions and beyond, and Peter Jarvis has suggested how the prophetic or utopian vision is central in "the education of desire," so I will not repeat what they have said here. What is central to this tradition, however, is the telling forth of God's word for a particular time and place, with the emphasis on present action rather than future events. For the prophets, what it means to "know God" is to "do justice, to love mercy, and to walk humbly with your God" (Micah 6:8), and conversely, God is known primarily through his liberating actions in history, and primarily in the paradigmatic act of the Exodus. God is explicitly named in this tradition as "Teacher" (e.g., Isaiah 30:20f): which means, not the dispenser of abstract truth, but the leader and guide, as well as the judge, of Israel, the one whose voice calls, saying, "This is the way; walk in it." The special significance of this tradition for a theology of education is its highlighting of the social and political dimensions of "knowledge of God" and its insistence on rooting all learning within a praxis of justice making.

The Gospel Jesus-Traditions

It is axiomatic that the Gospel traditions about Jesus will be of particular importance for a Christian theology of education. This is not only because of the centrality to faith of Christology per se but because Jesus' own praxis as a teacher provides such a rich and insightful perspective on the nature of both learning and teaching as human activities. It is surprising that none of the essayists in this collection have made anything more than passing reference to this tradition. Clearly it is impossible here to do more than hint at some of the theological themes that invite exploration, but I will suggest a few.

Jesus' teaching, especially as this is evident through his strikingly original use of the parable form, is marked, it seems to me, by at least three fundamental features. First, it is rooted in relationship and dialogue, arising out of particular encounters with individuals and addressing the particular situation from which the parable is drawn. While many of the Gospel parables have lost their original real-life setting, enough are preserved to suggest that Jesus' parables usually arose out of situations of controversy, conflict or, at the very least, debate. Second, Jesus' teaching is rooted in the everyday world and experience of his hearers, and yet it shocks his hearers into perceiving their experience in radically new ways. Far from being simple moral tales, contemporary literary analysis of the parables suggests that they function much more like riddles or jokes, through the use of surprise, hyperbole, and disruption of normality. Starting with the known and familiar everyday world of rural Palestine, the parables provoke a fresh perspective and a radical challenge by subverting that world in unexpected ways. Third, Jesus' teaching demands a response from his hearers and yet at the same time leaves them completely free. Again, rather like the joke, a parable invites an immediate response, and in the response the hearer makes an implicit choice either for or against the kingdom, as the gospel descriptions of the reaction of Jesus' original hearers make clear. Such theological reflection on the methodology of Jesus' teaching has much to offer of pedagogical significance.

Besides the methodology of the parables, the centrality of the kingdom, or rule, of God in Jesus' teaching needs to be taken seriously by a theology of education. All of Jesus' ministry and teaching is set within the context of the vision of the kingdom, and, however this is understood, it implies the setting of education within a community of radical equality and justice and, rather like the prophetic traditions, highlights the social and political commitments of education.

Theological Themes

When the Bible does not speak with one voice, it is hardly to be expected that theological traditions will either, and certainly there is enormous variety within the history of Christian theology. Yet, where the biblical traditions show little concern for systematic and comprehensive explication of faith, the opposite is true of Christian doctrine. Child of Greek philosophy as well as the biblical writings, Christian theology from post-biblical times has been marked by the attempt to state as clearly and systematically as possible the content and nature of Christian faith in terms drawn from surrounding culture. Thus, the doctrinal traditions of Christianity present very different kinds of resources to the biblical traditions: they are much more speculative and systematic in emphasis. Within the history of Christian theology, certain key themes or doctrines have provided a framework for the explication of Christian faith, and these will be briefly outlined here and a few comments made vis-a-vis their potential application to education.

Theology of Creation

The theology of creation is concerned with the purpose and nature of the created world as this is perceived by faith, the nature of God as creator and the nature of the relationship that obtains between them. Within theological circles there is a renewed concern to develop theologies of creation which are adequate to the contemporary ecological crisis. Classical theology has tended to emphasize the separation of God from the creation and the distinctiveness of the human species from other orders of creation, and to speak of humanity's role as that of exercising dominion over creation. Yet many now find this kind of language inadequate, and Matthew Fox (1983) speaks for many when he calls for a "Creation-centered spirituality" to replace the anthropocentric redemption/fall paradigm which has dominated Christianity in the West. Process theologians and others try to envisage a relationship between God and world which is marked by interconnectedness, mutuality and co-creatorship, rather than by distance and possession. All of this has much to say to educationalists, reminding us of the need to put our discourse about education firmly within a global and cosmic perspective, and suggesting that reality in its most basic constituents is profoundly relational and interconnected. Education which is not an instrument of ecological commitment and transformation is not faithful to the God whom people of faith name as "Creator."

Theological Anthropology

Within the broader framework of a doctrine of creation, theological anthropology is concerned to explicate a doctrine of the human person. Since the practice and philosophy of education are dependent on an understanding of the nature of personhood, this is clearly an area of fundamental concern to educators. Traditionally, Christian anthropology has taken as its starting point the biblical notion of humankind "made in the image of God," but the interpretation of this image has been conducted largely within a Platonist and hellenistic framework, with disastrous consequences. The dualistic Greek concept of the human person has been imported into Christianity, bringing with it an inherent distrust of the body and the senses, and an elevation of the "spirit" or the "soul" over the body, which is then understood as the true locus of human identity, the "divine spark" containing the image of God. Enlightenment rationality did little to reinstate more biblical notions of the person as total body-soul, but only emphasized all the more the identity of rational thought with the "essence" of man. Stubblefield reflects this understanding when he interprets the "imago dei" as meaning that "the soul is rational, uses language to communicate, and is given dominion over the earth". I have already indicated why I find this kind of account both inadequate and dangerous. Contemporary theology is concerned to recapture a more holistic understanding of personhood, emphasizing the essentially bodily and relational nature of human existence and understanding the notion of the *imago dei* more in terms of humanity's capacity for creativity which mirrors the divine outpouring of Godself in creation. Again, this is highly suggestive for educational praxis and discourse, offering a warning against excessively rationalist understandings of education and pointing towards an understanding of personhood which is rooted in community, relationality, bodiliness and creativity.

Soteriology and Christology

Soteriology refers to the doctrine of salvation (from the Greek *soter*, to save), which includes an analysis of the fallenness of the human condition from which salvation is necessary, as well as the means of salvation in Christ. Christology is thus closely related to soteriology, although classically a distinction has been made between the two on the grounds that soteriology is concerned with the *work* of Christ in salvation while Christology is concerned with the *nature* of Christ, especially in relationship to God. Thus, soteriology has given rise to theories of atonement, while Christology has issued in theories of incarnation and, more widely, the nature of the Trinity. Again, this is an area where one might expect much fruitful interchange between theology and education since, though the religious terminology is not generally used, education, too, is concerned with the "salvation" or "redemption" of the human being to the extent that it is concerned to promote the "fulfilment" or "development" of the full potential of the human being.

Christian theologies of redemption offer a variety of models of the root cause of the fallenness of the human condition, and propose different understandings of the work of Christ in saving humankind. A distinction is often made between "objective" and "subjective" theories of atonement, the former emphasising the objectivity of Christ's atonement and the latter laying stress on the subjective response of the believer to the Christ-event. Still, such distinctions are less important than the different analyses of the human condition and the nature of salvation suggested by soteriology. In terms of their educational significance, notions of human frailty, fallenness, alienation and ignorance provide a sobering corrective to an optimistic humanism which believes that education can achieve all. On the other hand, notions of incarnation, atonement, redemption, mediation, salvation and divinization provide a variety of models for understanding the salvific work of education, and perhaps offer fruitful ways of understanding the teacher-student relationship in particular.

Within Christology, different models for understanding the identity of Christ may also be suggestive for an analysis of the identity and role of the teacher. Traditionally, Christology has centered around the New Testament "titles" of Christ as Son of God, Son of Man, Lord, Messiah, and so on, and their development in patristic theology in the doctrines of incarnation and Trinity. More recent Christologies offer rather different models: Christ as the "man for others," the "human face of God," the liberator, the passionate justice-maker, to name a few. Both traditional and contemporary models may offer creative paradigms for understanding the work of the teacher. A fascinating use of the paradigm of incarnation in educational discourse, for example, is offered by Maria Harris in *Teaching and Religious Imagination*, a book which she describes as "an essay in the theology of teaching." Here she defines teaching as "the incarnation of subject matter in ways that lead to the revelation of subject matter" and develops this understanding in a number of original directions. Such a work not only offers many insights into the work of teaching, but also provides an exemplary model of what a theology of adult education might look like in practice.

Ecclesiology

Ecclesiology is concerned with a theological understanding of the nature of the church and its relation to both God and world. It is the area of theology which, perhaps more than any other, roots the life of faith firmly in a communal and historical context. It has both a "domestic" and a "missionary" orientation, that is, a concern with the internal life of the Christian community and a concern with the wider mission of the church in the world. As such, it offers an interesting parallel to educational discourse about the learning community, which must be concerned both with the domestic life of that community and its wider mission within society.

Ecclesiology offers a variety of models for understanding the community of the church, which is spoken of as the Body of Christ, the People, or family, of God, the Temple of God, the sign of the kingdom, the sacrament of history. These models offer different ways of understanding the tension between the glorious vocation and the human failure that characterize the life of the church. They might well be helpful in analyzing the nature of the educational community which, in many ways, shares similar tensions and concerns with the church. Both communities exist "at the margins" of society, functioning fully within it and reflecting many of its values, but at the same time, pointing to some other and future possibilities, offering a critique of the present limitations of the world. Both communities live with the tension of the domestic and the missionary, pulled one way and then the other by competing social and political forces, and attempting to maintain an integral balance between the two. Both communities are fueled by glorious vision yet live with a daily reminder of their all-too-human frailty. Ecclesiologies which try to speak meaningfully of this marginal situation of the Christian community might be a highly significant resource for a theology of education.

Eschatology

Eschatology is concerned with a doctrine of "the last things" (from the Greek *eschaton*, the end), and puts the whole of the theological enterprise in a radically transcendent, or we might say, utopian, perspective, which both relativizes and consummates the whole of human history and endeavor. Traditionally, eschatology has been concerned with a vision of heaven and hell and the "end times," though modern theologies have generally "de-mythologized" such terminology and prefer to think of eschatology as a dimension suffusing the whole life of faith, and not merely its end-point. Thus Moltmann (1967) speaks of eschatology as "the doctrine of the Christian hope," and asserts that "from first to last, and not merely in the epilogue, Christianity is eschatology, is hope, forward looking and forward moving, and therefore also revolutionizing and transforming the present." However eschatology is understood, it is clear that it offers a visionary language for speaking about the future possibilities of the cosmos, and, as such, provides a way of thinking about and speaking of the utopian ideals of education, as Peter Jarvis demonstrates in his final chapter. It provides a language which combines strong elements of crisis and judgment with elements of fulfilment, consummation and finality, offering both hope and warning to the religious community. Educational discourse needs such a language, perhaps as never before. At a time when the educational establishment is marked by a deep pessimism and frustration, a prophetic and visionary eschatology is urgently required which can "educate desire" and fuel present action for transformation.

CONCLUSION

The development of an authentic theology of education, to which the essays in this volume bear witness, is, I have suggested, long overdue in the English-speaking world. Yet some theological and philosophical traditions, some root metaphors and images, will serve better than others in this enterprise. I have suggested a range of those which I consider to offer fruitful starting points, as well as to highlight perceived limitations of some others. Agreement with this inevitably personal perspective on the part of readers is less important than the willingness to wrestle with, and the commitment to articulate as clearly as possible, in dialogue with one another, the fundamental precommitments which will shape a theology of education to serve our time.

REFERENCES

Fox, M. 1983, *Original Blessing: A Primer in Creation Spirituality*. Santa Fe, Bear & Company.

Francis, L. and Thatcher, A., eds., 1990, *Christian Perspectives for Education: A Reader in the Theology of Education*. Leominster, Fowler Wright.

Harris, M. 1987, *Teaching and Religious Imagination: An Essay in the Theology of Teaching*. San Francisco, Harper & Row.

Hull, J. 1984, 'What is theology of education?' in *Studies in Religion and Education*, London, Fowler Press, pp. 249–272. Also in Francis & Thatcher, op. cit.

Moltmann, J. 1967, *Theology of Hope*. London, SCM.

Moran, G. 1990, 'Alternative developmental images' in Fowler, J. W., Nipkow, K. E. and Schweitzer, F., eds., *Stages of Faith and Religious Development: Implications for Church, Education and Society*. New York, Crossroad, pp. 149–161.